PROJECT FEASIBILITY ANALYSIS

A GUIDE TO PROFITABLE NEW VENTURES

DAVID S. CLIFTON, Jr.

DAVID E. FYFFE

Georgia Institute of Technology

A WILEY-INTERSCIENCE PUBLICATION

JOHN WILEY & SONS, New York • London • Sydney • Toronto

This publication is designed to provide accurate and
authoritative information in regard to the subject
matter covered. It is sold with the understanding that
the publisher is not engaged in rendering legal, accounting, or other professional service. If legal advice or
other expert assistance is required, the services of a
competent professional person should be sought.

*From a Declaration of Principles jointly adopted by a
Committee of the American Bar Association and a Committee
of Publishers.*

Library of Congress Cataloging in Publication Data

Clifton, David S.
  Project feasibility analysis.

  "A Wiley-Interscience publication."
  Includes bibliographies and index.
  1. Industrial project management 2. Capital investments.
3. Marketing research. I. Fyffe, David E.,
joint author. II. Title.
HD47.5.C57   658.4'04   76–51321
ISBN 0–471–01611–X

Printed in the United States of America

10 9 8 7 6 5 4 3 2 1

To

Karen, Derek, and Mark
Opal, Larry, and Stephen
and
Jennifer Ann

PREFACE

Our interest in the subject of project feasibility analysis arises from experience in the preparation of many such studies for potential entrepreneurs, growing companies, and local development organizations by the staff of the Economic Development Laboratory, Georgia Institute of Technology, and from training activities conducted jointly with organizations in developing countries. We know that the preparation of a good project feasibility analysis is not an easy task and that the consequences of inadequate analysis are costly to individuals and businesses. Each year Dun and Bradstreet publishes reports of business failures.[1] The prospect for a new business venture is not encouraging, and 16 out of 17 companies fail. Many of them should never have been started and probably would not have been if a thorough feasibility analysis had been made.

This book attempts to present a step-by-step approach for the preparation of project feasibility studies. The business person or entrepreneur, the industrial development planner, and the loan officer have a common interest in one or more of the following questions:

- Is the proposed project financially profitable?
- How does the proposed investment appear when evaluated from the viewpoint of society?
- Does the proposed management have the necessary capabilities?

The process of project analysis presented in this book is a methodology, although not the only methodology possible, which provides answers to these questions.

[1] *The Business Failure Record, Monthly Business Failures, Quarterly Failure Report* (New York: Dun and Bradstreet, Inc.).

The book is addressed specifically to the business person, the entrepreneur, the industrial development professional, and, to a somewhat lesser extent, the loan officer who must pass judgment on investment proposals.

For the entrepreneur, this manual will help ensure thoroughness in evaluating the financial feasibility of his venture idea. Too frequently he becomes "super-committed" and loses much of his analytical objectivity. He may in fact seek only information favorable to his project and avoid negative data. According to loan officers, entrepreneurs frequently approach them with requests for funds and little except their own enthusiasm to support the request. The procedures presented in this book will result in an objective analysis and a well-documented investment proposal.

The importance of the industrial sector in economic development is widely recognized. Because of this importance, most countries have various organizations that provide development assistance. Among other activities, these organizations (1) attempt to identify and analyze opportunities for new industrial ventures and (2) provide assistance to entrepreneurs in the analysis of venture ideas and preparation of investment proposals for projects that appear to be feasible. While the primary objective of the entrepreneur or business person may be profit, the industrial development professional is likely to have multiple objectives. In addition to the commercial profitability of the business, he may wish to analyze investment alternatives with respect to characteristics such as the generation of employment, support of existing or planned industry, upgrading of employment opportunities, or the amount of foreign exchange saved. The book should be useful to these professionals.

Finally, the loan officer who must appraise investment proposals and pass judgment on their commerical worthiness also will find the book useful. Loan officers of both commercial and governmental lending institutions usually specify the information they require in order to analyze and appraise an investment proposal. Often the loan officer becomes directly involved with the business person in his efforts to obtain the necessary information for the investment proposal or loan application. In some instances the loan officer is also assigned the task of preparing an independent analysis.

Chapter 1 provides an overview of the process of project analysis, and Chapter 2 covers the generation and screening of venture ideas. Chapters 3, 4, and 5 deal with the elements that comprise the economic feasibility study—market analysis, technical analysis, and financial analysis. Chapter 6 presents a case study feasibility analysis. The discussion of social profitability analysis in Chapter 7 reviews items that are pertinent from a social viewpoint. Chapter 8 is concerned with financing the project and the preparation of the investment proposal, the document presented to the lending institution. The investment proposal includes the economic feasibility study or, in most instances, excerpts from it, as well as a statement of management capabilities.

The business person who wants to examine the economic feasibility of expansion (perhaps an addition to the product line or a new plant capacity) will find Chapters 3, 4, and 5 useful. If financing is being sought, Chapter 8 will be a helpful guide. These same chapters will assist the entrepreneur in evaluating the feasibility of a proposed new venture. In addition, he may be interested in the suggestions for the generation and screening of venture ideas discussed in Chapter 2.

The planner or industrial development specialist seeking to identify industrial opportunities for a specific region will find Chapter 2 helpful. If the planner is attempting to attract potential investors to the area, he probably will prepare economic feasibility studies, the techniques of which are covered in Chapters 3, 4, and 5. To complete the analysis, the planner will want to consider potential investments from the social viewpoint which is discussed in Chapter 7.

Loan officers will be concerned with the discussion of investment proposals in Chapter 8. Chapters 3, 4, and 5 will be of interest to them as well, since a thorough understanding of the techniques used and the assumptions made in the preparation of the information presented in the investment proposal is essential to appraise it properly. For government loan officers, Chapter 7, on social profitability, discusses the necessary techniques to determine if the project is in the best interest of the nation.

We should like to point out that most users of this book are not likely to perform all the steps of the market analysis, technical analysis, and financial analysis in the detailed manner described in Chapters 3 through 5. The amount of effort and detail that can be justified depends on the project size, the technological newness and complexity of the product, the number of technological alternatives, and the desired accuracy of cost estimates.

Some highly valued assistance was received in the preparation of this book. We are particularly grateful to the Institute for Small-Scale Industries at the University of the Philippines for permission to use the Clare Garments case, and we deeply appreciate the consent of Dr. Tze I. Chiang and the Economic Development Laboratory at the Georgia Institute of Technology to our use of the feasibility analysis of thermomechanical pulp mills in the Coastal Plains region of the United States. Finally, the initial notes on which this book is based stem from work done under an institutional grant from the U.S. Agency for International Development to the Georgia Institute of Technology. The authors take full responsibility for the statements and views contained herein, however, and they do not necessarily reflect the policies or positions of the Agency for International Development or the U.S. government.

DAVID S. CLIFTON, JR.
DAVID E. FYFFE

Atlanta, Georgia
October 1976

CONTENTS

Chapter One

OVERVIEW OF THE PROCESS FOR

PROJECT FEASIBILITY ANALYSIS

The term *"project,"* for our purposes, means the establishment of a new enterprise or the introduction of something new into an existing product mix. A project can encompass a wide range of possibilities, from a single piece of machinery to an entire plant. Project feasibility analysis, then, may involve an examination of the feasibility of a new business venture, major modifications of existing products, or product-line acquisitions.

Although the term "analyst" is used in the text in reference to the individual conducting the project feasibility study, in reality, the individual conducting the study is an entrepreneur, investor, professional industrial developer, planner, or loan officer. In fact, the text is oriented primarily to the entrepreneur who wants to evaluate a new business venture, which is the most difficult type of project to analyze.

A project feasibility analysis comprises a market analysis, technical analysis, financial analysis, and social profitability analysis. Frequently, the analyst is interested only in the commercial profitability and thus examines only the market, technical, and financial aspects of the project; the resulting study is referred to as an "economic feasibility study."

THE NATURE OF PROJECT FEASIBILITY ANALYSIS

In the broadest sense, every rational decision to make a new investment is

1

preceded by an investigation of the feasibility of the project, whether or not this is carried out in a formal manner. The larger the project and the greater the investment, the more formalized the investigation. Assurance is needed that the market exists or can be developed, that raw materials can be obtained, that sufficient labor supply is available, that local services vital to the project are at hand, and that the overall costs for plant equipment, labor, and raw material inputs will be of a certain order. Most importantly, it must be determined that income will exceed costs by a margin sufficient to make the project financially attractive.

However, if the project is small, the study format may be quite informal. Perhaps there will be no formal study at all and little accumulation of actual data. Nonetheless, the feasibility calculations will have to be computed and evaluated, even if in an informal manner, before the ultimate step of actual investment is taken.

STAGES OF PROJECT FEASIBILITY ANALYSIS

The analysis of a project involves a certain number of stages[1] during which its various elements are prepared and examined in order to reach decisions. The preparation of a project therefore can be seen as a series of activities culminating in the establishment of a certain number of studies and documents which permit decision making.

Project feasibility analysis is conducted in a given institutional frame which determines its nature and the number of economic agencies likely to be interested in it. Thus the nature and sequence of decisions concerning viability of the project and its financing are determined by various institutional policies as well as company objectives. Also, the range and accuracy of information necessary for decision making during different stages of a project depend on its inherent characteristics, such as size, degree of complexity, and risk. Therefore any attempt to describe a typical procedure for feasibility analysis must be general, because the decisions to be made and the information required vary among companies, institutions, and types of projects.

The process of project feasibility analysis, following the determination of the objective to be attained, can be divided into stages and steps. Figure 1.1 illustrates the main stages and the corresponding flow of types of studies needed to evaluate the project. For the purpose of clarity in presentation, no

[1] Adapted from United Nations Industrial Development Organization, "The Stages of Preparation and Implementation of Industrial Projects," *Industrialization and Productivity*, Bulletin No. 19 (New York, 1973).

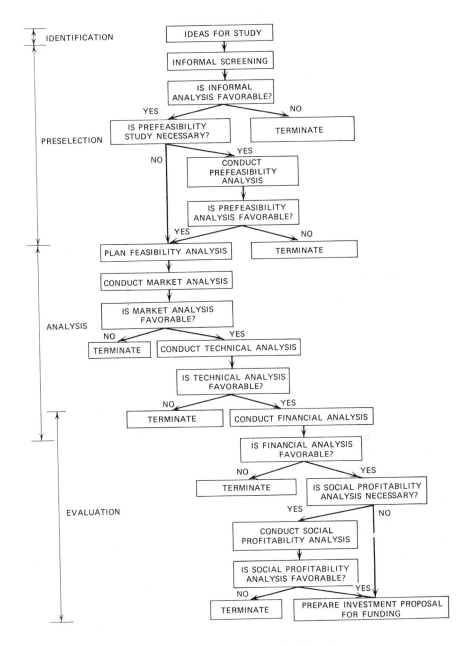

Figure 1.1 Project feasibility analysis flow chart.

3

feedback loops are shown on the feasibility analysis flowchart. For example, if the market analysis is unfavorable, the data may indicate that the objectives of the study should be redefined (i.e., redefine the product) rather than terminate the project.

Also, the feasibility analysis flowchart indicates that the market, technical, and other studies should be conducted in a certain order which is not always applicable. For example, a study of the feasibility of manufacturing charcoal indicated production in excess of consumption in the market area. The project analysis was not terminated, however, because information from the technical study being conducted simultaneously showed that, with modern charcoal technology, it was possible to penetrate the region's charcoal market through lower costs.

Before examining the stages of a project feasibility analysis, it should be emphasized that this method and the accompanying studies discussed below are suggested formats, since no standards exist. Every feasibility analysis is different, tailored to the subject area as well as to the potential audience. However, the basic documents usually necessary for project analysis have been identified. The nature of a given project may dictate that one or more of these documents be given more emphasis or be omitted.

IDENTIFICATION STAGE

The starting point of a project analysis is the establishment of the objective to be attained. This objective may be to prove that it is possible and desirable to add a piece of equipment to the existing plant, to manufacture a certain product or group of products, or to utilize certain resources.

Ideas for new products or diversification for a company can be generated in an informal and spontaneous manner from customers, distributors, competitors, salespeople, and others, or the entrepreneur can rely on a systematic process of idea generation.

For the planner, the product idea is more likely to stem from a survey of existing industry, sectoral, or interindustrial analysis, area resource surveys, or market studies. The proposed project may develop as a response to a need that appeared within the framework of industrial development planning.

PRESELECTION STAGE

In the preselection stage, a decision must be made as to whether it is advisable to examine in detail the feasibility of the project and, if so, to define the scope and estimate the cost of subsequent studies. Both the entrepreneur and planner want to ensure that the project is of sufficient interest in the technical-economic plane to justify an in-depth study, that is, that a feasible solution can be anticipated. Also, the entrepreneur wants to eliminate from further consideration ideas that are dissonant with either company objectives or resources. Likewise, the planner needs to ensure that the project conforms with the objectives of governmental strategy and plans. The information gathered during this stage assists in the identification of those aspects of the project that deserve special attention during subsequent research (e.g., market surveys, machinery evaluation).

The results obtained during the preselection stage are often compiled into a prefeasibility study. To permit decisions on the merit of the project, the prefeasibility study should include:

1. A description of the market (estimate of consumption, trends, present supply, price).
2. An outline of manufacturing processes and information concerning availability of main production factors (mainly raw materials).
3. An estimate of necessary investment and cost of operation.
4. An approximate estimate of profit.
5. Statement of anticipated major problems and risks.

ANALYSIS STAGE

At the analysis stage, the various alternatives in marketing, technology, and other considerations must be studied, and the findings, with supporting data, presented in a systematic form. For a particular project, there may be more than one possible technology to evaluate, and such factors as plant size, capital availability, raw materials availability, and labor skills and availability need to be considered.

The analysis of the feasibility of a project can be conducted at different levels of effort with respect to time, budget, and personnel, depending on the circumstances. A complete study contains a market, technical, and financial analysis and is referred to as an economic feasibility study. In some cases, such a detailed study is not necessary. For example, if the project's output has a confirmed buyer, then an in-depth market analysis is not required. In some instances, a partial study of the market or of the technologies satisfies the data requirements for decision making.

To permit a decision on the merit of the project, the project feasibility analysis should include the following studies.

Market Analysis

During the process of project feasibility analysis, market studies can be made separately or as a segment of the overall economic feasibility study. Market analysis can serve as a method for screening venture ideas and also as a means of evaluating a project's feasibility in terms of the market. In each of these instances, the market analysis involves the search for and analysis of data that can be used to identify, isolate, describe, and quantify the market. The basic difference in these market studies is that those conducted during the evaluation require a more extensive effort and in-depth analysis than those used for screening. A market analysis generally should contain:

1. A brief description of the market, including the market area, methods of transportation, existing rates of transportation, channels of distribution, and general trade practices.
2. Analysis of past and present demand including determination of quantity and value of consumption, as well as identification of the major consumers of the product.
3. Analysis of past and present supply broken down as to source (whether imported or domestic), as well as information which will assist in determining the competitive position of the product, such as selling prices, quality, and marketing practices of competitors.
4. Estimate of future demand for the product.
5. Estimate of the project's share of the market, considering the demand, supply, competitive position, and the project's marketing program.

Technical Analysis

The technical analysis of a project feasibility study serves to establish whether or not the project is technically feasible, and it also provides a basis for cost estimating. Equally important, it provides an opportunity to consider the effect of various technical alternatives on employment, ecology, infrastructure demands, capital services, support of other industries, balance of payments, and other factors. The technical analysis should contain a review of techniques or processes to be applied and should incorporate:

1. Description of the product, including specifications relating to its physical, mechanical, and chemical properties, as well as the uses of the product.
2. Description of the selected manufacturing process, showing detailed flow charts as well as presentations of alternative processes considered and justification for adopting the one selected.

3. Determination of plant size and production schedule, which includes the expected volume for a given time period, considering start-up and technical factors.
4. Selection of machinery and equipment, including specifications, equipment to be purchased and origin, quotations from suppliers, delivery dates, terms of payment, and a comparative analysis of alternatives in terms of cost, reliability, performance, and spare parts availability.
5. Identification of the plant's location and assessment of its desirability in terms of distance from raw materials sources and markets. For a new project, this part may include a comparative study of different sites, indicating the advantages and disadvantages of each.
6. Design of a plant layout and estimation of the costs of erection of the proposed types of buildings and land improvements.
7. Study of the availability of raw materials and utilities, including a description of physical and chemical properties, quantities needed, current and prospective costs, terms of payment, locations of sources of supply, and continuity of supply.
8. Estimate of labor requirements, including a detailed breakdown of the direct and indirect labor and supervision required for the manufacture of the product.
9. Determination of the type and quantity of waste to be disposed of, along with a description of the waste disposal method, its costs, and necessary clearance from proper authorities.
10. Estimate of the production cost for the product.

Financial Analysis

During the financial analysis of a project feasibility study the emphasis is on the preparation of financial statements, so that the project can be evaluated in terms of various measures of commercial profitability and the magnitude of financing required can be determined. The financial analysis requires the assembly of the market and the technical cost estimates into various pro forma statements. If more information on which to base an investment decision is needed, a sensitivity analysis or, possibly, a risk analysis can be conducted. The financial analysis should include:

1. For existing companies, audited financial statements such as balance sheets, income statements, and cash flow statements.
2. For projects that involve new companies, statements of total project cost, initial capital requirements, and cash flows relative to the project timetable.

3. For all projects, financial projections for future time periods, including income statements, cash flows, and balance sheets.
4. For all projects, supporting schedules for financial projections, stating assumptions used as to collection period of sales, inventory levels, payment period of purchases and expenses, and elements of production cost, selling, administrative, and financial expenses.
5. For all projects, financial analyses showing return on investment, return on equity, break-even volume, and price analysis.
6. For all projects, if necessary, a sensitivity analysis to identify items that have a large impact on profitability, or possibly a risk analysis.

EVALUATION AND DECISION STAGE

Decisions as to whether the project will be implemented must be made at this stage. For the entrepreneur, the studies conducted during the analysis stage of the project provide an assessment. If positive results are obtained, the entrepreneur, if seeking financing, will want to prepare an investment proposal. The planner or government official, however, having obtained positive conclusions from the economic feasibility study, will want to evaluate the project's social profitability. If an order of national development priorities exists, the project must be quantitatively assessed in terms of its social profitability. Finally, the investment proposal must be prepared and submitted to the lending institution and, in some instances, to the government body on whose approval execution of the project depends.

Social Profitability Analysis

The social profitability analysis, that is, an evaluation of a project's contribution to the economy, is primarily the concern of the government loan officer or planner. The techniques used to determine social profitability range from the very simple to the complex. In developing countries, the analysis often contains no more than an estimate of the project's employment impact or net foreign exchange benefits. To obtain an in-depth assessment of the social profitability, a cost-benefit analysis may be the desired approach. This involves:

1. Definition of the project in terms of technical description, alternatives that should be considered, and any pertinent constraints.
2. Enumeration of costs and benefits and an assessment of the validity and quantifiability of the listed costs and benefits.
3. Collection of the data needed to evaluate the costs and benefits.

4. Measurement of the costs and benefits of the project.
5. Presentation of results.

Investment Proposal

The purpose of the investment proposal or loan application is to convince a lender that the project is a desirable investment. This implies that it not only possesses the potential for profit, but that the proposed management team has the capabilities to achieve that potential. The investment proposal normally contains:

1. General information on the product, company history, nature of the industry, type of organization, organizational chart, and the reputation and qualifications of the existing or proposed management.
2. Description of the project, which usually consists of extracts from the economic feasibility study and includes information on such items as markets, production, selected manufacturing method (with detailed indication of the cost of equipment and operational expense), and financial statements.
3. Miscellaneous information, such as proposals concerning guarantees to be offered to a lending institution, steps taken and formalities completed toward implementation of the project, and technical partners envisaged or selected.

PROJECT IMPLEMENTATION STAGES

This text is concerned only with project feasibility analysis and does not deal with project implementation. However, the stages of project implementation are contracting, project designing, selection of materials, and construction.

Contracting

Methods of implementation, at this stage of the project, must be defined as contracts. Negotiations must be conducted with lending institutions on types of financing, with governments on possible site and fiscal incentives and, possibly, with a consulting engineering company concerning technical supervision. Negotiations with suppliers of materials and technical know-how are also important. Bids must be evaluated, technical and commercial conditions fixed, and the necessary contracts signed.

Project Designing and Construction

Industrial installation must conform with technical specifications and time schedules specified in the contract. Contract specifications should cover various activities such as preparation of plans and detailed technical studies, construction drawings, site development, construction work, deliveries, erection, tracts, and so forth. It should be noted that the drawing up of contracts does not always precede the preparation of plans and construction.

BIBLIOGRAPHY

Agency for International Development, Office of Engineering. *Engineering, Feasibility Studies, Economic and Technical Soundness Analysis, Capital Projects.* Washington, D.C., October 1964.

Cassell, Robert B. "Research for Industrial Development," in *Guide to Industrial Development,* ed. Dick Howard. Englewood Cliffs, N.J.: Prentice-Hall, 1972.

United Nations. "The Stages of Preparation and Implementation of Industrial Projects," *Industrialization and Productivity,* Bulletin No. 19. New York, 1973.

University of the Philippines, Institute for Small-Scale Industries. "Format for Project Feasibility Study." Quezon City, Philippines. n.d.

Chapter Two

GENERATION AND SCREENING OF

VENTURE IDEAS

The search for a potentially profitable product is a first step toward a successful venture. In fact, there are many examples to indicate that the product idea is the single most important factor in business success. After studying business successes and failures, Murphy[1] concluded that the "golden key" to success is, *"Get in the right business at the right time."*

The advice is simple; the accomplishment is not. Very few ideas result in successful business ventures. Even when introduced by well-established firms, new products frequently fail. *Business Week* magazine,[2] in a discussion of information supplied by A. T. Kearney, Inc., emphasizes the risks in product innovation.

> If a company brings out the ultimate in innovation, a new product in a new market, Kearney rates its chances at only 1 in 20. This might be the first blender for home use, say. Next on the Kearney scale is an old product moving into a new market—the home blender offered in the hospital field, for instance. Its chances are 1 in 4. A new product entering an old market has 1 chance in 2. This could be a home blender five times as fast as anything else on the market. Finally, there is the old or "me-too" product introduced in an old market. It has slightly less than 1 chance in 1.

It is quite likely that the entrepreneur already has a product idea in mind.

[1] Thomas P. Murphy, *A Business of Your Own, How to Select, Finance and Start It Successfully* (New York: McGraw-Hill, 1956), p. 4.
[2] "The Breakdown of U.S. Innovation," *Business Week*, Feb. 16, 1976, pp. 56–68.

11

In fact, his product idea may be responsible for the decision to strike out on his own in a business venture. Understandably, he may be so convinced of the merits of his idea that he fails to assess its potential objectively. Many new businesses fail for just this reason. Realistically, we can expect that most venture ideas will be eliminated by preliminary screening and that most of those remaining will fail to survive a careful feasibility analysis. In order to increase the likelihood of finding a successful product idea, as many candidates as possible should be considered. Those that appear most promising must then be subjected to a more detailed feasibility analysis. In the remainder of this chapter we discuss systematic approaches to product idea generation and methods to eliminate from further consideration ideas that have the least chance for success.

PRODUCT SELECTION CRITERIA

Before considering the matter of how to find venture ideas, it may be useful to examine some necessary requirements for a successful product. First and foremost, the new venture must compete favorably in its market in order to survive. It follows, then, that in the search for venture ideas both the entrepreneur and the industrial developer are looking for a product that meets one of the following criteria.

1. *The product serves a presently unserved need.* This situation may arise because heretofore (a) no one knew how to make a product to fulfill the need, (b) the need had been unrecognized and undeveloped, or (c) the need did not exist. Many new products and services fall into one of these three categories. The need for a small, hand-held calculator, for example, existed long before technology became available to provide it; and its sales have exceeded the most optimistic estimates of its producers. Similarly, needs related to health and medicine are now being met by products which, until the advent of recent technology, were impossible (e.g., pacemakers, artificial joints). The Water Pik, on the other hand, is an example of a product that was conceived as an answer to a need not recognized by the general public. Its acceptance has resulted from successful efforts to make the public *conscious* of a need. Obviously, both product development and market development are required. The risks are great and so is the potential for profit.

2. *The product serves an existing market in which demand exceeds supply.* That is, the product competes with similar or like products in a market where existing producers cannot serve the entire demand. In this situation, exist-

ing producers normally increase output to meet the demand unless certain factors (e.g., capacity, raw material availability) prevent such action. Therefore the reasons for apparent shortages must always be understood before a decision is made to start a new venture in the industry. A few years ago, for example, a Georgia entrepreneur was convinced that he had found a fantastic venture opportunity. Railroad ties for the construction of industrial sidings were in short supply, and their price was at least triple what it had been a year earlier. He priced the necessary production equipment and found the investment could be recovered in about 2 years. What he had not discovered, however, was that the railroad tie shortage had arisen because lumber was being drawn to an unusually high construction market. This market subsided within 9 months, and railroad ties returned to their previous price level.

3. *The product can successfully compete with existing similar products because of an "advantageous situation" such as one of the following.*

  - *Improved design.* Design innovation resulting in special features, improved performance, lower costs, better appearance, improved quality, or reliability may provide a competitive advantage.
  - *Lower price.* The ability to underprice competitive products and still make a profit depends on cost advantages in production, distribution, and/or selling. Such cost advantages may arise from input materials costs, labor costs, tax advantages, transportation costs, capital costs, or process innovations. In addition, cost advantage may be provided by government intervention through protective tariffs. This is frequently the case when the market is being served by imported products.

These criteria may serve both as a guide in the search for venture ideas and as a preliminary screen to indicate potential for success.

VENTURE IDEA GENERATION

Since good venture ideas are the "golden key" to success, we can expect them to be elusive. There are those who claim that good product ideas are the province of great research organizations and that the day of the entrepreneur is over. The many successful small businesses in every community provide obvious proof that this is not true. The entrepreneur is not looking for a technological breakthrough. He is looking for a situation in which he can invest capital and talent for profit and personal benefits. There are many alternatives that may serve his objectives and, the more ideas generated, the more likely he is to find one that will lead to success.

The important question is, "How can venture opportunities be identified?" Karger and Murdick[3] suggest two key approaches as follows.

(1) Look for a need and then the product to satisfy that need, or

(2) Find a product idea and then determine the extent of the need.

In the following sections we examine checklists which may be helpful in each of these two approaches. As you will see, it is not always possible to separate them completely.

Looking for a Need

Venture ideas can be stimulated by information which indicates possible need. This approach requires access to data and considerable analysis. However, if the perceived need is real, the product idea has a better than average chance of leading to a successful venture.

The need may be one now being served inefficiently at high cost, or it may be presently unserved. The first implies an obvious product. The second implies that a considerable amount of creative design and development may be required to arrive at a product that appears to satisfy the need.

Study Existing Industries. Many states and municipalities publish manufacturing directories which provide complete information on each manufacturer. Typical information given for each firm includes name, address, date established, officers, products manufactured, and number of employees. Listings are made by geographic area, municipality, and product Standard Industrial Classification (SIC) number. These directories are available from state development agencies or at large local libraries. These lists may be analyzed to suggest:

- Needs not presently met by local industry (i.e., products not produced). There may be justifiable reasons why certain products are not produced. However, it also may be that the basis for these reasons has changed and that you will be the first to recognize these changes.
- Inadequately served markets (i.e., inappropriately few manufacturers of a product for which demand should be high).
- Support needs (i.e., subcontracting of components, tooling, and services). Can any of these be supplied at a lower cost than at present?

[3] Delmar W. Karger and Robert G. Murdick, *New Product Venture Management* (New York: Gordon and Breach, 1972).

Examine Input Needs and Output of Existing Industries. Manufacturing directories also may be used to study input needs of existing industries. Opportunities may exist when:

- Materials, purchased components, or supplies are presently obtained from distant sources with attendant long lead times and high transportation costs.
- Specialized components that are common to several firms and now produced internally by each firm could be supplied at lower cost by a single producer because of economies of scale.

In addition, the outputs of existing industries and agriculture may be studied for venture opportunities based on further processing of product output or processing of wastes. The latter may provide particularly attractive opportunities, for it is indeed true that, "One man's trash is another man's treasure." Moreover, economic and technological changes may cause an idea that was previously unprofitable or impossible to be a prime candidate for a successful venture. How many millions of tons of sawdust, shavings, and wood scrap were burned before technology and economic pressure provided impetus for their use in particleboard, fireplace logs, pulp, and other products?

Analyze Population Trends and Demographic Data. The need for various types of products may be projected by studying population age shifts. It is possible, for example, to trace the economic effects of the "baby boom" of the 1940s, progressing from the growth in youth-oriented markets (toys, school-related products, youth clothing, etc.) to the unprecedented expansion of household-oriented markets (home furnishings, etc.) in the 1960s. Population age shifts should be carefully studied to determine how they will affect markets.

Study Development Plans and Consult Development Agencies. Industrial development organizations are busy in virtually every state, region, and locality, attempting to plan for and expedite industrial and economic growth. They analyze the available resources and shortcomings of their areas in terms of industrial development needs and identify venture opportunities. These organizations may have already conducted prefeasibility studies on various venture ideas. They generally are ready and willing to assist the potential entrepreneur with further technical and financial analysis, advice during proposal preparation, and the search for financing of the venture.

Examine Economic Trends. Changing economic conditions may create new public needs which can provide business opportunities. During the past two decades, for example, the public has become very aware of the value of time. As a result, demand for prepared food items, microwave ovens, and other time-saving products has increased greatly. More recently, rapid inflation has reduced the discretionary purchasing power of most families. Businesses that recycle, repair, or maintain are expanding. In the future, it is virtually certain that the squeeze will be on material resources. There has been a startling awakening to the rather obvious fact that we are using the earth's finite resources at a very rapid rate and that the end for some of them is easily within the lifetime of the earth's present inhabitants. The result is a scramble for products that are material- or energy-conserving. Old ideas for energy generation and conservation (e.g., wind-powered electric generators and flywheel energy storage systems) are being re-evaluated and new developments being pushed.

Information which may serve to stimulate ideas can be found every day in newspapers, business periodicals, trade publications, and technical journals.

Analyze Social Changes.   Every society undergoes continuous social evolution, with resulting changes in social values. In the United States, for example, changes have taken place in the perception of individual importance and self-awareness. There is a very apparent desire for leisure and recreational activities. The market for recreational vehicles, camping equipment, and other recreational products has been on the increase.

Over the past decade crimes against both persons and property have increased markedly. As a result there are new markets for such products as guard dog services, attack repellents, burglar alarms, and security locks. A specific example is the fake package of currency now commonly used in many banks to foil bank robbers. This device was developed by an entrepreneur who observed the need. With the assistance of the Engineering Experiment Station at Georgia Tech, he developed a device which, when activated as it passes through the bank exit, explodes after a 1-minute time delay. The device is placed in a fake package of currency in each teller's cash drawer. It is effective, and the entrepreneur is looking for other ideas.

Study the Effects of New Legislation.   Whether we like it or not, the fact is that government controls affect existing businesses and often create opportunities for new ventures. Examples of such legislation can be found in the areas of environmental controls, consumer protection, health, safety, and employee rights. The legislation may place requirements on existing companies which, because of economies of scale, can be more economically performed by newly established enterprises which provide the needed service or product to several affected firms. For the most part, needs arising because of government controls are service-oriented and require professional skills. Venture ideas and venture success depend heavily on a knowledge of operations in the affected industries.

Finding a Product

Each of the preceding suggestions for idea generation centers on the recognition of a *need* in order to arrive at a product idea. The suggestions that follow are product-oriented. They are intended to stimulate product ideas which may meet one or more of the criteria previously discussed. Their use should result in a large number of ideas which can be subsequently examined with regard to need. Very likely only a few will survive a preliminary screening. However, it is logical that, the more ideas generated, the better chance that there will be a few good ones. The following list should be useful to both the entrepreneur and the industrial development professional.

Investigate Local Materials and Other Resources. A good place to start any search for product ideas is an inventory of native resources. It is characteristic of developing regions that local resources are exported for processing. The region thus loses a valuable commodity and gains only a relatively small return. The benefits of employment and added value are, in effect, exported with the resource. If local materials are presently being shipped to distant plants for processing, it is likely that the local market, at least, can be served more economically by a local processing plant.

If local raw materials are not being utilized, study possibilities of applying new technology to produce new products. Scientific advances and new technology always create new opportunities for industrial projects.

Complete information concerning natural resources and how they are being exploited can be obtained from state and federal government agencies.

Examine Import Substitutions. Local manufacture of goods that are presently imported is attractive for several reasons:

- Generates employment.
- Keeps capital at home and thus improves the balance of payments.
- Provides markets for supportive goods and services.
- Increases the local industrial base.

Also, if local raw material resources are available, locally produced goods may be lower in cost than imports, since transportation costs are avoided.

The term "import" is usually applied to goods brought in from outside the country. These reasons therefore may appear to apply only to a developing nation. However, in a manner similar to developing nations, developing regions in every country import goods and have regional balance-of-payments problems. The benefits of local production listed above are applicable to any region. They may not have the same importance in a highly industrialized section of the nation, but they are certainly valid for a great many regions of the country which are still working to strengthen their industrial base.

Study Local Skills. The skills of local artisans may suggest products which could be profitably produced. This is particularly true in less developed nations and regions where surplus labor exists and handicraft skills have survived. The major markets for handicraft products are the export and tourist markets. Both bring outside dollars into the region.

Study Implications of New Technology. Advances in technology in any field often have applications for many products. Probably the most publicized examples are space-age electronics and the related technology in digital computers. Many examples of products resulting from advanced technology (e.g., calculators, digital watches, communications equipment) seem to indicate that such products are only for large corporations which can afford to invest large sums of money in development and marketing. However, this is not the case. Many small companies have been initiated by technically competent entrepreneurs (often former employees of the large corporations that developed the technology), which have carved out a special segment of the market. The key seems to be the identification of a product application not presently being served by any of the so-called giants, that is, gaps in product lines.

In addition to the opportunity to enter directly into the field, opportunities also may exist to utilize advanced technology products to improve old products or to create new ones. Semiconductor technology, which is the basis for most of the new electronic products, is becoming increasingly less expensive. What are the possible applications?

Use Industry Lists. Industry lists such as the Standard Industrial Classification of the United Nations may serve as helpful checklists to stimulate ideas and avoid overlooking a product idea. As noted previously, many states publish directories of manufacturers, which list all companies by location and SIC number. Some suggestions for using these lists to generate product ideas based on needs have already been discussed. In addition, industry lists may be used to stimulate ideas for product innovation.

Much has been written concerning methods to stimulate individual creativity in generating new product ideas. Osborn[4] offers a list of questions to stimulate creative ideas for new products. A similar list distributed by Dr. Herb True also is intended to aid the creative process.

MODIFY   Color, shape, sound, odor, motion, meaning.
REARRANGE   Sequence, pace, components, schedule, pattern.
OBVIOUS   Imitate, transfer, suggestive, copy.
REVERSE   Backward, upside down, direct opposite.
MAGNIFY   Units, action, price, higher, longer, thicker.
REDUCE   Miniature, omit, shorten, split, condense.
SUBSTITUTE   Ingredients, power, process approach.
ADAPT   Outright, related, reborn, new uses.
BASIC WANTS   Personalized, emulate, senses, anticipated.
COMBINE   Blends, units, assortments, ensembles, ideas.

Attend Trade Shows and Inventors' Expositions.   Industry trade associations introduce the latest and most advanced products to the trade at regional and national exhibits. Many of these shows are open to the general public and offer excellent opportunities to look for new product ideas and trends in the industry. The same approach used in the analysis of industry lists can be applied here to stimulate new product ideas.

An annual directory of trade shows, *Exhibits Schedule*, is available from Bill Communications, 633 Third Avenue, New York, New York 10017. Also, the convention bureau of any major city will be happy to provide a list of scheduled trade shows.

Inventors' expositions are also a likely place to obtain product ideas. The U.S. Patent Office holds an Annual Inventor's Day show at which hundreds of inventors display their wares and an "inventor of the year" is named by the Association for the Advancement of Invention and Innovation. Inventors' expositions are also held in many states. Dates and locations may be obtained by writing to the state department of industry and trade.

Published Sources of Ideas.   A large number of publications which may be useful in product idea generation are available at libraries or may be obtained

---

[4] Alex F. Osborn, *Applied Imagination* (3rd rev. ed.; New York: Charles Scribner's Sons, 1963), pp. 286–287.

from publishers. The number of such publications prohibits a detailed discussion of each. However, a partial list of sources is given below.

1. *International New Products Newsletter*, 24 Brockett Place, Marblehead, Mass.
2. *Design News Annual*, Cahners Publishing Co. Inc., 221 Columbus Ave., Boston, Mass. 02116.
3. *New Product News*, Dancer, Fitzgerald, Sample, 347 Madison Ave., New York 10017.
4. *Products List Circular.* Available from Patent Exchange, Inc., 26 Broadway, New York 10004.
5. *Patent Abstract Series*, U.S. Patent Office, Department of Commerce, 2021 Jefferson Davis Highway, Arlington, Va. 22202.
6. *Significant NASA Inventions Available for Licensing in Foreign Countries.* Available from the Superintendent of Documents, U.S. Government Printing Office, Washington, D.C. 20402.

The above checklist of suggestions should be useful to both the entrepreneur and the industrial development professional in the search for venture ideas.

Ideas and the Entrepreneur

Regardless of the approach used to find venture ideas, the entrepreneur must be certain that the final choice is consistent with his own personal interests, objectives, and capabilities. In his advice on "how to tell an opportunity from a millstone," Murphy[5] tells entrepreneurs: "You will find that real opportunity always has these three factors:

1. *It fits you*: Opportunity is personal. It utilizes your abilities, training, and inclinations.
2. *Access*: You must be able to get in. Sometimes this is a matter of licensing, more often a matter of financing.
3. *Potential*: The business must offer the prospect of rapid growth and high return on invested capital."

In order to find venture ideas that "fit," the entrepreneur should start with and be guided by the following self-analysis:

• What part of my present work do I enjoy most?

[5] Murphy, *op. cit.*

- What products and processes do I know most about?
- What hobbies or avocations interest me?
- What are the things that I have always wanted to do if I were not so busy making a living?
- What is my most important objective in a business of my own? Independence? Freedom? Financial gain?
- Which of the ideas generated in response to the first four questions meet the objectives listed in the fifth?

PRELIMINARY SCREENING

By using the preceding checklist, it is possible to develop a long list of potential venture opportunities. Obviously, it would not be realistic to conduct a detailed feasibility analysis or even a prefeasibility analysis for each idea on this list. What is needed is a preliminary screening to eliminate the many ideas that have little or no hope for success and to provide, if possible, a rank-ordering of the remaining few.

The screening can be conducted as a two-phase process. In the first phase venture ideas are eliminated on a go/no-go basis. A "yes" response to any of the following should eliminate the idea from further consideration.

- Are there restrictions, monopolies, shortages, or other causes that make any factors of production unavailable at reasonable cost? (Examples are scarce skills, energy, special materials or equipment, processes, and technology).
- Are the capital requirements excessive? If the project requires large amounts of unavailable capital, there is no point in further consideration.
- Are environmental effects contrary to government regulations or good public relations? (Examples are air pollution, noise, water pollution.)
- Is the project inconsistent with national policies, goals, and restrictions? (Examples are import restrictions, foreign exchange requirements, employment generation, industrialization plan.)
- Is there an effective monopoly in the industry which precludes the entry of new firms—particularly a small firm? If so, stay clear. It takes more than slingshots for modern-day Davids to fight Goliaths.
- Are there factors that preclude effective marketing of the product (e.g., need for an extensive sales and distribution system which you cannot provide)?
- Does the project support existing or planned industry?
- Will the project serve to upgrade employment opportunities, or will it commit human resources to unskilled, low-paid jobs?

Comparative Rating of Product Ideas

After elimination of obviously unattractive venture ideas, it is desirable to choose the best of those remaining for further analysis. Various comparative schemes have been proposed for rating venture ideas. In this section we examine factors that should be considered and some possible ranking methods.

Since most of the available literature deals with success, the analysis of causes of business failures is not well documented. For the most part, business post mortems state the cause of death as "poor management." While this is almost certain to be true, it provides no insight to help screen and compare venture ideas. Hilton[6] provides several short case histories which indicate the following major cases for failure of new product sales to reach a profitable level:

- Product design and development weaknesses.
- Failure to analyze the market realistically and estimate demand.
- Inadequate sales and distribution effort.

The above causes of failure provide only a partial basis for venture idea ratings. Realistically, in order for a product idea to lead to a successful venture, it must meet the following four requirements:

- An adequate *present market*.
- A predicted *growth market* (potential).
- *Competitive costs* of production and distribution.
- *Low risk* in factors related to demand, price, and costs.

A detailed analysis of market, market potential, costs, and risks requires considerable effort and expense which cannot be justified unless the product is a good candidate for a successful venture. At this point a checklist may be useful in making a subjective evaluation of product ideas.

Present Market. The size of the presently available market must provide the prospect of immediate sales volume to support the operation. Sales estimates should not be based solely on an estimate of the number of potential customers and their expected individual capacity to consume. Some factors that affect sales are:

[6] Peter Hilton, *New Product Introduction for Small Business Owners* (Small Business Management Series No. 17; Washington, D.C.: Small Business Administration, 1961).

- Market size (number of potential customers).
- Product's relation to need.
- Strength and dominance of competition.
- Quality-price relationship compared to competitive products.
- Service requirements.
- Availability of sales and distribution systems.
- Sales efforts required.
- Export possibilities.

Market Growth Potential.   There should be a prospect for rapid growth and high return on invested capital. Some indicators are:

- Projected increase in number of potential customers.
- Projected increase in need.
- Increase in customer acceptance.
- Product newness.
- Economic trends (favorable to increasing consumption).
- Social or political trends (favorable to increasing consumption).
- Competitive advantage.

Costs.   The costs of production factors and distribution must permit an acceptable profit when the product is priced competitively. The comparative rating process should consider factors likely to result in costs higher than those of competitive producers:

- Costs of raw material inputs.
- Labor costs.
- Distribution costs (e.g., excessive transportation, handling).
- Selling costs.
- Efficiency of production processes.
- Service, warranty, and customer complaint costs.
- Patents and licenses.

Risks.   Obviously it is impossible to look into the future with certainty, and the willingness to assume risk is the major characteristic that sets the entrepreneur apart. However, unnecessary risk is foolhardy and, while it may be difficult or impossible to predict the future, we can examine, with considerable confidence, the possible effect of unfavorable future events on each of our venture candidates. The following factors should be considered.

- Market stability in economic cycles.
- Technological risks.

- Import competition.
- Size and power of competitors.
- Quality and reliability risks (unproven design).
- Predictability of demand.
- Initial investment costs.
- Vulnerability of inputs (supply and price).
- Legislation and controls.
- Time required to show profit.
- Inventory requirements.
- Seasonal demand.
- Exclusiveness of design.

For purposes of preliminary screening, these factors can be subjectively evaluated. However, comparative rating of product ideas is facilitated by attaching a rating scale to each factor as in Table 2.1. For any given product idea, a rating score for each of the major considerations is obtained by averaging the subfactor ratings. An overall rating may be calculated as the sum of the averages for each major area. However, if any major consideration has a very low value, perhaps the venture idea should be rejected.

THE PREFEASIBILITY STUDY

The preliminary screening may leave several ideas which appear to be worthy of further study. Since a complete feasibility study is time-consuming and expensive, it may be desirable to perform a prefeasibility analysis in order to further screen the possible projects. The purpose of a prefeasibility study is to determine:

- Whether the project seems to justify detailed study.
- What matters deserve special attention in the detailed study (e.g., market analysis, technical feasibility, investment costs).
- An estimate of cost for the detailed study.

The last, while perhaps secondary, is nonetheless important. For many projects, the prefeasibility analysis may provide adequate evidence of venture profitability if certain segments are more carefully verified. With special needs identified, a study plan detailed by task can be constructed, from which personnel requirements, time, and costs can be estimated.

In the prefeasibility study emphasis depends on the nature of the product and the area of greatest doubt. In most cases market aspects and materials

Table 2.1 Comparative Rating of Product Ideas

1. Present market

Factor	10	5	0
• Market size (number of potential customers)	Product has widespread uses. Many prospective customers		Customers restricted to a special class. Few in number
• Product's relation to need	Product always needed. Satisfies basic need		Luxury product, not really needed
• Strength and dominance of competition	Competitors relatively small. Field not crowded		Well established, large competitors dominate the market
• Quality-price relationship	Special product features. Better value than competitive products		Carbon copy of products now on the market
• Service requirements	Product easily serviced. Service system available or easily contracted		Service needs unknown. No service facilities available
• Availability of sales-distribution system	Easily marketed through existing jobbers or wholesalers		Special sales and distribution system required
• Sales effort required	Product will literally sell itself. Repeat sales likely		Intensive sales effort required for every sale

- **Export possibilities**

  10 | Can be exported competitively Large international market
  5 |
  0 | Domestic market only

2. **Market growth potential**

- **Increase in number of potential customers**

  10 | Population trends indicate increasing customer population
  5 |
  0 | Declining customer population

- **Increase in need**

  10 | Projected increase in demand for associated products
  5 |
  0 | Declining demand for associated products

- **Increase in customer acceptance**

  10 | Demand is certain to grow as consumers become acquainted with product
  5 |
  0 | Multiple sales not possible Customer acceptance will have minimal effect on sales

- **Product newness and design protection**

  10 | New product. Can be protected by patent
  5 |
  0 | Difficult to protect. Can be easily copied

- **Economic trends**

  10 | Projected economic trends will increase demand and/or value
  5 |
  0 | Projected economic trends will seriously reduce demand and/or adversely effect costs

- **Social and political trends**

  10 | Trends appear stable and imply an increasing need
  5 |
  0 | Indicators unstable. Social or political changes could produce market decline

	10	5	0
• **Competitive advantage**	High value added. Industry not easily entered. Process innovations easily protected		Low value added. Easy to start new venture in this field

3. Costs

	10	5	0
• **Costs of raw materials**	Ensured supply of raw materials available at stable, low costs		Premium costs for raw materials because of location or availability
• **Labor costs**	Good supply of skilled labor available. Wage rates nominal		High wage-rate area. Will have to outbid present industry for needed skills
• **Distribution costs**	Distribution will not require large inventories and high handling costs. Transportation available		Large stocks must be maintained. Market widely dispersed
• **Selling costs**	Product easily sold with minimal sales effort		Large sales force needed Demand heavily dependent on sales effort
• **Efficiency of production processes**	New processes will provide long-term cost advantage		Processes standard. Competitor's costs unknown—may have a cost advantage

- **Service, warranty, and customer complaint costs**

  10 — Product needs little or no service. Warranty costs low
  5
  0 — Product service will require specially trained personnel Commercial service shops cannot handle

- **Patents and licenses**

  10 — No costs in this area. We hold patents
  5
  0 — License fees required

4. Risks

- **Market stability in economic cycles**

  10 — Market not greatly affected. Product needed in good times and bad
  5
  0 — Demand will drop quickly in bad times

- **Technological risks**

  10 — Technology stable or else product and processes easily modified in response to new technology
  5
  0 — Product locked to present technology. Technological advances are being made rapidly

- **Import competition**

  10 — Product nature precludes imports. No forseeable threat from imports
  5
  0 — Product requires imported raw materials. Labor content high. Easily shipped long distances

- **Size and power of competition**

  10 — No single competitor can affect market share substantially
  5
  0 — Powerful competitors could at any time reduce prices to capture market

Factor	10	5	0
• Quality and reliability	Proven quality and reliability		Product design not fully tested. Reliability unknown
• Predictability of demand	Demand estimates easily and accurately made. Data readily available		No data available for demand estimating. Estimate is largely a guess
• Initial investment costs	Relatively low investment. Can be liquidated at little or no loss		High investment required. Special buildings or machinery can be liquidated only with great loss
• Vulnerability of inputs	Raw materials widely available. No forseeable shortages		Raw materials in short supply and closely controlled
• Legislation and controls	Product does not affect health or environment. No controls likely		Product in area of controversy. Controls pending
• Time required to show profit	Cash flow projections indicate profit in first few months of operation		Profit delayed

29

● **Inventory requirements**

Short distribution chain
Inventory requirements minimal

10			5			0

Long lead times on input material. Customer needs require large finished goods inventories

● **Seasonal demand**

Steady demand in all seasons

10			5			0

Demand highly seasonable. Will not sustain full-time production

● **Exclusiveness of design**

Exclusive design not easily copied or "leapfrogged"

10			5			0

Design innovations easily accomplished. Not easy to maintain design leadership receive primary emphasis. The prefeasibility study may include some or all of the following elements.

1. *Product description.* The product's characteristics should be briefly described, along with possible substitutes which exist in the marketplace. Also, allied products should be identified, which can or should be manufactured with the product under study.
2. *Description of market.* The present and projected potential market and the competitive nature of the market should be delineated.

   - Where is the product now manufactured?
   - How many companies exist and how specialized are they?
   - What are the national production, imports, and exports?
   - Are there government contracts or incentives?
   - What is the estimated consumption?
   - What is the estimated product longevity or future consumption?
   - What is the price structure?

3. *Outline of technological variants.* The technology choices that exist for the manufacture of the product should be described briefly. Also, the key plant location factors should be identified:

   - Labor (quantity, special skills).
   - Proximity to markets and raw materials.
   - Transportation facilities and costs.
   - Water (quantity, quality, restriction).
   - Other (personal preference, competition, tax considerations, environmental controls, and so on).

4. *Availability of main production factors.* Production factors such as raw materials, water, power, fuel, and labor skills should be examined to ensure availability.
5. *Cost estimates.* Estimates should be made of the necessary investment costs and costs of operation.
6. *Estimate of profit.* The data gathered should include estimates of profits of firms manufacturing similar products or, if the preliminary data are extensive, an actual estimated profit for the project under study.
7. *Other data.* In certain cases, the following factors may be the most important in the evaluation of the suitability of a proposed product, especially in the case of the establishment of a new firm.

   - Local attitudes toward industry.
   - Educational, recreational, and civic data.
   - Availability of local sites.

The prefeasibility study can be viewed as a series of steps culminating in a document which permits determination of whether or not a complete detailed feasibility study should be made. It does not possess the depth the detailed study is expected to have, and the data usually are gathered in an informal manner. For example, information may be obtained by the following means.

- Interviews with salespeople.
- Interviews with individuals in government.
- Interviews with purchasers as they are identified.
- Literature search (state directories, census, indexes, association publications).
- Contacts with trade associations.

Since the prefeasibility study is a screening device, it should be discontinued at any point where information is uncovered indicating that the venture idea should be rejected.

BIBLIOGRAPHY

Alexander, Raphael. *Business Pamphlets and Information Sources.* New York: Exceptional Books, 1967.

Allen, Louis L. *Starting and Succeeding in Your Own Small Business.* New York: Grossett and Dunlap, 1968.

Baty, Gordon B. *Entrepreneurship: Playing to Win.* Reston, Va.: Reston Publishing Co., 1974.

Buchele, Robert B. *Business Policy in Growing Firms.* San Francisco: Chandler Publishing Co., 1967.

Cantin, Donald W. *Turn Your Ideas into Money.* New York: Hawthorn Books, Inc., 1972.

Dible, Donald. *Up Your Own Organization.* Santa Clara, Calif.: Entrepreneur Press, 1971.

Donham, Paul. *New Enterprise and Small Business Management.* Homewood, Ill.: Richard D. Irwin, 1959.

Kanopa, Leonard Jesse. *New Products, Assessing Commercial Potential.* New York: American Management Association, 1966.

Karger, Delmar W. *The New Product, How to Find, Test, Develop, Cost, Price, Protect, Advertise, and Sell New Products.* New York: Industrial Press, 1960.

Kaynor, Richard S., and Konrad F. Schultz. *A Practical Guide to Industrial Development.* New York: Praeger, 1967.

Klaasen, L. H. *Methods of Selecting Industries for Depressed Areas.* Paris: Organization for Economic Cooperation and Development, 1967.

Klatt, Lawrence A. *Small Business Management, Essentials of Entrepreneurship.* Belmont, Calif.: Wadsworth, 1973.

Liles, Patrick. *New Business Ventures and the Entrepreneur.* Homewood, Ill.: Richard D. Irwin, 1974.

McGuire, E. Patrick. *Generating New Product Ideas.* New York: The Conference Board, Inc., 1972.

Metcalf, Wendell O. *Starting and Managing a Small Business of Your Own.* Washington, D.C.: Small Business Administration, 1958.

Morrison, Robert. *Manufacturing Entrepreneurs Handbook.* Cleveland: Western Reserve Press, Inc., 1973.

O'Meara, John T., Jr. "Selecting Profitable Products," *Harvard Business Review*, Jan.–Feb., 1961, pp. 83–89.

Pessemier, Edgar A. *New-Product Decisions, an Analytical Approach.* New York: McGraw-Hill, 1972.

Slocum, Donald H. *New Venture Methodology.* New York: American Management Association, Inc., 1972.

Solomon, Morris, J. *Analysis of Projects for Economic Growth—An Operational System for Their Formulation, Evaluation, and Implementation.* New York: Praeger, 1970.

Chapter Three

MARKET ANALYSIS

During the process of project feasibility analysis, market studies can be performed separately or as a segment of the overall economic feasibility study. Market studies can serve as a method for screening venture ideas and also as a means of evaluating a project's feasibility. In each of these instances, the market study involves a search for and analysis of data that can be used to identify, isolate, describe, and quantify the market. The basic difference in these market studies is that those conducted during the evaluation require a more extensive effort and in-depth analysis than those used for screening.

STEPS OF THE MARKET ANALYSIS

The following analysis, conducted in an informal manner, illustrates the type of market information required to evaluate a project's market. A shoemaker located in a small village in a developing country is able to display his product to the local townspeople. He is in constant contact with his customers and can develop his product line in order to satisfy individual needs. The shoemaker, being acquainted with the characteristics of his particular market, can judge the type, size, style, and color of shoes desired by his customers. He then has to determine how many shoes to produce, how many people to hire, and what production equipment is required. He makes these decisions based on his knowledge of the market and his ability to forecast future market needs.

Should the shoemaker decide that he wants to specialize and produce only men's shoes, he will have to measure the size of the market for men's shoes in order to determine the market's potential. Knowing that he cannot sell to the entire market, he will have to determine the size of the segment of the market that he can capture.

The shoemaker's analysis of his market would follow certain steps. First, he would talk to his customers to determine present market size and characteristics. Then, he would project the market based on his knowledge of the village. The market analysis of course increases in complexity for a product with a regional, national, or international market. At these levels, the market is more dynamic and less stable than in the small village, and other factors, such as population movements, personal income changes, and competition, must be given consideration.

In compiling the market data, for whatever size market or type of product, it is helpful to follow an orderly procedure in order to be as efficient as possible. No one procedure for conducting a market study is always the best, but the following represents a general procedure which will be helpful as one attempts to analyze the market. Figure 3.1 outlines the process of market analysis by specifying the main steps involved.

DEFINE THE OBJECTIVES
OF THE STUDY

The initial step in the market component of an economic feasibility study is to set down in writing a preliminary statement of objectives in as much detail as possible. Obviously, the overall objective of the market analysis is to measure and forecast the market to determine if the project will produce the right product at the right time and at the right price. These questions are general, however, and the objectives must be spelled out in more detail if one is to produce a useful analysis. A good procedure is to structure the objectives in question form. When setting objectives, always keep in mind how the information will be used when it is obtained. This helps eliminate objectives that would not make a contribution to the market analysis.

For example, a small manufacturer has developed an improved pump based on a new principle of pumping which appears to offer many advantages over the machinery in use.[1] The new pump can handle a wider range of materials.

---

[1] George F. MacKenzie, "How to Make the Marketing Concept Make Sense," *Industrial Marketing*, March 1960, p. 58.

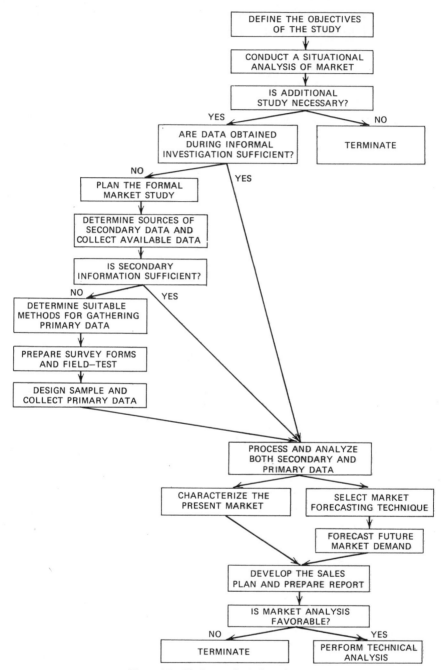

Figure 3.1 Market analysis flow chart.

However, the president of the firm lacks information about where and how to market the new pump. The objectives of the market analysis are to answer the following questions:

- What is the market area?
- What size and capacity pump should be manufactured?
- What models should be offered and to what industries?
- How many can they expect to sell to each industry annually?
- What price will ensure acceptance?
- What channels of distribution will prove most efficient?
- What individuals, by name, will be actual buyers?
- Who are the immediate sales prospects?

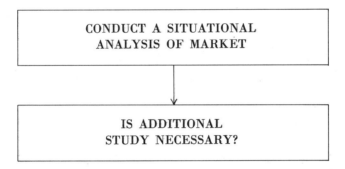

This step involves analyzing the product's relationship to its market by using readily available information. The information reviewed and each question asked will give the project analyst a "feel" for the situation surrounding the product. Since the analyst cannot be an expert on the product and market for every project he researches, this step contributes to his knowledge of the market so that he can conduct an analysis and converse with people using terms familiar to the industry. Involved in this stage is an informal investigation which includes talking to people in wholesale firms and outlets, brokers, competitors, customers, and other individuals in the industry. If the project involves an existing company, examining firm records and questioning people within the firm can assist in this step.

If this informal investigation produces sufficient data to measure the market adequately, the analysis need proceed no further. Also, in some instances, where time is critical or where the budget is a problem, the data gathered during the informal market analysis may be all that is available on which to base decisions. However, a more extensive formal investigation is usually necessary.

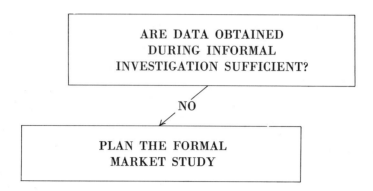

Seldom do the data obtained during the situational analysis answer all the necessary questions. This informal phase of the analysis provides the basis for a revision of the objectives, usually needed, and frequently indicates the most fruitful methods by which the market can be studied. With a precise statement of objectives, it is possible to plan in detail the types of information necessary, the sources from which it is to be gathered and, in general, a comprehensive program of study. This program should include a description of the tasks and methods by which each type of information is to be gathered. It should include not only a work schedule showing the time involved for each task, but also an estimate of costs likely to be incurred. The following project study outline illustrates the work that may be required for the pump manufacturer.

Task 1—Define Product-Market Area

The purpose of this task is to define the characteristics of the pump in such a way as to narrow the scope of the study (e.g., eliminate pumps used in aircraft) and to determine preliminary geographic boundaries for the market.

Task 2—Secondary-Data Search

A search through company files, telephone directories, trade publications, government documents, journals, and other sources is conducted to determine the known or suspected end user, industry groups, their mailing addresses, and the available market data on pumps.

Task 3—Design the Survey Instrument-Tabulation Formats

The purpose of this task is to design a questionnaire and cover letter in order to survey the identified end users. This survey instrument should provide market information to answer the objectives. Tabulation formats are also constructed to ensure that the questionnaire will provide the required data.

Task 4—Field-test the Survey Instrument

The purpose of this task is to test the questionnaire to see that it is understandable and practical and, if not, to incorporate any revisions necessary. A small number of companies is interviewed to fulfill this task.

Task 5—Conduct the Market Survey

The purpose of this task is to gather market data from the identified end users. A mail questionnaire is sent twice, with a period of 2 weeks between mailings.

Task 6—Edit and Tabulate the Returns

The purpose of this task is to aggregate present and future purchase quantities by state, pump specifications, and industry group. Other market data are also prepared, such as plant address, name and position of respondent, present and anticipated purchase of pumps, current delivered cost, supplier's shipping point, pump specifications, and problems with present suppliers.

Task 7—Final Report

The final report contains a statement of objectives, an explanation of marketing research procedures used, a statement of findings limited to the pertinent facts, a brief summary of the conclusions, and an appendix which contains survey forms, statistical tables, and individual plant data.

```
DETERMINE SOURCES OF
SECONDARY DATA AND
COLLECT AVAILABLE DATA
```

Market analysis is mainly a formal search for and analysis of data that will be useful in answering the questions listed as the objectives. The information needed may or may not presently exist. The sources of data available are either primary or secondary. Data that have been collected previously are called secondary data, while data that the analyst must gather for the first time are called primary data. In many instances, neither the research skills nor the budget necessary for collecting and using primary data is available. Heavy reliance is placed on using secondary data in measuring both present and future markets.

Secondary sources are published materials available from company files, libraries, government agencies, universities, trade and professional agencies, and the like. Secondary information sources may provide sufficient data so that the market analysis need proceed no further. If not, new data must be obtained.

Caution should be used when working with secondary information, because it has been prepared by different individuals for many different purposes. According to Kotler, the project analyst should check secondary data for impartiality, validity, and reliability.

Impartiality is a quality not so much of the data as of the person or organization supplying it. The researcher generally can assume that government statistics and the data furnished by the larger commercial organizations are free from any conscious slant or bias. On the other hand, some of the data published by private organizations, such as trade associations and chambers of commerce, may be selected to cast the organization, industry, or area in a favorable light. The issue may not be one of conscious fabrication but of the selection of statistical measures and samples that create a one-sided picture.

Validity raises the question of whether a particular number or series is a relevant measure for the researcher's purposes. A historical series of steel list prices would not be a completely valid measure of the actual prices paid for steel, because the steel market has been characterized by gray prices in different periods. Company data on shipments to various regional warehouses may not be a completely valid measure of sales in each region, because often warehouses transship stock to other regions to meet unanticipated surges in demand.

Reliability raises the question of how precisely sample data reflect the universe from which they are drawn. A randomly drawn sample of 4,000 housewives is likely to give a more accurate picture than a random sample of 400 housewives. Before using reported studies, management should examine the sample size and the degree of precision it implies.[2]

If the market study involves an existing firm, the necessary data may be found in the firm's own records. These records, however, are seldom in a form suitable to meet the needs of the market study, and extensive analysis is often required, if the records are usable at all. Another type of secondary data, commercial information, can be purchased from marketing information firms who collect market data on a continuing basis. A. C. Nielson Company and Market Research Corporation of America are examples of such companies who provide market studies or data to subscribers.

Usually, an analysis of the company's records, if possible, is not very productive, and commercial data are very expensive to obtain unless available at the local library. Fortunately, the analyst has other secondary sources from which to gather data. The availability and type of secondary data vary for different countries. For example, if one were interested in chemical business information sources, a large number of publications not discussed below would be helpful.[3]

The usual practice is to classify most secondary sources of information by type, such as government publications, registration data, buyers' guides, trade directories, trade and professional associations, investment and brokerage firms, university research organizations, and periodicals.[4] For the purpose of this book, however, it seemed more practical to categorize the various types of information one might need in conducting a market analysis and to list the secondary sources most helpful for attaining the information in each category. It is hoped that this format will be more helpful to the analyst. One disadvantage of this method is that some sources of secondary data perhaps should be listed under more than one heading. For example, trade associations are listed under the subject heading "Identifying Customers and Competitors" because through their newsletters and similar publications they are one of the main sources for this type of data. However, trade associations often are able to provide other useful data such as current marketing conditions. Also, the sources

[2] Philip Kotler, *Marketing Management*: Analysis, Planning and Control (2nd ed. © 1972) pp. 315–316. Reprinted by permission of Prentice-Hall, Inc., Englewood Cliffs, New Jersey.
[3] See Barbara Lawrence, "Preliminary Project Evaluation—Any Technologist Can Do It," *Chemtech*, Nov. 1975, pp. 678–681.
[4] For a description of some of these publications, see Harper W. Boyd, Jr., and Ralph Westfall, *Marketing Research: Text and Cases* (3rd ed.; Homewood, Ill.: Richard D. Irwin, 1972) Chap. 6.

listed below deal primarily with information for the United States, but there are comparable data sources for many other countries. In order to become familiar with secondary data sources for another country, one should check the marketing bibliographies.[5]

Price and Cost Data

Prices change quite rapidly in today's economy. Therefore it is often necessary to contact trade associations, manufacturers, or suppliers directly to obtain accurate prices. Some of the published sources of information for items such as the cost of raw materials and competitors' prices are listed below.

- *Commodity Prices: A Source Book and Index*, Paul Wasserman and Diane Kemmerling, compilers (Detroit: Gale Research Co., 1974). Alphabetical list of more than 300 commodities, showing periodicals in which their prices appear and the frequency of publication.
- *Americal Metal Market* (New York: Americal Metal Market). Covers market statistics, production, and prices.
- *Chemical Marketing Reporter* (New York: Schnell Publishing Co.). Price lists for chemicals in large lots, f.o.b. New York. Also articles on subjects such as markets, prices, and mergers.
- *Wholesale Prices and Price Indexes* (Washington, D.C.: U.S. Bureau of Labor Statistics). Monthly report on wholesale price movements, including statistical tables and technical notes.

Historical Consumption, Production, and End Uses

Statistical data on past consumption, production, and end uses are numerous, and those reviewed below represent a selection of the major sources. A thorough literature search will reveal other data sources for the specific product under consideration. For instance, if the product under study were a metal, *Metal Statistics: The Purchasing Guide of the Metal Industry*, which contains a profile, exports, imports, prices, production, sales, and shipment information for metals would be appropriate. Also, although some government publications are shown below, the *American Statistics Index*, discussed later, should be consulted to identify other pertinent government publications.

- *Standard & Poor's Industry Surveys* (New York: McGraw-Hill, Inc.).

[5] See, for example, Gordon Wills (compiler), *Sources of U.K. Marketing Information* (London: Thomas Nelson and Sons, Ltd., 1969).

Limited industry coverage, but in-depth coverage of such areas as general outlook, financial data, composite industry data, market data, and statistical data.

- *Agricultural Statistics*, U.S. Department of Agriculture (Washington D.C.: U.S. Government Printing Office). Contains prices, uses, production, supply, and distribution.
- *Minerals Yearbook*, U.S. Bureau of Mines (Washington D.C.: U.S. Government Printing Office). Contains general discussion and statistical data on production, consumption, and resources.
- *Current Industrial Reports*, U.S. Department of Commerce (Washington D.C.: U.S. Government Printing Office). Reports presenting current industry data on production, shipments, inventories, consumption of materials, exports, and imports for about 5000 manufactured products.
- *Census Reports, Census of Agriculture, Census of Construction Industries, Census of Selected Service Industries, Census of Wholesale Trade, Census of Governments, Census of Housing, Census of Manufactures, Census of Mineral Industries, Census of Transportation*, U.S. Department of Commerce (Washington D.C.: U.S. Government Printing Office). Although the data in these publications are usually several years old, they sometimes constitute the most detailed or the only information available.

Projected Consumption, Production, and End Use

Often projections on consumption, production, and end users are available for the product under study. Such information can be used as a means of checking the analyst's own projections or incorporated into the market analysis as it exists. If the analyst incorporates the data as it exists, he should be sure to examine all assumptions used in making the projections and the date the projections were made.

- *Predicasts* (Cleveland: Predicasts, Inc.). Information for the world is covered in *Worldcasts*. Abstracts of published forecasts in single-line format showing subject, base period data, short- and long-range forecasts, and the reference. Arranged by SIC code with subject guide (e.g., consumption, shipments, production, imports).
- *U.S. Industrial Outlook 1975 with Projections to 1980*, U.S. Department of Commerce (Washington D.C.: U.S. Government Printing Office, 1975). The 1975 edition contains detailed analyses of more than 200 manufacturing and nonmanufacturing industries. Flowcharts show relationships of major industry groups to their suppliers and consumers.

Current Marketing Conditions

Since the market information available is usually out of date, it is necessary to obtain a feel for the current market situation. Trade journals and the publications listed below are sources of such information.

- *F & S Index of Corporations and Industries* (Cleveland: Predicasts, Inc.). Areas outside the United States are covered in *F & S International Index*. Each entry contains a brief description of the contents of the article. Arranged by company and SIC code with subject guide (e.g., organizations, resources and resource use, market information, costs and prices, financial data).
- *Business Periodicals Index* (New York: H. W. Wilson Co.). A cumulative author-subject index to periodicals of general interest published in the United States.

Identifying Customers and Competitors

To find mailing addresses, telephone numbers, and company officers, and to identify a company that makes a specific product, one should consult trade directories, telephone directories, and buyer's guides.

- *Encyclopedia Associations*, 9th ed., Margaret Fisk (Detroit: Gale Research Co., 1975). This guidebook lists associations, their addresses, their telephone numbers, and descriptions of their scope, activities, and publications.
- *World Guide to Trade Associations* (London: R. R. Bowker Co., 1973). This handbook lists associations, their addresses, and their telephone numbers for Europe, Africa, America, Asia, and Oceania.
- *Thomas Register of American Manufacturers and Thomas Register Catalog File* (New York: Thomas Publishing Co.). Contains a list of products and services, company addresses, telephone numbers, company officials, a brand-name index, and catalogs of companies.

Economic, Population, and Employment Data

Basic data on economic indicators, population, or employment are frequently needed during a market analysis. Some of the sources providing such data are listed below:

- *County Business Patterns*, U.S. Department of Commerce (Washington, D.C.: U.S. Government Printing Office). Series of state reports showing the number, employment, and payrolls of businesses and manufacturing establishments by SIC code for each county and Standard Metropolitan Statistical Area (SMSA).

- *Census of Population*, U.S. Department of Commerce (Washington, D.C.: U.S. Government Printing Office). Presents official population figures broken down by area and subject (e.g., race, urban-rural, age). For updated information, check *Current Population Reports*.
- *Survey of Current Business*, U.S. Department of Commerce (Washington, D.C.: U.S. Government Printing Office). Comprehensive report on economic conditions and business activity.
- *Business Conditions Digest*, U.S. Department of Commerce (Washington, D.C.: U.S. Government Printing Office). Report compiling about 300 statistical time series on the economy.
- *1972 OBERS Projections, Regional Economic Activity in the U.S.*, U.S. Department of Commerce and U.S. Department of Agriculture (Washington, D.C.: U.S. Government Printing Office, revised April 1974). Contains data, both historical and projected, from 1929 to 2020.
- *Survey of Buying Power* (New York: Sales Management). Contains figures on population, household, income, retail sales, and merchandise line sales for the nation, states, SMSAs, and countries.
- *Statistical Abstract of the United States*, U.S. Department of Commerce (Washington, D.C.: U.S. Government Printing Office). Contains data on population, vital statistics, labor force, income, prices, power, mining, and many other subjects.
- *United Nations Statistical Yearbook* (New York: United Nations). Data on population, labor force, history, industrial production, trade, transport, and other items.
- *Sources of European Economic Information* (Boston: Gower Press, 1974). Reference access to key sources of published economic information for 16 countries.

General References

The following publications should be consulted for required information not found in other sources.

- *American Statistics Index: A Comprehensive Guide and Index to the Statistical Publications of the United States Government* (Washington, D.C.: Congressional Information Services). This report is the master guide and index to the statistical publications of the U.S. government.
- *Monthly Catalog: United States Government Publications* (Washington,

D.C.: Superintendent of Documents). The reference to all types of government publications.

• *Statistics Sources*, Paul Wasserman and Joanne Pasear, 4th ed. (Detroit: Gale Research Co., 1974). Contains a list of selected sources along with a subject listing.

Unless the analyst has a specific procedure, the list of secondary-data sources can be overwhelming. The example of the pump manufacturer can be used to illustrate how the data search may be conducted. A good place to begin the literature search is the Office of Management and Budget, *Standard Industrial Classification Manual, 1972* (SIC). Every product made has a SIC number which is used frequently in publications. Eight categories of pumps are listed, and the one of interest is "SIC 3561—Pumps, Hydraulic."

The analyst next wants to obtain current information on the market for pumps. Scanning the *Encyclopedia of Associations*, he discovers that four pump associations are located in the United States, of which only the Hydraulic Institute seems appropriate. Listed under SIC 3561 in the *F & S Index of Corporations and Industries* are various current articles, some of which are listed below:

• Pumpmakers see rosy market future.
• Pumps and compressors new orders data, 1975.
• Pumps shipments projections, 1975.
• Pumps and compressors exports projections, 1980.
• Hydraulic pumps specifications examined by manufacturer, model.
• Pumps, compressors and blowers total demand by end use, 1985.

A quick glance at the *Business Periodicals Index* and the *Readers' Guide to Periodical Literature* reveals that these publications can provide nothing on the subject of pumps that is of use.

With several articles on the current market for pumps, the analyst turns to the collection of historical data. Looking in the *American Statistics Index 1975*, he finds no listing for pumps. Pumps (SIC 3561) make up a segment of the more general category "SIC 35—Machinery, Except Electrical" which is included in the overall category "Manufacturing." Using those subject headings, the analyst finds several publications, such as the *Census of Manufactures* and an annual publication, *Current Industrial Report on Pumps and Compressors*. In the government documents section, the analyst checks the *Monthly Catalog: United States Government Publications* for nonstatistical publications on pumps.

In addition to the historical data collected, projections for the pump market are also of interest. *Predicasts* lists over 40 sets of projections for such items as employment, productivity, production, shipments, imports, exports, expenditures by different end users, and new orders. In addition, *U.S. Industrial Outlook 1975 with Projections to 1980* contains a section on pumps and compressors. This example illustrates the procedure used in a secondary-data search, and the search can be continued further, depending on the information required.

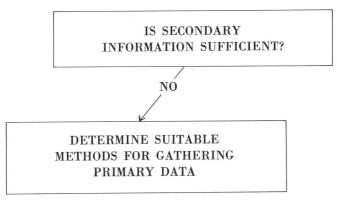

If secondary-data sources do not provide the data necessary to answer the questions outlined as the objectives, primary data must be collected. Primary sources are new data which the analyst usually obtains from a survey of people involved with the product, such as competitors, government officials, trade associations, buyers, and users.

The collection of primary market data can be accomplished utilizing several survey techniques either in conjunction or separately: mail questionnaire, telephone interview, and personal interview. The time available to conduct the survey, the budget, the desired reliability, and the research skills available are factors that help determine the selection of the appropriate survey technique. Another factor that influences the choice of technique is the type of market. For instance, a different technique is indicated where the end users of the product are in the industrial market where the number of firms to be surveyed may be small, as compared with a product in the consumer market. Also, the type of market data needed can help determine the survey technique. If the questionnaire is very technical, it may require an interviewer with an engineering background to administer it. The objectives of the analysis should always be kept in mind in selecting the appropriate procedures for collecting the necessary data of the desired quality in the most efficient manner. Table 3.1 presents a guide to data collection methods under alternative survey conditions. The advantages and disadvantages of the different survey techniques are discussed in the following sections.

Table 3.1 A Guide to Preferred Data Collection Methods under Alternative Survey Conditions

Conditions of Survey				Possible Data Collection Methods[a]			
Funds	Time	Certain Precision Required	Type of Data	Personal Interview	Mail	Telephone	Comments on Method
Restricted	Restricted	Yes or no	Few items			×	Assuming telephone population representative
Restricted	Restricted	Yes or no	Much information	×			If funds permit
Restricted	Ample	Yes	Few items		×	×	Assuming telephone population representative
Restricted	Ample	Yes	Much information	×——	×		Nonrespondent follow-up needed
Restricted	Ample	No	Few items		×	×	
Restricted	Ample	No	Much information	×			
Ample	Restricted	Yes or no	Few items	×		×	Assuming telephone population representative
Ample	Restricted	Yes or no	Much information	×			
Ample	Ample	Yes	Few items	×		×	Assuming telephone population representative
Ample	Ample	Yes	Much information	×			
Ample	Ample	No	Few items	×	×	×	
Ample	Ample	No	Much information	×——	×		Either joint or one method alone

[a] A line connecting two crosses represents joint use of two data collection methods. Otherwise two crosses in the same line indicate that either method can be used.

Source. Robert Ferber and P. J. Verdoorn, *Research Methods in Economics and Business* © The Macmillan Company, 1962, p. 212.

Mail Questionnaire

The mail survey is most effective when specific limited answers are needed, a good mailing list is available, and it is not important to have a high response rate.

In circumstances where it can be used effectively, the principal advantages of the mail survey are its low cost and convenience. Even when the cost per valid response is considered, the mail survey is less expensive than the other two methods, especially when the number to be surveyed is large. One individual can administer and control the mail survey from his office, making it more convenient than personal interviews, where frequent trips to and from interviewees are necessary. Some other advantages of the mail survey as compared with other survey techniques are: wider geographic distribution is possible; the respondent has more time to obtain the requested data; and the necessary data can be obtained more quickly than with personal interviews.

The response rate for a mail survey is usually between 20 and 30% for the first mailing. This can be increased to 50 to 60% if there are three mailings; and with incentives it is possible to increase the response rate to an even higher level. The time needed to conduct a mail survey naturally depends to a certain extent on the survey size. However, the minimum time required for one mailing, excluding preparation time, is 2 weeks, while the time necessary for three mailings usually is approximately 6 to 8 weeks.

The major drawback of the mail survey is that a substantial proportion of those surveyed do not respond. Without knowing the answers of the nonrespondents, the analyst cannot be certain that the data are not biased. Bias is not usually as severe a problem if the basic objective of the market analysis is to quantify the market. However, in other areas of market research, such as consumer motivation, the bias created by a large number of nonrespondents can pose more serious problems. Frequently, telephone interviews of selected nonrespondents can provide sufficient information to determine whether their responses are significantly different from those of persons who answered the mail survey.

Some of the disadvantages of the mail survey are associated with mailing lists. They are sometimes out of date; they may not include the names of individuals or provide the desired company officers (e.g., purchasing agent); and they frequently contain only a segment of the group that is to be surveyed. In fact, it is not always possible to construct a usable mailing list.

The survey instrument itself can also cause problems. For example, the questionnaire cannot be too long. A one-page questionnaire on the reverse side of the cover letter results in a higher response rate than a six-page questionnaire. This is especially true for businesspeople who have a limited amount of time as compared with at-home consumers. Another difficulty with the mail survey is that the subject matter may be too complex to structure into such a format.

Even with all the disadvantages of the mail questionnaire, it is probably the primary survey technique used to collect data for the market analysis, especially in the industrial market. Therefore the following discussion on the construction of the mail questionnaire is provided.

The overall appearance of the questionnaire should not be crowded, nor should it appear lengthy when the individual first glances at it. A long questionnaire can be made to appear much shorter to the respondent if the questions are grouped. For example, question 1 can be subdivided into parts *a*, *b*, and *c*. There are also several ways to structure the questions which result in a higher response. Yes-no or multiple-choice questions, which are easy to answer, improve the response. Open-ended questions, those in which space is left for the respondent to write an answer, should not be avoided altogether, but should be used only when this type of question will yield the most information. The open-ended question is often valuable because it can make the analyst aware of problems he did not know existed and can provide insights into the market. An open-ended question is always used when the number of possible responses is so large that it cannot possibly be structured as a multiple-choice question.

In the development of the questionnaire, care also should be taken to avoid questions that are difficult to answer or which require the respondent to make calculations. This does not imply that the respondent cannot be asked to check his files for information, if the analyst is sure the information exists.

It is important to remember one's own experience with questionnaires. If the questionnaire took too much effort, if a particular question was difficult to understand or answer, or if the questionnaire did not apply to one's area of interest, it probably was thrown away. This illustrates the importance of the cover letter. A clear statement of the purpose of the survey is essential in the cover letter and, if applicable, a statement as to how the respondent can benefit or further an area of his own interest should be included. An appeal to the respondent's ego in the cover letter also is helpful in obtaining responses to the questionnaire. For instance, in the case of the market analysis for pumps a request for data from the respondents as "experienced authorities" who can be of assistance may be included.

Finally, there are several points to remember when wording a mail questionnaire: The average American adult has a reading ability approximately equal to the ninth grade; the comfortable reading level is 2 years less, that is, the seventh grade; reading has little to do with intelligence; and it is not necessary to avoid repeating a word more than once. Edward L. Thorndike's *Twentieth Century Dictionary* lists the 30,000 most used English words and gives their meanings in order of public understanding, and his book, *The Teacher's Word Book of 30,000 Words*, lists the most used words and tells who is familiar with them.[6]

Personal Interviews

Personal interviews can be used to collect a wide variety of market information. Various personal interview techniques have been developed for the collection of different types of market data. For our purposes, the discussion is limited to those interview techniques that help fulfill the objectives of identifying and quantifying the market for the project's output. The depth interview and projective techniques are examples of other types of interviews used in motivation research to discover the factors influencing human behavior.

Personal interviews can be classified as structured, partially structured, or unstructured. In the structured interview, the questions to be asked are formulated in advance. The interviewer is instructed to ask each question exactly as it is worded, in an exact order, and to offer no additional explanations or comments. The procedure used in the structured interview results in the collection of specific information, and the replies are comparable. However, this advantage must be balanced against the possible loss of information because of the inflexibility of the procedure, which places limits on the use of the interviewer's insight and tends to prevent additional remarks by the respondent which might be of value.[7] As Wilson notes, the structured interview is essentially a tool of consumer marketing research and is effective and inexpensive to use when massive interviewing takes place, where the quality of interviewers is highly variable and not always accessible, and where the respondents are subject to a relatively superficial examination.[8]

The partially structured interview is the personal interview technique that is the most appropriate in conducting a market analysis for a project feasibility study. The interviewer has specific questions to ask and is allowed to use his own judgment in the timing and sequence of questions. There may be a list of

---

[6] Adapted from Paul J. Bringe, "A Basic Guide to Better Direct Mail Copy," *Industrial Marketing*, Sept. 1958, pp. 63–66.

[7] Herbert H. Hyman et al., *Interviewing in Social Research* (Chicago: University of Chicago Press, 1954), p. 30.

[8] Aubrey Wilson, *The Assessment of Industrial Markets* (London: Hutchinson & Co. Ltd., 1968), p. 166.

general topics to be covered during the interview. The freedom the interviewer has permits him to lead the respondent into key questions the respondent might neglect to answer. He also can probe to clarify incomplete responses.

The unstructured interview is a general discussion between the interviewer and respondent, which is oriented toward, but not directed to, certain topics. This technique is of primary interest to the analyst during the initial stage of the analysis, when he is trying to obtain a feel for the market. This is because during the unstructured interview the respondent often makes unsolicited comments about the market situation, competitive products, and the like, which neither he nor the interviewer could have anticipated as being important.

No matter what interview technique is used, the following requirements have to be met to ensure a successful interview: a thoroughly briefed interviewer, a well laid-out plan for coverage of the subject matter, and a careful selection of proper respondents.

In general, the advantages of personal interviews are: they are a more flexible method for gathering data; the length of the interview can be varied; this method yields the highest response rate; elaboration is possible in some instances; and the interviewer can use visual aids or present complex material to the respondent.

The most serious drawbacks to personal interviews are the time required for contact, travel, and interviewing, and the cost. Personal interviews are the most expensive of the different survey techniques, especially when the geographic spread of those to be surveyed is great. The personal interview also presents problems involving the training, supervision, and control of the interviewers, as well as the scheduling of interviews. Finally, it should be remembered that even the use of personal interviews does not make certain that all the necessary market data will be obtained.

Telephone Interviews

Telephone interviews are another means for gathering the data necessary for the market analysis. The techniques for personal interviews discussed previously are, for the most part, applicable to telephone interviews. Telephone interviews frequently are used in conjunction with either mail surveys or personal interviews. For instance, with mail surveys the telephone interview is sometimes used as a means to survey the nonrespondents.

The telephone interview offers the speediest means of obtaining market data, and its cost falls between that of the mail survey and the personal interview. Another advantage of the telephone interview is that it tends to command

attention, thereby offering access to individuals who might otherwise be difficult to reach. It also is more flexible than the mail questionnaire and allows
wider geographic coverage than the personal interview.

Of course, the primary disadvantage of the telephone interview is that not
everyone has a telephone. In consumer research this is of importance, because
using telephone interviews would create a bias unless ownership of telephones
is one of the criteria. However, in research involving businesses, there would
not be such bias because telephones are necessary in modern business operations.
The telephone interview is usually short, and therefore the respondent's comments may not be as extensive as with other survey methods.

> # PREPARE SURVEY FORMS AND
> # FIELD TEST

Whatever the survey technique used to obtain the market data, a survey
instrument has to be developed. The structure of the questionnaire depends on
the type of survey technique used, as already discussed to some extent, in the
preceding sections. However, during the design of any survey instrument the
objectives of the market study should be kept in mind to help eliminate ex-
traneous questions and to make certain that all necessary questions are included. It is also advantageous when developing the questionnaire to design
the tabulation forms. This ensures that the questions on the questionnaire will
provide the information they were intended to supply.

After a questionnaire has been designed, it must be field-tested. Field-
testing is especially useful because it tests the wording of the questionnaire to
see that it conforms with the vocabulary of the individuals being interviewed.
No matter how good an analyst thinks his questionnaire is, it still should be
field-tested for the following reasons.

- To make sure the questions are clear and in proper order.
- To find out whether or not the instructions to the respondents or interviewers are adequate.
- To uncover any problems that may arise in the course of editing, coding,
  and tabulating the questionnaires.[9]

The method for field-testing is simply to try out the questionnaire on a

[9] William T. Stanton, *Fundamentals of Marketing* (New York: McGraw-Hill, 1964), p. 56.

small number of people similar to those who will be interviewed. It is best to let the analyst do some interviewing. By observing the reactions and answers of a few respondents, he may be able to anticipate a number of unforeseen problems.

DESIGN SAMPLE AND
COLLECT PRIMARY DATA

Thus far in the market analysis, the analyst has specified the types of necessary data and the means of acquiring these data in order to satisfy the objectives of the study. At this point, he must decide whether to survey all the consumers of the product (referred to as the universe) or to select only a sample. The process of selecting the consumers to be surveyed is called sampling. In most surveys it is impractical in terms of both cost and time to conduct a complete enumeration of the universe. However, in some cases, especially in an industrial market analysis, the number of customers who comprise the universe is so small that a complete survey is feasible.

The primary objective of any sampling procedure is to obtain a sample, subject to limitations of size, which will reproduce the characteristics of the universe as nearly as possible. The sampling operation involves the definition of the universe and the sample design. This discussion is to acquaint the reader with the sampling procedure, so that he will be aware of the major considerations involved.[10] There are various organizations which, for a fee, provide assistance or actually conduct the survey. Because of the expertise required, it may be advisable to utilize their services.

Definition of the Universe

The definition of the universe is determined entirely by the research objectives of the market analysis. Defining the universe may present no problem, or it may require many decisions.

The case of the pump manufacturer illustrates some of the problems that arise in defining the universe. The market can be defined as the consumers of

---

[10] For technical discussion on sampling, see William G. Cochran, *Sampling Techniques* (New York: Wiley, 1953) or Taro Yamane, *Elementary Sampling Theory* (Englewood Cliffs, N.J.: Prentice-Hall, 1967). For marketing-oriented discussion, see Boyd and Westfall, *Marketing Research: Text and Cases* (3rd ed; Homewood, Ill.: Richard D. Irwin, 1972).

pumps located in the South. This includes power plants, chemical processing plants, pulp and paper plants, and water and sewer works. This may be an accurate definition of the market, but it is not a sufficient basis for a sampling design. However, even though this definition of the universe as the end users of pumps is not exact, it has narrowed the survey by eliminating from consideration other possible universes such as firms making pumps or retail-wholesale outlets.

The definition of the universe for the pump manufacturer is not precise for the following reasons. The industry groups identified as consumers of pumps are not specific and need to be better defined. For example, to what group does the chemical processing industry refer? Since the chemical processing industry is not considered a separate industrial category in the SIC manual, the industry groups that compose the chemical processing industry should be identified by SIC number. Also, the geographic area referred to as the South is not clearly defined. Does the term "South" refer to the Bureau of Census definition, the Southeastern Federal Region, or the company's sales area?

In the consumer market analysis it is usually not as difficult for the analyst to define the universe accurately. Often, an examination of published demographic and other data is all that is necessary both to define and to locate the universe of interest. For example, to define the universe for a product aimed at the retirement market, demographic data can be used to locate the market by identifying such states as Arizona and Florida. Demographic data can also provide data as to the size and other characteristics of the retirement market.

Sample Design

The sample design involves identifying the sampling units, constructing a complete list of sampling units, selecting the sampling method, and specifying the sample size.

Sample Units.   The market analysis is most often concerned with such sample units as individuals, households, and business establishments. For a product aimed at the retirement market the sampling unit would be an individual over the age of 55. In selecting individuals as sample units difficulty may arise if those surveyed are not the actual purchasers of the product. Lists can be gathered from several sources, and their completeness depends on the product and market area to be covered. Telephone directories, trade association lists, industry directories, and government documents are some of the sources for lists.

Compiling a list for the pump manufacturer involves scanning the state manufacturing directories for the southern states to identify names of company officers as well as telephone numbers and mailing addresses for the appropriate end-user groups. The environmental protection agencies for each of the southern states can be contacted in order to obtain a listing of water and sewer works. The most common problems found with using directories from each state are that they vary in reliability. Some may have inadequate coverage of industry; there may be inaccuracies due to incorrect assignment of companies to industry groups (SIC numbers); and the frequency of directory publication varies among states, so that some may contain obsolete data. These are the types of problems that may occur in the construction of any list of sample units.

It is possible to select a sample even when no sample list exists and there is no practical means of constructing one within the limitations of the budget. Multistage sampling is one of the techniques that can be employed. In the illustration of the retirement market, for example, since a list of individuals over 55 is not available, such a list can be constructed through the use of multistage sampling which involves making several random decisions. To construct a list for the retirement market, one can first list the states and then randomly select a few states for the survey, similarly choosing counties within the states, towns within the counties, blocks within the towns, and individuals over the age of 55 within the blocks. In this way, every individual in the country over the age of 55 has an equal chance of being selected.

Another alternative, if a sampling list does not exist, is to construct a quota sample. To accomplish this, however, the major characteristics of the universe and their proportions must be known. The accuracy of the survey will depend to a large extent on the accuracy with which these characteristics can be isolated in the quota frame. According to Davies, it has been found that in consumer surveys, if the basic characteristics age, sex, marital status, and geographic location are accounted for, these characteristics will provide a reliable basis for estimating other commonly found characteristics.[11]

Select the Sampling Method.   After the decision has been made to use sampling, one must decide which sampling method to use. The two main types are probability and nonprobability sampling. The basic difference between the two is that only probability sampling provides a measure of the reliability of the sample estimate. Factors such as cost, time available, and required reliability

[11] Anthony H. Davies, *The Practice of Market Research* (London: William Heinemann, 1973), p. 53.

influence the choice of sampling method. It is not uncommon in market analysis to use a combination of methods.

In probability sampling the chance, or probability, of being selected for the sampling is known for every unit of the universe. Four common probability sampling procedures are: simple random sampling, stratified random sampling, systematic random sampling, and simple cluster sampling. In all probability sampling procedures the units are chosen strictly at random and the sampling operation is, therefore, objectively controlled and independent of the person conducting the study.

Nonprobability sampling methods do not allow every unit in the universe a known probability of being included in the sample. Here the process of selection is at least partially subjective and someone must decide what units to survey. With this method it is not possible to determine the reliability because probabilities cannot be assigned to the units objectively. The judgment sample and quota sample are examples of nonprobability sampling methods.

The selection of the sampling method depends, to a large extent, on whether the market analysis involves the consumer or industrial market. These markets definitely call for different sampling procedures.

In the consumer market it is often the practice to separate the sampling procedure into two or more stages. In the first stage selection is made, usually on a probability basis, of the areas that the survey will cover.

In the next stage, using either random or quota sampling methods, the actual selection of the sampling units is made for the previously selected areas. Because the consumer market is more homogeneous than the industrial market, the analyst is more likely to use probability methods when conducting a consumer market analysis. The industrial market is typically characterized by a small number of firms which account for a large proportion of the industry's output. It is necessary in an industrial market analysis to identify the significant firms and to separate them from the universe. This selection from the universe consists of an arbitrarily selected stratum and therefore precludes the possibility of constructing an unbiased total sample. The procedure in industrial market analysis is to separate the universe into two strata: one for which 100% coverage is required and one for which probability sampling can be used. The results, when suitably weighted, combined, and projected, have been shown to produce an answer within an acceptable degree of accuracy.

Such a sampling procedure illustrates the importance of nonprobability sampling. The quota sample, a type of nonprobability sampling, depends on the stratification of the sample in terms of certain known characteristics of the universe. It attempts to secure equal representation by dividing the universe into more homogeneous segments, selecting units at random from each of these strata and combining them to form a total sample.

Specify Sample Size.   Sample size can be determined by using a rule-of-thumb measure or by a computation using sampling theory. The calculation of sample size based on sampling theory is possible only for probability sampling. Even when using sampling theory it is not always possible to determine if the sample size selected is the best.

Although probability sampling is primarily oriented toward the consumer market analysis, it is also desirable to adapt, to the extent possible, the features of probability sampling to the industrial analysis as well, as illustrated in the preceding discussion.

The market analysis can involve estimating the percentage of consumers in the universe who probably will purchase a new product on the basis of the percentage from the sample who replied that they would do so. The sample size that yields this desired percentage with the required precision at the minimum cost should be selected. Precision refers to the desired accuracy of the percentage. Will the objectives of the market analysis be satisfied if the percentage is correct within 10%? The sample size selected is determined by two factors which are often conflicting: the data collection process and the need for a sample of sufficient size to ensure the desired accuracy.

The data collection process can affect the size of the sample in that a large sample may require considerable time to implement, and thus it may not be consistent with the desired time frame for the study. One must also be sure that the sample size is consistent with the budget and labor available to take the sample. As Zaltman and Burger have indicated, the economics of the personal interviewing situation might preclude the use of sampling theory for calculation of sample size.[12] The typical market research agency often does not even consider a sample size of less than several hundred interviews, because sample sizes below this minimum cannot cover the expenses of interviewer training.

The sample must include a sufficient number of responses to ensure that the information has the desired accuracy. For example, in a new product analysis, in addition to determining the percentage of consumers who will purchase the product, it is also necessary to characterize this subgroup of potential customers. In other words, the original sample may have to be broken down into

---

[12] Gerald Zaltman and Philip C. Burger, *Marketing Research Fundamentals and Dynamics* (Hinsdale, Ill.: Dryden Press, 1975), p. 397.

subgroups—purchaser and nonpurchaser—and these subgroups into subgroups so that, as this breakdown occurs, the number of responses in a subgroup declines. Each subgroup to be analyzed requires a certain number of responses of its own to obtain the desired accuracy. Therefore the size of the original sample must be large enough to allow accuracy in analysis of the smallest subgroup.

A common practice when making a stratified analysis is to establish minimum strata sizes. The minimum strata size is established at over 30 observations because of the central limit theorem.[13] When probability sampling is not used, the sample size computation involves the numerical addition of the desired number of interviews in each stratum, since the interviewing procedure is structured to obtain the necessary information for each stratum.

Another factor that influences the size of the sample is the type of sampling method employed. For the example of the heterogeneous universe, stratified random sampling, if used in place of simple random sampling, can reduce the required sample size.

The number of units that must be surveyed in order to achieve the desired accuracy is influenced by the factors already discussed. Formulas have been derived to calculate the sample size when probability sampling is used. Random sampling theory is used to illustrate the calculation of sample size for two frequently used parameters: percentages and averages. It should be remembered that usually more than one item is measured in a survey and therefore the sample size must be calculated for every item for which a degree of precision is desired in order to determine the critical or largest sample size.

The market analysis might involve estimating the percentage of consumers who indicate that they will purchase a new product. In this instance, the desired precision for this percentage must first be determined. Suppose that the objectives of the market analysis indicate that $\pm 10\%$ accuracy is sufficient. Since there is no way to be absolutely certain that the sample drawn in the survey will yield a percentage within the permissible error of $\pm 10\%$, the analyst must determine how certain he wants to be of selecting a sample that falls within this desired range. Two of the most commonly used levels of assurance of probability are "significant," which means that there are 19 chances out of 20 (or a probability of 0.95), and "very significant," which means that there are 99 chances out of 100 (or a probability of 0.99) that the sample selected for the survey will not exceed the $\pm 10\%$ desired accuracy.

Assume for this illustration that 95% reliability is sufficient. To simplify

[13] *Ibid.*, p. 317.

matters, assume further that the sample size is small in comparison with the universe and that the percentage to be computed is normally distributed. The problem, then, is to find the sample size n so that the precision d of the percentage will be within $\pm 10\%$ with a reliability of 95%. Using a normal probability table, the number of standard error units z that corresponds to the required reliability of 95% is found to be 1.96.

The appropriate formula for determining the sample size in simple random sampling is:

$$n = \frac{p(100 - p)z^2}{d^2}$$

A difficulty in using the formula to estimate sample size arises at this point because the analyst must have some idea of the universe who will purchase the product. After much deliberation, or possibly a small survey, assume that the percentage p is estimated at 80%. Then, by substituting figures into the formula, the sample size can be derived:

$$n = \frac{80(20)(1.96)^2}{10^2} = \frac{6146}{100} = 615$$

This means that a random sample of 615 consumers should give an estimate with a 95% probability that the sample percentage is within the $\pm 10\%$ range.

Another frequently used measure for which it is often necessary to calculate size is the average of the universe for a given precision and given reliability. When using this measure, a preliminary estimate of the standard deviation of the universe mean (σ) is required before the following formula can be used to calculate the sample size (n).

$$n = \left[\frac{z\sigma}{d} \right]^2$$

Practical problems are encountered which limit the use of this type of formula to calculate sample size. For example, it is necessary to be able to estimate a characteristic of the universe. For instance, for percentages, an estimate of the percentage is necessary, while to calculate an average, an estimate of the standard deviation of the average is required.

In some market analysis applications it is possible to deal with these problems by using sequential sampling. In sequential sampling, a series of samples is drawn at random from the universe, and the desired percentages, averages, or other values are calculated and then evaluated to see if they are acceptable. If not, another survey is conducted and its results are added to the original data, and so on until the desired accuracy is obtained.

PROCESS AND ANALYZE BOTH SECONDARY AND PRIMARY DATA

Processing the data involves editing, coding, and tabulating. The effort involved in processing the gathered data depends to an extent on whether they are secondary or primary data and, in turn, whether the survey instrument used was the mail questionnaire, the personal interview, or the telephone interview. Also, more effort is required to process data collected during the unstructured interview than during the structured interview. The analysis of the data can be divided into two general areas which relate to the objectives of the study, market measurement and market forecasting, both of which are discussed later.

Editing and Coding

The primary purpose of editing and coding the survey instrument is to process the data into categories. Preliminary categories for responses should have been established at the time the survey instrument was constructed, to ensure that the information requested would satisfy the objectives of the market analysis.

An initial screening of the survey is conducted as the responses are received. This quick editing of the survey instrument separates responses that obviously present problems. For example, a response may be illegible, contain information that is obviously incorrect, or lack critical information. If such problems are identified at an early stage of the survey, it is possible to try to obtain critical information.

The final editing of the survey instrument is more extensive and requires skill as well as an in-depth familiarity with the overall intent of the survey and the reasoning behind the questions. Based on a thorough knowledge of the survey and the common sense to recognize obvious problems, the editor's task is, where possible, to remove inaccurate answers, complete partial answers, decipher illegible handwriting, fill in blanks (no answers), reconcile numerical contradictions in answers, and convert numerical data to common units (e.g., barrels to gallons). The editor also determines the final categories to be used in calculations. For example, a complete list of the responses to an open-ended question may become so long that it is of little value. As the data are processed, however, the editor gains insight into the answers and eventually is able to structure the responses into categories that reveal the most information.

After leaving the editor to be coded, the data should be in such a form that no questions are needed to clarify them. Depending on the size of the survey, the editor may also code the questionnaires.

Tabulating

Tabulating the survey instrument involves determining the number of items that fall into the various categories. Straight tabulation is merely the summation of the responses to a question, while cross-tabulation involves relating the answers to one question to another.[14] Hand tabulation can be used if the size of the survey is not large, and if only a few cross-tabulations are desired. Another factor in deciding whether to use hand or machine tabulation is the type of summary statistics to be calculated. The use of hand tabulation presents no problem when percentages and averages are adequate for the analysis. However, when correlation analysis or measures such as standard deviation are necessary, machine tabulation has distinct advantages. The decision to use hand or machine tabulation should be made at the time the survey instrument is designed, because at that time it is sometimes possible to include the appropriate information so that the keypunching can be done directly from the questionnaire, eliminating the need for a keypunch form.

> ## CHARACTERiZE THE PRESENT MARKET

With the secondary and primary data processed and tabulated, the analyst is in a position to characterize the market for the product. The data must be analyzed to provide information on market size, market share, market growth patterns, market channels, and other market characteristics.

Market Classification

The market comprises all individuals and organizations who are actual or

---

[14] See Hans Zeisel, *Say it With Figures* (5th ed. rev.; New York: Harper & Row, 1968).

potential consumers of a product. Classification of the market for a product is important because it may indicate the best procedure to use in estimating the market size. There are several different ways to classify the market.

The basic types of markets are consumer, industrial, middleman, and government. Characteristics of the product, such as durable or nondurable, as well as established product or new product, can be used to classify the market. The product can be discussed in terms of its market demand, market share, and market potential for both present and future markets. The market analysis can be described in terms of one or more of the above classifications. In the pump illustration, for example, the market analysis can be described in terms of a new durable product for the industrial market, to ascertain the present and future market demand and market share.

Measure the Present Market

Market measurement is the development of quantitative estimates of demand. In quantifying the present market, the analyst is interested in measuring the market demand, the market share and, possibly, the market potential for the product. A brief examination of these terms is followed by the actual methods used for developing this information.

To determine the market demand for a product, the analyst must specify the geographic area, the groups of consumers being studied, the units of measurement being utilized, and the time period covered. The marketing demand for a product depends on political, social, and economic conditions, sometimes referred to as the marketing environment and the level of industry marketing effort. Market potential is a concept sometimes employed to determine the size of the market if the industry level of marketing effort is at a maximum for a given marketing environment. The market share is the share of the market demand that a firm can capture, and it is influenced by the firm's marketing effort relative to the effort put forth by its competitors.

Define Market. In calculating the market demand, it is necessary to ascertain whether the product is for the total market or for a segment of the market. A market segment refers to a subsegment of a total market which can be identified by specific characteristics. The concept of market segments is important in a market analysis, because the analyst must be careful to include all market segments that constitute the total demand for the product and, similarly, to exclude market segments for which the product is not appropriate or to redefine the product line and customize the product for these market segments. The introduction of a distinct feature, different quality, or style in a product aimed at a specific market is referred to as product differentiation. Such product differentiation, although advantageous in that it allows deeper penetration into the market, has drawbacks in increased costs in such areas as product design, production, and inventory.

In the industrial market, segmentation may be by industry type, size, and location; for the consumer market, common characteristics by which markets are segmentized include income, age, and family size. Two major benefits are derived when the market segments applicable for a product are determined. It assists in defining the market, which in turn makes the task of determining market size somewhat easier. Instead of struggling with a vague, hard-to-define market, the analyst may be able to separate the market into easily defined segments, which simplifies the task of determining market size.

Estimate Market Size. It is usually necessary to estimate the total market as a means of arriving at an estimate of the firm's share of that market. However, quantification of the total market is not absolutely necessary if data are available, perhaps as a result of primary-data collection, that indicate sufficient sales for the firm.

The difficulty involved in estimating the market varies. For example, estimating the market for a new product usually presents more problems than for an established product. This is because estimating present total markets is done largely through the collection and analysis of published data. When published data on total demand are inadequate, the analyst may have to depend primarily on information and opinions obtained from primary-data sources. Measuring the present market consists of collecting bits and pieces of information from many different sources and using imagination and judgment to combine them in such a way that a total picture emerges.

The total market can be estimated by using either direct data or corollary data.[15] The direct data method refers to the situation in which information on the product under study is available. The corollary data method involves using data that are related to, but different from, the product.

Data for the past and present market for a specific product occasionally can be obtained from secondary-data sources. Limitations encountered when using secondary information are that sometimes it varies in coverage (e.g., sales for only trade association members), it may be dated, the figures may be reported for areas (e.g., states, census regions) that are not compatible with the geo-

[15] Boyd and Westfall, pp. 758–760.

graphic market area, or the market may be quantified in shipments or production rather than consumption. Nevertheless, if the data for the specific product cannot be used directly, they often provide a means for constructing bridge factors (e.g., sales for trades association members divided by their employers gives a sales-per-employee factor), which aid in estimating the market.

One method of estimating the market, when data for a specific product are unavailable, is to use data for a broader category. This naturally assumes that the proportion of the specific product related to the broader category is known with some degree of probability. For example, *Sales Management* publishes annual estimates of sales by product classes such as food, building materials, and general merchandise.

The corollary data method for estimating the market is based on establishing a relationship between the product under study and another item (variable) for which information is available. This method is more likely to succeed if the product and the variable have a closely related demand, that is, if the demand for one is derived from the other or if it is a complementary demand. This procedure is particularly applicable in industrial markets, where the demand for the product is derived from the products with which it is included and ultimately depends on consumer demand. For example, the market for leaf springs in the Southeast is primarily dependent on the mobile home industry. Even though no data exist on the market for leaf springs, information on the production of mobile homes, by state, does exist, and therefore the market for leaf springs can be estimated. In this particular case, inquiry showed that the majority of mobile home manufacturers purchase undercarriages with the leaf spring already attached. However, the southeastern market can still be estimated using the corollary data method, since the manufacturers of undercarriages are also located in the Southeast. In this example, the relationship between the product under study, leaf springs, and another variable, mobile homes, is not difficult to establish. However, this is not always the case.

Another method of estimating the market is to use a combination of primary and secondary data. Using the pump illustration, the total market can be estimated in the following manner. The mail questionnaire survey of the industry groups (SIC categories) provides data on the sales of pumps and the employment size of the firms surveyed, which yield bridge factors, dollar sales per employee, for each of the industry groups. With the use of *County Business Patterns*, which provides employment data by industry group at the county level, the total market for pumps can then be estimated.

An estimate of the market for a consumer good can be obtained in a similar manner. The survey reveals the relationship between purchase data for the product and consumer characteristics such as family income. Then, by consulting *Survey of Buying Power*, which provides data on family income by categories at the county level, an estimate of the total market can be made.

Estimate the Market Share

If the analyst estimates the total market for the product, he must further quantify the firm's share of this market. There is no specific computational procedure that can be used to estimate market share. Estimating the market share is a decision based on analysis of the information available. Several factors—product quality, pricing, production cost, competitor's locations, and many others—should be examined to ascertain the market share. The location of competitors and price are two of the factors that allow the analyst to determine the degree of market penetration that can be achieved.

Competition. Some knowledge of the competition is helpful when estimating the market share. An ideal situation exists if information is available concerning the production capacity of the competition as well as their shipments both inside and outside the market area. Such information rarely exists, however, so the analyst must rely on such information as employment size, or possibly sales, to determine the extent of the competition.

One procedure for estimating market share is illustrated by a feasibility study on locating a charcoal briquette plant in Georgia. Although charcoal briquettes may be shipped throughout the nation from a single plant, information is desired as to what share of the market this proposed plant could expect in its freight advantage area, defined as the Southeast. An estimate of the demand for charcoal briquettes was made for each of the states in the six-state Southeast. Information on production capacities and the sources of raw materials (specifically, whether boiler, char, lump, or loose charcoal, which vary in cost) used to prepare the charocal briquettes was available for the five charcoal briquette plants located in the region. Based on the estimated market in each state, the estimated production, and the location of existing briquette plants in these states, the market share that the proposed plant could possibly capture was estimated for each state.

Pricing. So far, no mention has been made of the role of price in determining market demand or in determining the firm's share of the market. The relationship between price and demand is referred to as the elasticity of demand. This elasticity is defined as the percentage change in quantity demanded divided by the percentage change in price, and it is an indication of the percentage responsiveness of quantity to price.

In general, derived demand has less price elasticity than direct demand if one assumes the existence of substitutes. This implies that a manufacturer of industrial goods is not often able to expand his market substantially through the use of price reductions. This does not mean, however, that he cannot increase sales through price reductions below the current market levels.

Direct demand is generally responsive to price change in most sectors of the consumer goods industry. For this reason, through price reductions, an industry can substantially increase its share of consumer spending at the expense of other industries, just as a firm can improve its share at the expense of another firm.

Although these general statements on the elasticity of demand provide the analyst with some insight, for the majority of market studies sufficient time, data, or funds are not available to conduct a sophisticated analysis of the relationship between price and demand. The market demand is simply determined with the price information limited to a presentation of the current and, perhaps, historical price structure for the product.

In addition to presenting the price structure, the analyst should provide some insight into how, in the past, competitor's prices have changed with the entry of a new firm into the market and, when substitution is possible, the price structure of substitute products. The price information gathered thus far then should be examined to see if the price of the product under study is indeed competitive. The relationship between the output and production costs from the technical analysis, coupled with administrative costs, indicates whether or not the proposed product can be produced at a competitive price.

Market Growth Patterns. An examination of the past demand for a product plotted against time results in curves showing certain typical characteristics of their growth patterns. In market measurement, especially forecasting, it is helpful to be able to recognize the type of growth pattern for a specific product. The existence of the historical growth pattern for a product is an aid in selecting the type of forecasting technique. Versions of three typical growth patterns, somewhat idealized, are illustrated.

The growth pattern shown in Figure 3.2a represents one extreme, that is, products whose sales move in a steady pattern. Forecasting is relatively easy, with comparatively smooth growth (or decline) characteristics.

The growth pattern shown in Figure 3.2b represents the opposite extreme. This highly volatile growth pattern indicates the influence of erratic and/or

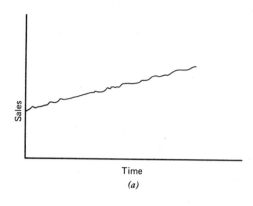

Time

(a)

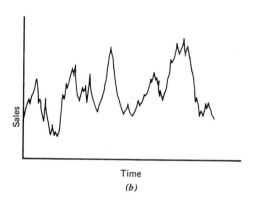

Time

(b)

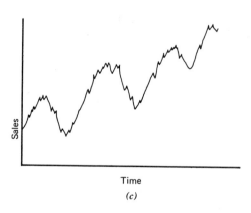

Time

(c)

Figure 3.2 Market growth pattern. (a) Steady growth pattern. (b) Highly volatile pattern. (c) Pattern of trend, cycle, and season.

Source. Philip Kotler, *Marketing Management*: Analysis, Planning, and Control (2nd ed. © 1972), p. 215. Reprinted by permission of Prentice-Hall, Inc., Englewood Cliffs, New Jersey.

nonrecurrent forces in the market. The growth of products showing these
characteristics is the most difficult to forecast.

The growth pattern shown in Figure 3.2c represents products whose growth
patterns fall between the two extremes. Demands for these products vary
appreciably but in a systematic manner, and there is recognizable regularity
in the forces acting on the sales of these products. This growth pattern can be
broken down into components of trend, cycle, and season. Trend forces contribute to the long-term shift (up or down) in sales. The large wavelike forms in
the pattern are the result of cyclical forces, and the smaller "sawtooth" effects
indicate seasonal forces. The term "season," incidentally, has come to refer to
any pattern of recurring movement with a periodicity of less than 1 year, and
not to the effects of the weather alone. Erratic forces may also be present but
not obvious at first glance. Trend-cycle-season patterns of growth are amenable
to forecasting techniques.

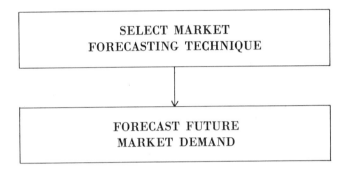

The current market demand for the product, the past market demand
growth pattern, and other market characteristics influence the choice of an
appropriate forecasting technique. The budget available, the time required to
develop the forecast, and the desired accuracy are other factors that influence
the selection of a forecasting technique.

The budget and time required to construct a forecast based on a survey of
end users is naturally more expensive and takes longer than a forecast
based on the assumption that the market will grow at the same rate as in the
previous year. The accuracy of the forecast depends heavily on the data available, as well as on certain market characteristics.

The market forecast for a new product for which there is no historical
statistical information is much more difficult, as well as more likely to be in
error, than a market forecast for a product for which such information is
available. The forecast for an industrial product where the customers are a

relatively small number of industry groups for which production figures have been published is apt to be more accurate than a forecast for a consumer product where customers compose a segment of the population that is difficult to identify and whose tastes are likely to change frequently. The geographic boundaries of the market area influence the accuracy of the forecast because data are more readily available at the national level than for smaller areas, and any method used to disaggregate the data to the smaller area increases the possibility of error.

The characteristics of the market also can influence the difficulty as well as the accuracy of the forecast. For example, it is much more difficult to forecast automobile sales, where the market exhibits a tendency toward wide year-to-year fluctuations, than to forecast future sales in the food industry, which exhibit a steady annual growth rate.

The general procedure employed to forecast market demand varies from product to product. The objective of the market forecast is to project the sales of the product or products for the desired time period. This sales projection is used in the technical analysis to construct a production schedule and to determine inventory requirements. A common practice is to forecast the market on an annual basis and then divide to obtain a monthly forecast. In cases in which seasonality of sales is important, the forecast interval should be monthly, or the production schedule, inventory requirements, and subsequential work flow analysis will yield erroneous results. The forecast is usually for a period of from 3 to 5 years into the future. Consideration, then, must be given to long-range influences on the market, such as number of households, which cause slow gradual trend changes, as well as short-range factors, which may cause fluctuations of sales along the long-term trend line.

The actual procedure used to forecast sales may begin with an examination of expectations of general economic and business conditions from which the market demand can be derived; or the procedure may involve forecasting the market demand using historical data; or it may use past sales of the firm to project future sales. The procedure discussed for estimating the product's sales is the most general in applicability. It consists of estimating market demand for the product and then determining the market share the proposed project is likely to capture.

A range of forecasting techniques can be used to estimate the market demand. If the data are adequate, and time and budget offer no constraints, it is sometimes possible to utilize sophisticated techniques to project future markets. Often, however, when the data are inadequate, the general direction of the market is all that can be ascertained.

The forecasting techniques that can be used to assemble and process the data into projections can be divided into four categories: those based on judgment, those based on surveys, those based on time series analysis, and those based on correlation analysis. It is not unusual to use a combination of techniques to derive the final forecast. Statistical forecasts, that is, time series and correlation analysis, are frequently used to provide baseline estimates of future market demand. These baseline estimates provide a starting point for considering factors which, although not important in the past, may be influential in the future. Such factors are used to alter the baseline market projections in a subjective manner.

Judgment Forecasts

Judgment forecasts are based on intuitive reasoning and subjective evaluations. However, a forecast of market demand based on judgment alone is not an appropriate technique. Seldom does the analyst possess sufficient experience with or knowledge of a product to make an accurate judgment forecast. Furthermore, the market analysis will be subject to the evaluation of others who are unlikely to accept a forecast based entirely on the judgment of the analyst, no matter how excellent his reputation. Judgment forecasts, however, are used in conjunction with other forecasting techniques. For example, as previously mentioned, a baseline forecast derived from a statistical technique may be altered because of specific factors the analyst believes to be important.

Survey Forecasts

Forecasts can be based on surveys of individuals involved in the market. Groups frequently surveyed are customers, distributors, salespeople, executives, and experts. The data are collected by using one of the survey techniques, such as mail questionnaires, personal or telephone interviews, or a group interactive method. Such forecasts are susceptible to the errors of statistical surveys such as nonresponse, as well as faulty judgment and uncertainty or ignorance among those surveyed. Such surveys, however, are useful in the identification of causal variables which provide insight into the market or need to be considered in the correlation analysis.

Survey of Buyer Intentions. This type of survey can consume a great deal of time and money depending primarily on the number of potential buyers, if all are to be surveyed, or the desired accuracy of the sample, if a sample is to be used. This approach also is dependent on how open the buyers are when reporting their intentions. Surveys of buyer intentions, however, have proved to be helpful in forecasts involving major consumer durable goods as well as industrial goods. The major obstacles that affect the accuracy of surveys of buyer intentions are that some buyers do not know their future intentions, some are unwilling to respond, and some, for various reasons, do not carry out their intentions.[16]

Kolter has pointed out that the effectiveness of survey forecasting increases to the extent that the buyers are few in number, the cost of reaching them effectively is small, they have clear intentions which they are willing to disclose, and they act on their original intentions.[17] A survey of buyer intentions, then, is most applicable for industrial products, for consumer durables, and for new products for which no data are available.

Sales Force Composite. If the project analysis involves an existing firm, the sales forecast for the firm can be made by taking a composite of the opinions of the sales force. This method is especially appropriate if the product under consideration is similar to the existing product line of the firm. The advantage of this forecasting technique is that estimates are made by individuals in close contact with local market demands. The major limitation to using a sales-person's estimates is that the individual salesperson tends to be either overly optimistic or pessimistic, depending on the economy, and this necessitates adjustments to his forecast. Also, salespeople are often unaware of basic economic developments affecting the firm's growth.

Executive Composite. Similar to the sales force composite, the executive composite gathers individual opinions on which to base an aggregate forecast. The major advantage of the executive composite technique compared with the sales force composite is that the opinions of executives involve broader economic considerations as well as a wider range of activities, because executives in the firm have different specialties and head different departments.

After the estimates have been collected from each executive, some method must be used to average them into meaningful information. Occasionally, the chief executive of the firm may make a final decision after a careful review of all estimates, or he may bring the executives together for discussion and modification of the estimates.

---

[16] Robert W. Eckles and Ronald L. Carmichael, *Market Research for Small Firms* (Rolla. Mo.: Extension Division, University of Missouri-Rolla), p. 11.
[17] Kolter, p. 211.

Expert Composite. A survey of expert opinions is similar to both the sales force composite and the executive composite. This forecasting technique surveys experts found in the firm's distribution channels, appropriate government agencies, trade and professional associations, and private institutions as to their opinions on the future demand for a product.

When data concerning the demand for new or existing products are scarce or nonexistent, a forecast based on a survey of experts is especially apropos, particularly since it can be made quickly and inexpensively. A more lengthy procedure, such as the Delphi method, also can be used. The Delphi technique attempts to crystallize group opinions or judgments of experts unidentified to each other through the use of written questionnaires in an iterative process. As the iterations continue, a convergence of estimates usually occurs.

Independent Forecasts Composite. The analyst can examine existing forecasts and arrive at a composite forecast by adjusting these forecasts in terms of his assessment of the individuals who made them, the forecast procedures used, and their applicability. The use of this forecasting technique provides baseline forecasts, and it is especially applicable to forecasts involving industrial products where the end-using industries have been identified and previous forecasts exist.

Time Series Forecasts

Forecasts based on time series analysis, as well as those based on correlation analysis, discussed in the next section, are statistical techniques that can be used only when historical data for the product are available. Statistical forecasting techniques rely on the basic assumption that past growth patterns will continue into the future. In the case of time series analysis, or trend analysis as it is often referred to, the past and future markets for the product are treated only as a function of time, with no consideration of other factors such as price or income changes which also influence demand. Because factors other than time influence demand, time series forecasting contains an inherent weakness which usually limits its usefulness to the immediate future, for example, 1 to 3 years, depending on the product. After this period of time, time series projections are sometimes treated as baseline projections and are altered accordingly, using other forecasting techniques.

The market data used to make projections with time series analysis should be considered raw data. The data for the product covering a specific period of time consists of secular trend (long-term trend), cyclical variations, seasonal variations, and irregular variations. Each of these can be seen as a separate entity if the pattern of such factors has been well developed. Then trend, cyclical, and seasonal components can be projected to determine the future market demand.

Secular Trend Analysis. Extrapolation of the market trend can be accomplished using two simple techniques which are most appropriate for conditions involving steady growth patterns and short-range forecasts.

- The market during the next time period is assumed to be equal to the market during the time period most recently past.
- The rate of change between the last two time periods is figured, and this rate of change is then applied to the most current time period to obtain a forecast for the future period.

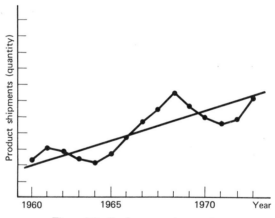

Figure 3.3   Product growth over time.

The best procedure when fitting a growth trend to historical data is to plot the past history of the market on a chart against time. An examination of the graph will show whether the growth pattern is steady, highly volatile, or trend-cycle-season.

If the market growth curve exhibits a general upward trend, approximating a straight line, even though the line tends to zigzag as in Figure 3.3, a straight line can be drawn and continued into the future to obtain a future estimate of the market.

The straight line in fact can be drawn in freehand. The use of the mathematical technique of least squares to fit a trend line to the plotted data points is best, however, since it eliminates guesswork. With the mathematical equation determined by least squares, the future market demand can then be obtained by substituting the future year into the equation.

If the long-term trend line of the market is not a straight line, the least-squares recession line will not be appropriate. There are several growth trends, or curves, such as parabola, exponential, or S-type from which to choose. If the analyst has access to computerized statistical programming packages, the market data can be fitted to several growth curves easily, and the curve that gives the best fit selected.[18]

Seasonal and Cyclical Variations. The forecast based on market trend does not include seasonal and cyclical elements that cause fluctuations around the trend line. If the forecast interval under consideration is annual, or if monthly data on the market are unavailable, seasonal adjusted market data are impossible to obtain. Furthermore, if the forecast interval is annual, the seasonal factor does not need to be considered.

The easiest way to calculate a seasonal monthly index is to average all the figures for a specific month, say June, and then divide each of these averages into the overall monthly average.

Another technique is the ratio-to-moving average. For example, sales for a given month can be compared to a moving average which, because it encompasses a 12-month period, contains no seasonal effects. The ratio of the actual value for a given month to the moving average gives a percentage indication as to how that month compares to data from which seasonal influence has been eliminated. The ratios for a given month over several years can then be averaged in order to obtain indexes of seasonal variation which, when applied to the trend-cycle component, yield a forecast that includes the seasonal element.

The cyclical pattern can be isolated by removing the seasonal and trend factors from the raw data. The resultant data should produce a relatively smooth undulating curve, similar to a sine wave. The extrapolation of the cycle into the future can be accomplished by projection of the old cycle. However, this does not take into account factors that may influence the cycle in the future. To simplify the analysis, the trend and cycle elements are often considered together. The projected trend-cycle forecast can be used as a baseline forecast which may be adjusted.

---

[18] For extensive discussions on techniques used for time series analysis, see Robert Ferber (ed.), *Handbook of Marketing Research* (New York: McGraw-Hill, 1974) and Robert Parsons, *Statistical Analysis: A Decision-Making Approach* (New York: Harper & Row, 1974), Chaps. 24–28.

Exponential Smoothing. Exponential smoothing is a time series technique which can produce efficient and economical short-range forecasts of up to 12 months. With exponential smoothing the greatest weight or influence is assigned to the most recent data.

Correlation Analysis

Correlation analysis is the most objective of any of the forecasting techniques discussed so far in that it helps to identify and to measure the direct relationships between the market and other variables. Correlation analysis determines the degree of relationship between the market, the dependent variable, and the independent variable, such as personal income, and indicates to what extent a linear or other equation describes or explains the relationship between the variables. In so doing, it provides a statistical relationship that permits predictions.

Correlation analysis is best used when the emphasis is on long-term trends. It is not as appropriate for short-range forecasts where cyclical or seasonal factors can distort the correlation. If the analyst can discover one or more factors that influence the product's demand, if he can determine the quantitative relationship between these factors and the product, and if he can then forecast the factor or factors, he can use correlation analysis to forecast the market for the product.

The variable to be forecasted, for example, the shipments of pumps, is referred to as the dependent variable. Independent variables explain, statistically, the changes in the variable to be forecasted. In this case, one independent variable could be new plant and equipment expenditures. Pump shipments are related to new plant and equipment expenditures; shipments tend to rise when new plant and equipment expenditures increase and to fall when expenditures decrease. Correlation analysis can be used to determine the nature of this relationship. That is, if new plant and equipment expenditures increase 10%, by what percent do pump shipments increase?

This example illustrates one limitation to obtaining forecasts by correlation analysis. If forecasts for suitable independent variables are not available, or if the relationship with the dependent variable is not lagged (i.e., pump shipments are related to new plant and equipment expenditures for the previous year), forecasts cannot be made.

The most common technique used in correlation analysis is linear correlation analysis; therefore the relationship between the dependent and independent variables must be linear. When examining a linear correlation, which involves only two variables, to determine its suitability a scatter diagram similar to Figure 3.4 is first prepared.

The scatter diagram is then studied for indications of stability in the relationship between the data. A high degree of correlation is evident if a straight or regression line can be drawn so that all points are quite close to it. This seems to be similar to trend analysis, except that here the comparison is between two sets of data rather than one set of data against time, as in trend analysis. The greater the distance between the points and the regression line, the poorer the correlation. Poor or no correlation exists if the points are widely dispersed and, accordingly, the factor is eliminated from the study.

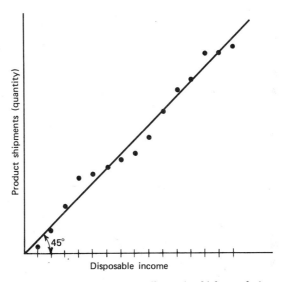

Figure 3.4 Scatter diagram illustrating high correlation.

Mathematical approaches to measuring the degree and nature of the relationship can also be used. The equation for measuring the degree of correlation yields r the coefficient of correlation. The extent to which the independent variable can explain the market is indicated by the degree of correlation value r, and the value of r ranges between $+ 1$ and $- 1$. Any value close to $+ 1$ and $- 1$ indicates a good correlation, while any value near 0 indicates a poor correlation.

In principle, multiple correlation or multiple regression is more like single correlation, the only difference being that, with the former, the market is correlated simultaneously with two or more independent variables (e.g., personal income, number of households), to explain the dependent variable (e.g., product shipments).

DEVELOP THE SALES PLAN AND PREPARE A REPORT

At this point in the market analysis, the sales forecast for the project has been developed. This sales forecast is an estimate of the sales expected for the product, given existing economic conditions, competitors, and the level of marketing effort. The basic procedure used to determine the sales forecast was to project the total market size and then to estimate the part of the market the project could capture. With this information the sales plan can be developed.

Sales Plan

The sales plan or sales budget combines the sales projections with the planned commitments of resources for advertising, promotion, and selling to obtain the expected sales volume. The sales plan encompasses three elements: the promotion and advertising plan, the selling expense plan, and the marketing plan.

Marketing Plan

The marketing plan shows the units and dollars of sales revenue by products and by geographic area, usually quarter by quarter for the first year, and thereafter on an annual basis. The marketing plan is very important because the product requirements specified in it must be converted to manufacturing requirements such as labor and raw materials.

Although the sales projection provides the basis for the marketing plan, other considerations such as the level of advertising and promotion and selling expenses influence the level of sales volume.

Some confusion may arise from the fact that the sales projections contain a level of marketing effort and therefore should be included in the marketing plan without further alteration. This is true if there is no management or proposed management for the project under study. However, the level of marketing effort contained in the sales forecast is usually based on the assumption that the level of effort in the past will continue in the future, or on a published figure for the specific industry being studied. Where management activity exists, the sales forecast represents a technical input which is subject to managerial judgment and strategy on the level of market effort; hence the resultant marketing plan.

Advertising and Promotion Plan

The advertising and promotion plan contains the type, as well as the costs, of promotional programs and media advertising required to generate the expected sales volume. The primary interest to the analyst is the levels at which these activities should be conducted. As previously stated, if a management or proposed management exists, they specify the level of advertising. However, for some projects the analyst has to consult published data to determine the relationship between the levels of sales generated by different levels of advertising for the industry under study. The data usually provide advertising information such as the advertising sales ratio by firm size in each industry.

Selling Expense Plan.   The marketing plan also provides the basis for calculating sales expenses. Selling expenses are all the expenses, except advertising, incurred in contacting customers, delivering products to them, and collecting money. There are two principal categories of sales expenses: those that vary directly with output and those that are constant for a given level of sales.

Selling expenses that vary directly with sales are sales commissions, distribution costs, and packaging costs. Sales commissions are calculated as a percentage of sales. The regional distribution of sales provided by the marketing plan and the appropriate freight rates allow the estimation of distribution costs. The type of packaging as well as its cost must be decided, so that the packaging costs can be calculated.

Some selling expenses, such as salespeople's salaries, traveling, and entertainment, are constant for a given level of sales and are usually considered annual appropriations.

Final Report

The levels of effort with respect to budget, time available to conduct the market analysis, and data availability are factors that influence the type of final report presented. Market research reports can vary from very short (6 to 10 pages) to lengthy studies, depending on the depth of analysis conducted.

Whatever the length, the market study should contain a statement of objectives, explanation of research approach, and findings or conclusions. The statement of objectives should clearly state the background of the market analysis, indicate the market area and product being researched, and point out the data expected to materialize from study. The explanation of the research approach is for the benefit of those who are expected to take action based on the report, as well as for those who may not be well versed in marketing research procedures, and should contain an outline of the various steps taken in gathering and interpreting the data. Survey forms, questionnaires, and other tools may be referred to here, but should be placed in the appendix. The findings, that is, the actual material gathered, should be presented skillfully without bias.

The report should contain a brief summary of the most significant conclusions drawn from analysis of the findings.

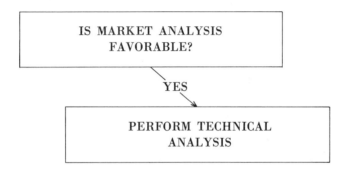

A decision can be made at this stage as to whether or not the remainder of the project analysis should be conducted. If the market study reveals an inadequate demand for the product or other characteristics of the market which would severely hamper the product's chances of success, the feasibility analysis can be terminated.

BIBLIOGRAPHY

Boyd, Harper W., Jr., and Ralph Westfall. *Marketing Research: Text and Cases.* 3rd ed. Homewood, Ill: Richard D. Irwin, 1972.

Bringe, Paul J. "A Basic Guide to Better Direct Mail Copy," *Industrial Marketing*, Sept. 1958.

Chambers, John G., Satinder K. Mullick, and Donald D. Smith. *An Executive's Guide to Forecasting.* New York: Wiley, 1974.

Cochran, William G. *Sampling Techniques.* New York: Wiley, 1953.

Davies, Anthony H. *The Practice of Marketing Research.* London: William Heinemann, 1973.

Eckles, Robert W., and Ronald L. Carmichael. *Market Research for Small Firms.* Rolla, Mo.: Extension Division, University of Missouri-Rolla, n.d.

Enrick, Norbert Lloyd. *Market and Sales Forecasting: A Quantitative Approach*. San Francisco: Chandler, 1969.

Ferber, Robert (ed.). *Handbook of Marketing Research*. New York: McGraw-Hill, 1974.

Ferber, Robert, and P. J. Verdoorn. *Research Methods in Economics and Business*. New York: Macmillan, 1962.

Hyman, Herbert, et. al. *Interviewing in Social Research*. Chicago: University of Chicago Press, 1954.

Kotler, Philip. *Marketing Management*. 2nd ed. Englewood Cliffs, N.J.: Prentice-Hall, 1972.

Lawrence, Barbara. "Preliminary Project Evaluation—Any Technologist Can Do It," *Chemtech*, Nov. 1975.

MacKenzie, George F. "How to Make the Marketing Concept Make Sense," *Industrial Marketing*, March 1960.

Parsons, Robert. *Statistical Analysis: A Decision-Making Approach*. New York: Harper & Row, 1974.

Parten, Mildred. *Surveys, Polls and Samples: Practical Procedures*. New York: Cooper Square Publishers, 1966.

Petry, Glenn H., and Stanley F. Quackenbush. "The Conservation of the Questionnaire as a Research Source," *Business Horizons*, **17**, No. 4 (Aug. 1974), pp. 43–47.

Reichard, Robert S. *Practical Techniques of Sales Forecasting*. New York: McGraw-Hill, 1966.

Stanton, William T. *Fundamentals of Marketing*. New York: McGraw-Hill, 1964.

Wentz, Walter B. *Marketing Research: Management and Methods*. New York: Harper & Row, 1972.

Wills, Gordon (compiler). *Sources of U.K. Marketing Information*. London: Thomas Nelson, 1969.

Wilson, Aubrey, *The Assessment of Industrial Markets*. London: Hutchinson, 1968.

Yamane, Taro. *Elementary Sampling Theory*. Englewood Cliffs, N. J.: Prentice-Hall, 1967.

Zaltman, Gerald, and Philip C. Burger. *Marketing Research: Fundamentals and Dynamics*. Hinsdale, Ill.: Dryden Press, 1975.

Zeisel, Hans. *Say It with Figures*. 5th ed. rev. New York: McGraw-Hill, 1968.

Chapter Four

TECHNICAL ANALYSIS

The technical analysis must establish whether or not the project is technically feasible and, if so, make tentative choices among technical alternatives and provide cost estimates as follows.

- *Fixed investment.* The cost of land, building, and auxiliary installations, and of equipment and installation.
- *Manufacturing costs and expenses.* The costs associated with production. These costs are direct material, direct labor, and factory overhead.
- *Start-up costs and expenses.* Costs over and above normal manufacturing costs, which may occur during plant start-up. Examples are increased overtime, rework, scrap, and learning costs.

From the viewpoint of the industrial developer, it also provides an opportunity to examine the projected effects of various technological alternatives on employment level, infrastructure demands, support of other industries, balance of payments, and ecology.

In order to provide cost estimates, tentative choices must be made among technical alternatives such as:

- Level of production technology.
- Raw material inputs.

- Equipment.
- Methods.
- Organization.
- Facilities location and design.

The technical analysis is vital to the final decision to carry out the project or to abandon it and is an important part of the business plan.

DEPTH OF THE TECHNICAL ANALYSIS

In this chapter is described a step-by-step procedure for a detailed technical analysis which will provide a basis for accurate cost estimates. In any particular study, it is unlikely that all these steps will be performed in the manner described. The amount of effort and detail that can be justified depends on the project size, the technological newness and complexity of the product, the number of technical alternatives (e.g., processes, methods, materials), and the desired accuracy of cost estimates. It is conceivable, for example, that in the case of a well-established product, standard production processes are well known, the choices of technical alternatives are obvious, and adequate cost estimates are available from industry sources. In such cases it would indeed be foolish to expend extensive effort on the technical analysis. The majority of new ventures, however, do not fit this description. Most of them contain novel features, or else they would not be worth consideration. For many new ventures economic feasibility is dependent on process innovations as yet untried and unproven, and the technical alternatives are numerous and complex. In these cases, technical feasibility must be established and, depending on the size of the project, detailed systems design and planning may be needed to ensure accurate cost estimates.

While it is true that the time and effort expended on the technical study must be related to the factors listed above, the risks of inadequate studies must be understood. Mistakes in technical analysis are most often due to inadequate preliminary analysis of technological requirements, failure to consider alternatives, and neglect of "secondary" factors such as material handling, inventory requirements, maintenance, and social facilities for employees. The inadequacy of the technical analysis is a potential source of serious errors which can result in financial problems if not failure of the new venture. The lack of thoroughness may result in costly trial-and-error modifications of facilities and processes when the plant begins production and/or failure to reach planned levels of productivity. The underestimation of secondary factors involving a large increase in investment may lead to the necessity of abandoning the project.

Aside from these problems, an inadequate technical analysis also produces misleading cost estimates. The estimates of total investment, working capital requirements, start-up costs, and manufacturing costs are particularly vulnerable to error if the technical analysis is poorly done. However, a well-done technical analysis is never a waste of time if the venture proves to be economically feasible and the decision is made to initiate the project. In this case, much of the planning for production facilities and systems will have been done. The acquisition of these facilities and systems can begin without delay.

PRELIMINARY INFORMATION REQUIREMENTS

Information that must be available to start the technical analysis is:

1. Product information.

   - Design and performance specifications.
   - Quality level.
   - Service requirements.

2. Market information.

   - Sales forecast.
   - Delivery service requirements.
   - Customer locations.

3. Materials information.

   - Specifications.
   - Availability.
   - Delivery lead time.
   - Source locations.

4. Other.

   - Capital availability.
   - Labor availability.

The product information should have been developed when the venture idea was selected, and perhaps clarified and refined during the market analysis. The required sales- and customer-related information is obtained from the market analysis, and specifications for raw materials, availability, and other materials information are derived from the product specifications.

STEPS OF THE TECHNICAL ANALYSIS

The flowchart of a technical analysis is shown in Figure 4.1. Individual steps
are discussed in the following sections of this chapter.

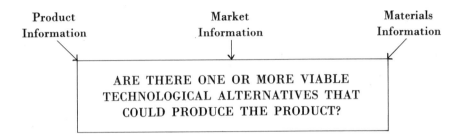

The first step in the technical analysis is to determine the alternatives
available to produce the product. The purposes of this step are (1) to avoid the
unquestioned use of an inappropriate level of technology and (2) to ensure that
all alternatives are considered. The alternatives may be fundamentally different processes, but more likely they differ only in the degree of mechanization.

Except for proprietary processes, the production technology for established
products is generally well known to the field and is available from trade associations and their publications. Other excellent sources are the manufacturers
of production equipment. Even for new products, production technology may
be available "off the shelf" if the materials and production operations are
similar to those for existing products. However, the analyst must be alert to
opportunities for the development of new technology which may provide
lower costs or a better product.

This search for alternative levels of technology is particularly important in
feasibility studies for projects in developing countries in order to avoid the
transfer of inappropriate technology from capital-intensive countries. For
example, the level of technology for producing iron castings in a country where
capital is extremely scarce (particularly foreign exchange with which to purchase imported machinery) and labor is readily available at $1.50 per day must
be different than in a country where capital is plentiful but labor is priced at
$50 per day. It would be a mistake, however, to conclude that labor and capital
costs are the only factors that affect the level of technology decision in such
cases. Quality requirements, particularly in goods to be produced for international trade, are also an important factor. Generally speaking, lower technology (i.e., labor-intensive) has trouble consistently producing goods of high

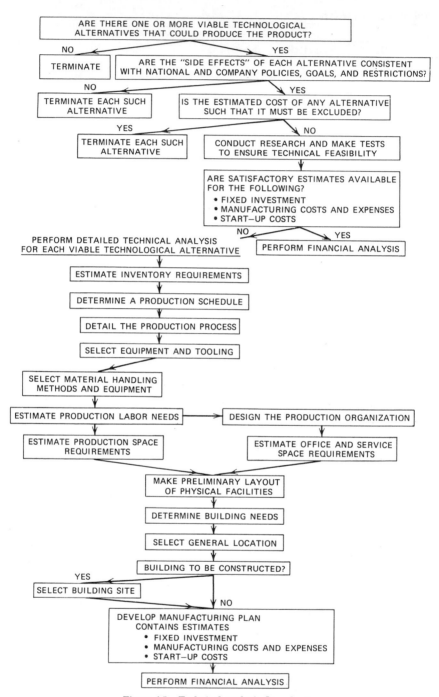

Figure 4.1 Technical analysis flow chart.

quality for world markets. For this reason, mechanization may be required even in a labor-intensive environment.

The important point in this step is that we are concerned with identifying alternatives capable of doing the job and none should be overlooked.

YES

ARE THE "SIDE EFFECTS" OF EACH ALTERNATIVE
CONSISTENT WITH NATIONAL AND COMPANY
POLICIES, GOALS, AND RESTRICTIONS?

This is the first of several steps in the process of eliminating alternatives that are inappropriate for producing the product. Note that the question refers to alternative levels of technology and not to the venture itself. Similar questions concerning the venture should have been answered in the initial screening.

Factors to be considered "side effects" include:

- Contribution to employment.
- Requirements for scarce skills, expatriots.
- Energy requirements.
- Environmental effects.
- Capital requirements.
- Need for imported equipment.
- Support of indigenous industry.
- Multiplier effect of the venture operation.
- Safety and health hazards.

These are not simple issues, and their evaluation is not easy. However, they are often the subject of official governmental concern, as evidenced by legislation and/or administrative policy. The project analyst must be well informed concerning such legislation and policy, and each technological alternative must be examined to ensure that there are no violations.

YES

IS THE ESTIMATED COST OF ANY ALTERNATIVE
SUCH THAT IT MUST BE EXCLUDED?

Even at this early stage, it is possible to examine rough estimates and reject alternatives that are clearly above the cost limits established for the project.

NO

CONDUCT RESEARCH AND MAKE TESTS TO ENSURE TECHNICAL FEASIBILITY

New products that depend on utilization of new technology for production obviously require tests and research to ensure that such technology is available in a suitable state of perfection. In the case of old products, venture success may hinge on a competitive advantage derived from such factors as a change to lower-cost raw material and process improvements to increase productivity. Examples of research and tests which may be needed are:

- Laboratory or pilot-plant tests of various raw material inputs.
- Research to develop processes or to adapt existing technology.
- Tests to verify adequacy of production process performance under local environmental conditions.

ARE SATISFACTORY ESTIMATES AVAILABLE FOR THE FOLLOWING?
- **FIXED INVESTMENT**
- **MANUFACTURING COSTS AND EXPENSES**
- **START-UP COSTS AND EXPENSES**

Estimates of these costs and capital needs are required for the financial analysis. If satisfactory estimates can be obtained from competitors, friends, trade sources, government data, or elsewhere, they may be used without going through a costly detailed technical analysis. A word of caution is in order, however. Two of the most frequent causes of new-venture failure are underestimation of fixed investment costs and failure to allow for working capital. If rough estimates are used for the financial analysis, they should be used with conservatism. In most cases, a detailed technical analysis should be made in order to estimate costs and capital needs more accurately.

PERFORM DETAILED TECHNICAL ANALYSIS
FOR EACH VIABLE TECHNOLOGICAL ALTERNATIVE

ESTIMATE
INVENTORY REQUIREMENTS

The primary purpose of inventories is to absorb the shocks of fluctuating demand. They serve as a "buffer" between the production (supply) function and the customer (demand) and permit the supply function to operate in an economic fashion even though demand is irregular both as to timing and quantity. Finished goods inventories, for example, permit quick delivery to the customer and controlled, level production in the plant. The disadvantage of inventories is that they cost money. For most firms, inventories represent a sizable investment which could otherwise be earning a direct cash return. However, failure to maintain adequate inventories also costs money in the form of lost sales and production interruptions.

Types of Inventories

Inventories are stocks of goods held in anticipation of use or sales. They are classified as follows.

- *Raw materials and purchased parts.* These are inputs to the production processes. Such inventories are necessary because (1) it is usually impossible to obtain deliveries that exactly coincide with production needs, (2) savings can be obtained by purchasing economic lot quantities, and (3) it is sometimes desirable to hold stocks in anticipation of price increases.
- *Work in process.* In-process inventories are the stock of partially complete product in the plant. These inventories are necessary to ensure smooth and continuous operation of production processes and to facilitate production scheduling.
- *Finished goods.* Finished goods inventories are stock that is available for shipment to customers. The need for finished goods inventories arises in two ways. First, since actual demand will almost certainly be different from forecasted demand, there is a need for a "safety stock" to ensure that customer orders can be filled without delay. Second, forecasted demand can fluctuate widely—particularly in seasonal-type goods such as lawn furniture, sports equipment, and toys. However, it is not generally desirable

to have the same wide fluctuations in production. Thus, in order to stabilize the work force and reduce capital requirements, products are produced during periods of low demand and held in inventory to be available for periods of high demand. These inventories are called "stabilization stock" and serve to keep production at a planned rate.

- *Supplies.* These are stocks of items used indirectly in production (e.g., sandpaper, glue, cleaning compounds) or in the management and maintenance of the plant.

Estimating Inventory Requirements

In an ongoing firm, optimal inventory levels are calculated to minimize the combined costs of holding inventory and inventory shortages. These calculations are based on historical data and depend on how much the actual demand fluctuated from forecasted demand. However, the entrepreneur or his technical analyst is not, at this point, concerned with optimal inventory levels. What is needed is a realistic estimate of the various inventory needs in order to arrive at (1) production schedules, (2) cost estimates, and (3) an estimate of working capital requirements. It is better to *overestimate* inventory needs than to ignore or underestimate. As a rule of thumb, it is suggested that inventory levels equivalent to 1 month's demand (i.e., one-twelfth of the forecasted annual demand) be allowed. If it is known that, in a particular case, this is inappropriate, adjustments should be made. For example, if raw materials are to be supplied by distant vendors and lead times are highly variable, a 2-month inventory may be more appropriate.

DETERMINE A PRODUCTION SCHEDULE

The production schedule is a specific manufacturing program which includes production for safety stock and may reflect efforts to operate at a planned constant production rate. It forms the basis for subsequent analysis and cost estimating.

In order to develop the production schedule it is necessary to begin with the projected production requirements. This does not mean a simple estimate of total sales over the year. What is needed are estimates of monthly or quarterly sales. Such estimates should be available from the market analysis. Unless the company produces only to specific customer orders, the actual production plan is arrived at by adjusting these estimates to reflect inventory changes.

Figure 4.2 illustrates the use of stabilization stock for production leveling.

In this case there is no initial inventory, and the production schedule for the first 4 months is set at 400 units per month to permit inventory buildup. Production for the remainder of the year is constant at 350 units per month, even though forecasted sales reach a seasonal high of 400 during months 6 and 7. At the end of the year the inventory level is near the desired safety stock level, and a new production schedule should be based on forecasted sales for the next year.

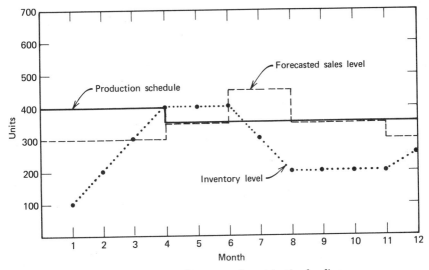

Figure 4.2   The use of inventory for production leveling.

If the nature of the product is such that each job is designed and produced to a specific customer order, only components that are common to many such jobs can be produced for inventory. In this case, the production plan is determined by the forecasted orders during a given time period and the desired delivery times.

DETAIL THE PRODUCTION PROCESS

The production process is the sequence of operations, moves, and inspections by which raw material inputs are converted to a finished product ready for the customer. While it is not necessary to design the plant completely in order to estimate costs, it is necessary to choose production methods and equipment and material handling methods and equipment, and to make at least tentative decisions concerning layout, inventory needs, and personnel requirements.

These factors affect both investment and manufacturing costs. The accuracy and completeness of cost estimates depend on how thoroughly the production process is detailed and analyzed.

The process chart is a useful means to detail a production process and ensure thoroughness in the technical analysis and cost estimating. An example chart is shown in Figure 4.3. The symbols used and their meanings are:

OPERATION. Any activity that results in a physical or chemical change in the product or component; also assembly or disassembly.

TRANSPORTATION. Any move that is not an integral part or an operation or inspection; also the prepositioning of a part in preparation for a subsequent operation or inspection.

INSPECTION. Any comparison or verification of characteristics against a quality or quantity standard.

DELAY. Any time period during which the component or product is waiting for an operation, inspection, or transportation.

STORAGE. Holding of the component or product for authorized removal.

Printed forms of the type shown in Figure 4.3 are readily available from most engineering bookstores, or the chart may be simply drawn with the appropriate symbols. Construction of the chart begins by filling in the heading to identify properly the part or assembly. Each production step is then recorded in the proper sequence and numbered. In addition to the number in the left-hand column of the chart, each symbol of the same type (e.g., each individual operation, transportation, inspection, delay, or storage) is numbered consecutively. The numbered symbols are then connected, so that the process steps can be easily followed. Each chart should follow the production steps for a single component from raw material to completion. Separate charts should be used to describe the assembly of components into subassemblies or finished products.

The information to be recorded in columns 4, 5, 6, and 7 depends on the purpose for which the chart is used. These include:

• Production equipment planning.
• In-process inventory planning.
• Space requirements planning.

PROCESS CHART

PART NAME_____Rotor Shaft 24K365_____

PROCESS DESCRIPTION _____Machine and Grind_____

DEPARTMENT _____Machining_____

PLANT _____#3_____

RECORDED BY____R.G.L._____ DATE___June 4_____

SUMMARY		NO.
○ OPERATIONS		
⇨ TRANSPORTATIONS		
☐ INSPECTIONS		
D DELAYS		
▽ STORAGES		
	TOTAL STEPS	
	DISTANCE TRAVELED	

STEP	Operations Transport Inspect Delay Storage	DESCRIPTION OF Proposed METHOD				
1	○⇨☐D▽	1/2" steel bar stock from storage				
2	①⇨☐D▽	cut to length and chamfer				
3	○⇨☐D▽	at cut-off machine				
4	○⇨☐D▽	to lathe				
5	②⇨☐D▽	cut retaining ring grooves				
6	○⇨☐D▽	at lathe				
7	○⇨☐D▽	to grinder				
8	③⇨☐D▽	grind O.D.				
9	○⇨①D▽	check surface finish, O.D. and roundness				
10	○⇨☐D▽	at grinder				
11	○⇨☐D▽	to milling machine				
12	④⇨☐D▽	mill end flat				
13	○⇨②D▽	check depth of flat				
14	○⇨☐D▽	at milling machine				
15	○⇨☐D▽	to rust protection treatment				
16	⑤⇨☐D▽	apply rust protection				
17	○⇨☐D▽	to shaft inventory				
18	○⇨☐D▽	at shaft area				
	○⇨☐D▽					
	○⇨☐D▽					
	○⇨☐D▽					
	○⇨☐D▽					

Figure 4.3

- Materials-handling equipment planning.
- Production labor planning.

Each of these is discussed at the appropriate step of the technical analysis.

SELECT EQUIPMENT AND TOOLING

Production equipment and tooling selection is facilitated by the process chart. For each operation, determine the alternative methods and equipment to accomplish the work. Also, consider the possibility of grouping several operations which offer the opportunity of being more economically performed if they are done at the same work station. Next, select the best alternative for the operation or group of operations.

Information concerning manufacturing processes and equipment can be obtained from:

- Existing manufacturers of the product.
- Trade publications.
- Trade associations and organizations.
- Equipment manufacturers.

Undoubtedly, the existing manufacturers with whom your plant competes will not be eager to supply information. However, you may obtain information from distant companies with whom you do not compete. Trade associations are listed in the *Encyclopedia of Associations*[1] which is available at most large libraries. These organizations are an excellent source of information concerning production methods, equipment, and suppliers of equipment. Once equipment alternatives have been identified, manufacturers can be located with the assistance of the *Thomas Register of Manufacturers and Thomas Register Catalog File*.[2] Equipment manufacturers are of course anxious to provide information concerning their products.

"Do's and Don'ts" for Equipment Selection

- Don't transfer methods and technology directly from another environment without modification and testing.

[1] Margaret Fisk, *Encyclopedia of Associations*, 9th ed. (Detroit: Gale Research Co., 1975).
[2] *Thomas Register of Manufacturers and Thomas Register Catalog File* (New York: Thomas Publishing Co., 1975).

- Do consider the following factors which may affect the choice of equipment and tooling.

  (*a*) Output capacity.
  (*b*) Quality capability.
  (*c*) Labor requirements (quantity and skill).
  (*d*) Convenience and simplicity of use.
  (*e*) Downtime expected.
  (*f*) Maintainability.
      Availability of repair parts.
      Skill needed to repair.
  (*g*) Input material requirements.
  (*h*) Materials handling requirements into and away from the machine.
  (*i*) Set-up difficulty.
  (*j*) Expense to install and debug.
  (*k*) Power, air, water, gas, or other utilities required.
  (*l*) Life expectancy and salvage value.
  (*m*) Risk of obsolescence.
  (*n*) Noxious by-products of operation.
  (*o*) Imported or locally produced.

- Do consider the "side effects" discussed earlier.
- Do consider all alternatives and make the decision only after a sound engineering economic analysis.

Economic Analysis of Equipment Alternatives

For most operations there are alternatives for accomplishing the required work. Usually, the alternatives differ with respect to initial investment, useful life, and operating costs. A typical example is shown in Table 4.1. Suppose both alternatives 1 and 2 have the capacity to meet production requirements and are equal in all respects except as shown in the table. Which machine should be chosen? The answer is not at all obvious. Certainly we cannot just add the cost figures and compare the total costs over the life of each alternative, for two reasons: (1) the length of life is not the same, and (2) the cash flows are not equivalent. Neither can we obtain an average yearly cost for each alternative by dividing investment cost by expected life and adding this to the annual operating and maintenance costs, since the cash flows are not equivalent. We can, however, compare the alternatives on an *equivalent annual cost* basis if we recognize the time value of money and choose an appropriate interest rate. Suppose, for example, that an annual interest rate of 15% is appropriate. Then, assuming that investment expenditures are initial expenditures and that all

Table 4.1   Economic Comparison of Equipment Alternatives

		Alternative 1		Alternative 2
Investment (I)			$24,300	$25,700
Purchase price	$20,000		$22,500	
Installation costs	1,700		1,500	
Transportation costs	1,100		1,200	
Tests and debugging	500		500	
Equipment operating costs				
(annual costs)		$13,450		$12,700
Labor	$ 9,500		$ 9,500	
Power and utilities	750		500	
Supplies	1,200		1,200	
Scrap and rework	2,000		1,500	
Maintenance costs	Year 1:	$1,000		
	Year 2:	1,200		
	Year 3:	1,400	Maintenance contract	
	Year 4:	1,750	at $1,500 per year	
	Year 5:	2,000		
Expected life	5 years		7 years	
Salvage value (S)	$2,500		$3,500	

other costs are paid at the *end* of each year, the alternatives can be compared as follows:

1. *For each alternative calculate the annual amount over the life of the alternative which is equivalent to the initial investment I less the salvage value S if interest is 15% per year.* These equivalent annual amounts are denoted by A_1 and A_2. Calculation of A_1 and A_2 requires the use of an interest factor:

$$(A/P, i, n) = \frac{i(1 + i)^n}{(1 + i)^n - 1}$$

where i = annual interest rate and n = expected life in years.

This factor is explained in the Appendix and values are tabulated in Table A.3. Using the interest factor for $i = 15\%$ and $n = 5$ from Table A.3, calculations are made as follows.

Alternative 1

$A_1 = (24,300 - 2500) \, (A/P, 0.15, 5)$
$ = 21,800 \, (0.298)$
$ = \$6496.40$

Alternative 2

$$A_1 = (25,700 - 3500) \, (A/P, \, 0.15, \, 7)$$
$$= 22,200 \, (0.240)$$
$$= \$5328.00$$

2. *For each alternative calculate the annual interest on the salvage value.*

Alternative 1

Annual interest on salvage value = 2500.00 (0.15)
$$= \$375.00$$

Alternative 2

Annual interest on salvage value = 3500.00 (0.15)
$$= \$525.00$$

3. *For each alternative calculate the uniform annual operating costs.* Since these are given as uniform annual costs, no calculations are required.

Alternative 1

Uniform annual operating costs = \$13,450.00

Alternative 2

Uniform annual operating costs = \$12,700.00

4. *For each alternative calculate the uniform annual costs that are equivalent to the nonuniform maintenance costs.* This calculation requires first that the non-uniform costs be expressed as a present value amount as explained in Appendix A and that this amount be multiplied by the appropriate interest factor to obtain the uniform annual cost. The interest factors for present value,

$$(P/F, \, i, \, n) = (1 + i)^{-n}$$

are tabulated in Table A.2.

Alternative 1

Present value of maintenance costs:
$$PV = 1000(P/F, \, 0.15, \, 1) + 1200(P/F, \, 0.15, \, 2) + 1400(P/F, \, 0.15, \, 3)$$
$$+ \, 1750(P/F, \, 0.15, \, 4) + 2000(P/F, \, 0.15, \, 5)$$
$$= 1000(0.870) + 1200(0.756) + 1400(0.658)$$
$$+ \, 1750(0.572) + 2000(0.497)$$
$$= 870.00 + 907.20 + 921.20 + 1001.00 + 994.00$$
$$= \$4693.40$$

Uniform equivalent annual disbursements:

$$EAD = 4693.40 \ (A/P, \ 0.15, \ 5)$$
$$= 4693.40 \ (0.298)$$
$$= \$1398.63$$

Alternative 2

Maintenance costs are given as uniform annual costs of $1500.00 per year.

5. *Calculate the total uniform equivalent annual costs for each alternative.*

	Equivalent Annual Cost	
	Alternative 1	Alternative 2
Investment less salvage value	$6,496.40	$5,328.00
Interest on salvage value	375.00	525.00
Operating costs	13,450.00	12,700.00
Maintenance costs	1,398.63	1,500.00
Total	$21,720.03	$20,053.00

The alternatives can now be compared on an equivalent basis, and it is clear that alternative 2 is better.

A more complete discussion of the economic comparison of investment alternatives, including the advantages and disadvantages of various comparison bases, is given in the Appendix. Also, several excellent books on the subject provide in-depth presentations.[3]

Use of Process Charts for Equipment Planning and Cost Estimating

The process chart is a very useful means of systematically planning the number of machines needed and the tooling requirements, and of obtaining estimates of equipment and tooling costs. Starting with a chart having only columns 1 and 2 completed, add headings for columns 4, 5, 6, and 7 as shown in Figure 4.4.

In the "description" column, briefly specify the equipment and special tools selected for the operation. In column 4, list the unit cost of the equipment,

[3] Suggested texts in this area are Thuesen, Fabrycky, and Thuesen, *Engineering Economy* (5th ed.; Englewood Cliffs, N.J.: Prentice-Hall, 1977), and F. Grant and W. Ireson, *Principles of Engineering Economy* (5th ed.; New York: Ronald Press 1970).

including special installation costs and any other one-time costs which should be included as capital equipment costs. Next, list the costs of tooling in column 5. Column 6 is used to record the output capacity, that is, units per hour or per shift. Output capacity can be obtained from the manufacturer. However, the manufacturer's rating usually represents maximum output under ideal conditions at 100% machine efficiency. Under normal operating conditions, output is likely to be about 90% of the rated capacity. Next, obtain the number of machines needed by dividing total production requirements for the operation by the estimated output capacity for one machine and use the next highest whole number. For example, if the production requirements are 200 units per day (one shift) and one machine can produce 125 per day, two machines will be required.

(1) STEP	Operation Transport (2) Inspect Delay Storage	(3) DESCRIPTION OF Proposed METHOD	(4) Equipment Cost	(5) Tooling Costs	(6) Output Capacity	(7) Number Req'd.
2	①◻▷◻◻▽	Gisholt Automatic Lathe 12k10	$12,000	$500	600	1
5	②◻▷◻◻▽	LeBlond Lathe	10,500	500	450	1

Figure 4.4   Process chart for equipment planning and cost estimating.

The total equipment costs for operation 1 can now be calculated by multiplying the number of machines by the unit equipment costs. Tooling costs can be obtained by multiplying the number of machines by the tooling costs for each machine or work station.

SELECT MATERIAL HANDLING METHODS AND EQUIPMENT

As the process chart can verify, material handling is an important part of the production process. Transportation of material usually follows each operation and inspection and comes out of each storage. Each transportation is certain to require labor and may require containers and handling equipment. Handling labor costs therefore are likely to be a significant proportion of manufacturing costs, and handling equipment may represent a sizable investment.

Material Handling Equipment Planning

Since all material and product moves are shown on the process chart, it is an easy matter to use the chart as an aid in estimating handling equipment and labor needs. For each move, consider the weight and physical characteristics of the material to be moved and the estimated distance of the move. Based on these considerations, make a preliminary choice of handling method (e.g., hand, hand truck, roller conveyor, forklift truck) and enter the description of material moved and handling method in column 3, as shown in Figure 4.5. In column 4, estimate the distance moved, and in column 5, the number of pieces handled. In column 6, record an estimate of the time required, and in column 7, the number of workers required if the handling method requires labor.

(1) STEP	(2) Operation Transport Inspect Delay Storage	(3) DESCRIPTION OF Proposed METHOD	(4) Distance Moved	(5) Number of Men Involved	(6) Pieces Handled	(7) Time Required per Move
1	$\bigcirc$①$\square\ D\ \nabla$	5-Ton Overhead Crane	25m	1	100	10min
4	$\bigcirc$②$\square\ D\ \nabla$	Roller Conveyor in Trays	4m	0	–	–

Figure 4.5 Process chart for material handling equipment selection and labor cost estimating.

When these estimates have been made for each move, summarize the time required for the use of each type of movable handling equipment in order to determine the number needed. For example, if a hand truck is to be used for a total of 14 hours per day, two will be needed on a one-shift operation. The requirements for fixed-path equipment, such as a roller conveyor, also can be obtained from the chart. Simply note the moves for which such equipment is to be used and estimate the distances. Having obtained these equipment estimates, the next step is to obtain cost estimates from equipment vendors.

Considerations in the Selection of Material Handling Equipment[4]

- Consider manual methods first. If manual handling is unsafe, too slow, or too expensive, consider mechanical equipment.
- Use equipment and containers that cannot damage parts being handled.

[4] Adapted from James M. Apple, *Plant Layout and Materials Handling*, Second Edition Copyright © 1963, The Ronald Press Company, New York, p. 214.

- Design equipment to carry materials in a position to save space and handling.
- Use equipment that does not require fixed floor space.
- Install only safe equipment.
- Wherever possible, use gravity for material movement.
- When loading or unloading time is a factor, use equipment in which the power unit can be separated from the load unit.
- Plan to keep equipment operating as much of the time as is practical.
- Use adjustable conveyor drives to provide flexibility in changing production schedules.
- Use standard equipment rather than special-design equipment.
- Provide alternative handling methods in case of breakdown.
- Consider all characteristics of the move before selecting the equipment.
- Do not exceed equipment capacity.
- Do not overmechanize.
- Install material handling equipment that is flexible and can serve a variety of uses or applications.
- Increase flexibility by means of accessories and attachments.
- Remember unit handling cost is reduced as the number of pieces handled at one time is increased.
- Select equipment on the basis of overall cost, not first cost.
- Maintain the lowest possible ratio of equipment investment to units of materials handled.
- Provide for handling of process scrap.
- Provide for handling and storage of defective work in process to avoid mixing with good product.

Types of Material Handling Equipment[5]

Material handling equipment is available for virtually any handling job regardless of its simplicity or complexity. From a functional standpoint, handling equipment can be classified according to the area it can serve: fixed path (conveyors), limited area (cranes and hoists), and unlimited area (trucks).

Conveyors transport material or parts along a fixed path from point to point or around a closed loop. The items being moved may be carried in containers or holders which are a permanent part of the conveyor system or in removable containers. The conveyor may be powered, in which case a moving chain, cable, or belt transports the load, or they may depend on gravity for material movement.

[5] Adapted from James M. Apple, *Material Handling Systems Design* Copyright, © 1972 The Ronald Press Company, New York, pp. 115–117.

Some situations in which conveyors find most frequent application are the following:

- High-volume production where the same sequence of operations is performed on each unit.
- Movement of units from one machine or operation to the next to avoid manual handling.
- Paced production in which each operation in the process is designed to require approximately the same time and the conveyor speed is set to move units at the proper pace.
- In-process storage carried overhead on the conveyor. Overhead conveyors also conserve floor space.
- Highly mechanized systems which provide for automatic counting, inspection, positioning and feeding parts to machines, and so forth.
- Processes for which manual handling may be impractical (e.g., paint dipping, solvent cleaning, annealing).

Common examples of conveyors are:

Roller conveyor	Monorail trolley
Belt conveyor	Bucket
Chute	Pneumatic

Cranes and hoists transfer material from one point to another in a fixed area over which the crane or hoist can be moved. Portable hoists are generally set up and operated at fixed locations and are not moved while loaded. This equipment is typically used to handle very heavy loads.

Some situations in which cranes and hoists find most frequent applications are:

- Handling heavy parts into a machine or workplace where manual handling would be slow or dangerous.
- Handling intermittent loads which may vary in size and/or weight.
- Handling loads to great heights and stacking for storage or retrieval from storage.
- Transferring material that is hot or for other reasons cannot be handled manually.

Common examples of cranes and hoists are:

Overhead traveling crane	Hoist
Gantry crane	Stacker crane
Jib crane	

Industrial trucks may be powered or hand-operated and are used where versatility is needed. Loads are containerized or palletized for convenience in pickup and release after transport. Hand trucks and forklift trucks can be used for a great variety of handling needs and are probably the most used material handling equipment.

Situations in which industrial trucks are used are:

- Movement of palletized or containerized material in warehouses.
- Transport of material from operation to operation in a job shop.
- Movement of finished product to storage or shipping.
- Loading or unloading of freight cars and over-the-road trucks.
- Movement of heavy loads over varying routes when demand is intermittent.

Common examples of industrial trucks are:

Forklift truck   Manual lift truck
Platform trucks   Hand stacker
Two-wheeled hand truck

ESTIMATE PRODUCTION LABOR NEEDS

The questions that must be answered concerning production labor needs are:

- How many employees are needed?
- What skills must these employees possess?

The process chart is useful in answering these questions with regard to both direct production labor and material handling labor.

Material handling labor can be estimated using the process chart used to estimate handling equipment needs. For example, suppose an overhead crane is to be used to move bar stock from storage to the cutoff and chamfer operation, and that production is 400 units per shift (8 hours). It was previously estimated that one worker would be involved and that the move would take 10 minutes (Figure 4.5). The total work-hours per day are obtained as follows.

$$
\begin{matrix} \text{Total work-} \\ \text{hours per} \\ \text{day} \end{matrix} = \begin{matrix} \text{number of} \\ \text{workers} \\ \text{involved} \end{matrix} \times \frac{\text{production per shift}}{\text{pieces handled}} \times \frac{\begin{matrix}\text{minutes required}\\\text{per move}\end{matrix}}{60}
$$

$$
= 1 \times \frac{400}{100} \times \frac{10}{60}
$$

$$
= 2/3 \text{ work-hour per shift}
$$

The total work load is obtained by performing these calculations for each move and summing the results. Dividing by the number of work-hours in the shift provides an estimate of labor needs. It should be noted that this estimate is only approximate. We have not considered the possibility that some material handling tasks can be performed by production operators without reducing their output (e.g., during machining time), and we have assumed 100% efficient utilization of labor. In spite of these deficiencies, the estimate is adequate for purposes of cost estimation.

(1) STEP	(2) Operation Transport Inspect Delay Storage	(3) DESCRIPTION OF Proposed METHOD	(4) Skill Class	(5) Output per Hour	(6) Required Production	(7) Man Hours Required
2	①⇨□D▽	Cut to Length and Chamfer	1	80	400	5
5	②⇨□D▽	Cut Retaining Ring Grooves	1	60	400	6 2/3

Figure 4.6   Process chart for estimating production labor requirements.

Production labor requirements also can be estimated with the help of the process chart. Using a chart as shown in Figure 4.6, consider each operation and briefly describe the task the worker must perform. In column 4, enter an estimate of the skill required for this task, and in column 5, the estimated production output per hour. Next, enter the required production per shift. In the last column, enter the number of work-hours needed. This figure is obtained by dividing the production requirement (column 6) by the output per hour (column 5).

An estimate of the total personnel needs for each skill class can now be obtained by summing the work-hour requirements for the skill class and dividing by the hours per shift. Labor availability and average wage rates for various skills are frequently available from state departments of labor. As in the case of material handling labor, this is an imprecise estimate but adequate for labor cost estimation.

DESIGN THE PRODUCTION ORGANIZATION

This step is for the purpose of determining the number and type of supervisory and staff employees required in the production organization and is necessary in order to estimate factory overhead. The number of such positions depends on the type and size of the business. However, the following functions are ordinarily associated with production operations (in addition to the direct production labor) and are usually considered part of factory overhead:

- Receiving.
- Packaging and shipping.
- Maintenance.
- Tool room.
- Inspection.
- Methods analysis.
- Janitorial.
- Production planning and control.
- Supervision.

Some of these responsibilities may be assigned to production employees and production supervisors in small firms. The above list should serve as a checklist to ensure that the planned organization can carry out the required activities and that labor cost estimates are not understated.

ESTIMATE PRODUCTION SPACE REQUIREMENTS

Production space is defined to include all space directly used in the production of the product. Thus it includes:

- Work station areas.
- Inspection areas (if done at separate stations).
- Storage areas.

The process chart also facilitates calculation of production space estimates.

Work Station Areas.   Using the process chart, compute the total square meters per operation. Include the following areas.

- Machine space.
- Auxiliary equipment (benches, etc.).
- Operator space.
- In-process material storage.

Multiply this subtotal by 150% to obtain an estimated area for each machine (this provides for spacing, aisles, etc.). Then add the space for all operations to obtain the total space needed for work stations.

A rule of thumb sometimes used in lieu of computations is 10 to 15 square meters per machine for a typical machine shop.

Inspection Areas. Allow sufficient space for an inspector and his work area. Also allow storage space for material waiting for inspection, material inspected and found acceptable, and material inspected and rejected.

Storage Areas. Using the process chart, estimate the quantity of material and space requirements at each indicated storage area. Add these to obtain a total.

ESTIMATE OFFICE AND SERVICE SPACE REQUIREMENTS

In addition to production space estimates made in the preceding step, it is necessary to estimate space requirements for all other activities of the business. Highly accurate calculations are not necessary, but a reasonable estimate of total space is needed in order to estimate building construction or rental costs. The following checklist of administrative and service functions will be found useful.

- **General administrative.**

    Administrative offices.
    Conference rooms.
    Reception rooms.

- **Marketing.**

    Sales.
    Customer service.
    Market analysis.

- **Financial.**

    Financial accounting.
    Personnel accounting.
    Cost accounting.
    Auditing.

- **Personnel.**

  Wage and salary administration.
  Health.
  Safety.

- **Product engineering.**

  Design and development.
  Research.
  Drafting.

- **Manufacturing staff services.**

  Purchasing.
  Manufacturing engineering.
  Quality control.
  Methods and standards.
  Production control.
  Facilities engineering.
  Maintenance.
  Receiving and shipping.
  Tool room.
  Tool crib.

- **Plant services.**

  Showers and lavatories.
  Lunchroom.
  Utility rooms (heating, air conditioning, power, compressors, etc.).
  Plant protection.

As in the case of production space requirements estimation, these estimates should include provision for planned expansion needs.

MAKE PRELIMINARY LAYOUT
OF PHYSICAL FACILITIES

The preceding steps have resulted in estimates of space requirements for production activities, offices, and services. The total of these figures provides an estimate of the floor space requirements. The total floor space requirements, however, may be affected by the relative arrangement of production and other areas. Certainly material handling needs are affected by relative placement of different production activities (e.g., machining, assembly, testing). Moreover, size alone is not sufficient to determine building needs and costs. Some production activities require special building construction. Overhead cranes, for example, usually require high bays. Heavy presses require special footings and isolation mounting. If such needs are overlooked, fixed investment costs are likely to be underestimated.

It is not necessary to make a detailed equipment layout at this step. What is needed is an efficient arrangement of the space units required by individual production activities and other functions. This is a preliminary step for a detailed plant layout which will be done if the business venture proves to be financially feasible.

The procedure for making an area allocation layout is described at length in most plant layout books.[6] It is summarized in the following steps.

- *Establish activity relationships.* Certain production functions and other activities *must* be near each other. Shipping and receiving, for example,

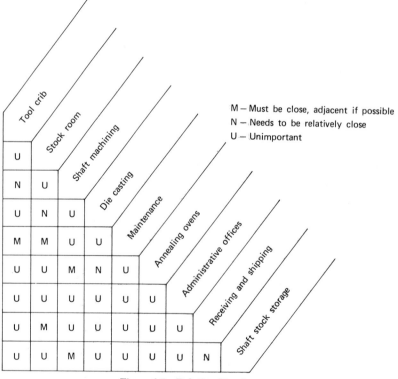

Figure 4.7   Relationship chart.

[6] See Apple, *Plant Layout and Material Handling* (3rd ed.; New York: Ronald Press, 1976).

must be near the stock storage area. Other activities *should* be near each other, and for some the relative location is unimportant. These relationships can be shown on a relationship chart similar in construction to the mileage chart shown in Figure 4.7. The cell showing the proximity relationship between any two activities is located by following the *column* under the first activity until it intersects the *row* corresponding to the other activity. Enter in this cell the code letter indicating the proximity needs of the two activities.

- *Arrange individual areas to meet relationship needs.* Using rectangular templates to represent the various production, office, and service space needs previously estimated, arrange the areas by trial and error to conform with the relative closeness shown by the relationship chart.
- *Draw the finished area allocation diagram to scale and label the various areas.*
- *Draw the material flow pattern to show direction of product flow through the production processes.*

A sample space allocation diagram is shown in Figure 4.8.

DETERMINE BUILDING NEEDS

The estimates of space requirements and the space allocation diagram indicate the overall floor space and desired dimensions. However, floor space alone may be an inadequate specification. Consideration also must be given to structural needs resulting from specific production processes and/or material handling. For example:

- High bays and adequate column support for overhead cranes.
- Multistory construction to facilitate gravity flow of materials.
- Special flooring construction for heavy production equipment.
- Shock and vibration isolation of certain areas where delicate processes are to be located.
- "Clean rooms" or other controlled-environment areas.
- Soundproof wall construction.
- Explosion-proof wall construction.
- Heavy-duty columns to support overhead handling and storage systems.
- Large areas of unobstructed floor space.
- Heavy-duty electrical service.
- Fuel storage for peak demand periods.

Any of these special needs affects the cost of building construction or rental and must not be overlooked.

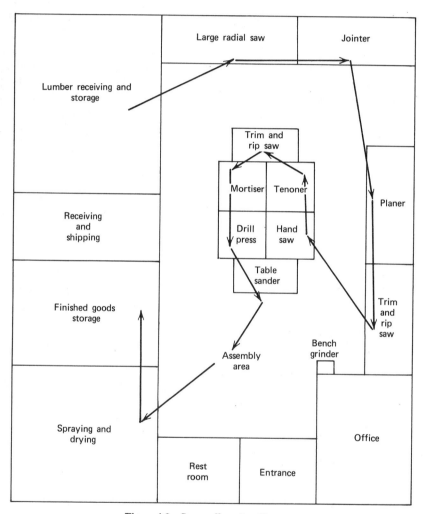

Figure 4.8 Space allocation diagram.

SELECT GENERAL LOCATION

This step is concerned with the choice of a geographic region or area as opposed to a particular site. A frequently used approach is to place primary emphasis on the criterion of minimum total transportation costs. The calculations are relatively simple. Generally, there are several potential location areas, and a hypothetical center is selected for each. Using data obtainable for this center, the total cost of raw material transportation and finished goods transportation (based on projected sales distribution) is calculated. The locations are then rank-ordered with respect to total transportation costs. The final choice is then influenced by consideration of the following factors.

- **Market factors.**

    Market growth potential.
    Locations of competitors.

- **Legislation and taxation.**

    Incentives for new industry.
    Environmental controls.
    Labor laws.
    Workmen's compensation insurance laws.
    Unemployment tax.
    State and local taxes.

- **Labor factors.**

    Prevailing wage patterns.
    Living costs.
    Availability of skilled and unskilled labor.
    Union militance and labor attitudes.
    Productivity.

- **Power availability.**

    Adequacy, including peak-load restrictions.
    Rate structure and cost.
    Reliability (standby requirements).

- **Water.**

    Availability of water.

Hardness and chemical content.
Drainage and sewer facilities.

- **Gas and other fuels.**

  Availability.
  Reliability of the supply, including peak-load restrictions.
  Cost.
  Specifications.

- **State and local government.**

  Attitude toward industry.
  Influence of business leaders in local government.

- **Waste disposal.**

  Process waste.
  Sanitary Waste.
  Public treatment facilities.
  Treatment facilities that must be provided by company.

- **Supporting industry and services.**

  Tooling.
  Potential subcontractors.
  Plant services (e.g., janitorial, plant protection, food service).

- **Community factors.**

  Quality of schools.
  Adult education availability.
  Cultural activities.
  Recreational facilities.
  Civic pride.
  Climate.
  Local transportation.

Obviously, this is an extensive set of factors which influence industrial location. The major force is of course cost. As pointed out, transportation costs are relatively easy to compute and are often the overriding cost consideration. However, the cost consequence of most of the factors listed above can be estimated if it is sufficiently important. If, for example, a potential location lacks adequate gas availability during peak usage months, the incremental cost of purchasing and storing liquefied petroleum gas should be estimated.

In general, the procedure described above tends to locate plants

- Near the raw material source if materials cost is a major factor in the total cost of the finished good or if materials are difficult and costly to transport.
- Near the market if the finished product is difficult or costly to transport.
- Near labor sources if the labor content is a major factor in the total cost of the finished product

Some industries do not have predominating elements among materials, transportation, labor, or distribution and can locate virtually anywhere with essentially the same costs for these elements. Such industries are described as "footloose."

BUILDING TO BE CONSTRUCTED?

Following the determination of building needs and the selection of a general location, the decision to lease or build must be made. Leasing avoids the capital investment in land and buildings and may be desirable for a new enterprise which expects to have difficulty raising capital. Also, it may be possible to arrange for the local industrial development authority to construct the facilities and lease them, at a nominal fee, to the new firm. This is sometimes done in order to attract new industry to the region. If suitable facilities can be found, leasing may be very attractive.

However, it may not be possible to find a building that meets the needs of the new company, and any compromise may result in higher production costs. Also, it may be difficult to convince the owners to make needed modifications unless the lease is long-term, and the new company may not wish to make such a commitment. Rent payments, unlike depreciation, are actual cash flows which must be met. During the start-up period, there is a need to keep such cash flows as low as possible.

In short, the choice between leasing and building should be based on economic and risk analyses. The final decision, however, may be dictated by the availability of capital.

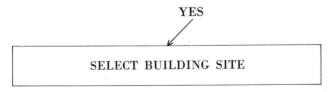

YES

SELECT BUILDING SITE

If investment and manufacturing costs can be estimated with sufficient accuracy with only the general location specified, it may be unnecessary to consider a specific site until financial feasibility is established and funding obtained. However, since many costs are likely to depend on specific location, this step is discussed.

Consideration of alternative sites is best done with the confidential assistance of a reputable realtor in commercial property. Land prices tend to increase drastically when word goes out that a piece of property is under consideration for a new plant. Moreover, there is often considerable anticipation and therefore disappointment when a particular property is not selected for the plant site.

The following checklist will be found useful in site selection.

- **Size factors.**

    Isolation requirements.
    Site layout (i.e., one building or several buildings, storage, etc.).
    Parking facilities.
    Landscaping objectives.
    Expansion plans.

- **Location factors.**

    Energy requirements (natural gas, electricity, coal, fuel oil, liquefied petroleum gas) versus availability.
    Waste disposal (cooling water, process, and sanitary waste).
    Transportation (highway, rail, water, and air).
    Water (cooling, process, and potable): quantities needed, specifications, and availability.
    Local government, laws, and regulations.
    Local taxes.
    Topography.
    Soil analysis.
    Proximity to suitable residential areas.
    Zoning patterns.

DEVELOP MANUFACTURING PLAN
CONTAINS ESTIMATES
- FIXED INVESTMENT
- MANUFACTURING COSTS AND EXPENSES
- START-UP COSTS

As stated at the beginning of this chapter, one of the principal purposes of the technical analysis is to provide cost estimates. It must be emphasized again that these estimates are crucial to the financial feasibility decision. The financial analysis and resulting estimate of financial profitability rest entirely on sales estimates and cost estimates. Obviously the accuracy of project financial performance can be no better than the accuracy and thoroughness of cost estimates.

Cost estimates obtained from the technical analysis fall in three major classifications:

1. *Fixed investment* consists of the cost of land, buildings, and related system, as well as production equipment and furnishings.

2. *Manufacturing costs* are made up of the following.

   - Direct material—material or components used in production, which are measurably identifiable with individual product units.
   - Direct labor—labor directly associated with production operations.
   - Factory overhead—includes material and supplies consumed in production but not measurably identifiable with individual product units (referred to as indirect material), all labor that is not direct labor (indirect labor), and other expense items related to production.

3. *Costs of start-up* are "nonnormal" manufacturing costs and expenses due to initial operating difficulties. These costs are frequently overlooked because of failure to recognize and allow for the usual problems in plant start-up. In fact, manufacturing costs at start-up are likely to be 33 to 50% higher than normal. Failure to provide for these extra costs may result in working capital shortages and threaten the life of the new business while it is yet in the birth process.

A checklist of elements in each of these cost classifications is given below.

1. Fixed investment.

   - Land.
   - Buildings and associated systems.

       Electrical supply.
       Plumbing.
       Air supply to pneumatic tools.
       Safety and security systems.

   - Other construction.
   - Production equipment (including freight in, installation, and debugging).
   - Materials handling equipment.
   - Furniture and fixtures.
   - Office machines.
   - Vehicles.

2. Manufacturing costs.

- Direct material (including freight in).
- Direct labor.
- Factory overhead—labor.

  Inspection and quality control.
  Supervision.
  Material handling.
  Maintenance.
  Shop clerical.
  Sorting and repair.
  Tool room.
  Packaging.
  Janitorial.
  Staff salaries.
  Tool crib attendants.

- Factory overhead—other costs.

  Maintenance and repair parts.
  Fuels.
  Power.
  Water.
  Packaging material (if not considered direct material).
  Office supplies in shop.
  Janitorial supplies.
  Indirect product material (e.g., paint, glue).
  Rent.
  Security.
  Taxes.
  Fringe benefits to employees.
  Depreciation.
  Training.
  In-process inventory carrying charges.
  Insurance.
  Scrap.
  Telephone.
  Obsolete material.
  Depreciation.

3. Costs related to start-up.

- Training costs.
- Rework.

- Overtime.
- Scrap.
- Extra costs resulting from inefficiencies and delays.
- Consultants' fees.
- Travel.

All of these costs which are applicable to the project must be forecasted to obtain monthly estimates during the preproduction period and the first year of operation. Quarterly or perhaps annual projections are usually required for the next 4 years of operation.

FIXED AND VARIABLE COSTS

In addition to the preceding classification, costs must be classified as *fixed* or *variable* in order to examine the effect of volume on profitability. Fixed costs are independent of volume or production. They may be further broken down into two types as follows.[7]

- *Depreciation charges.* The amounts charged annually as representing the cost of investments made in earlier periods. There is no actual cash outlay by the enterprise.
- *Structural outlays.* These are related to the productive capacity of the enterprise rather than to the actual level of output. They include the salaries and associated outlays for management and supervisory staff, and such overhead expenses as rents, real estate taxes, interest, insurance, and advertising. These expenditures must be made for some time, even if production volume drops substantially.

Variable costs are expenses directly related to production (cost of labor inputs, raw materials, power, maintenance, etc.).

This classification of costs as fixed and variable is of course often arbitrary and depends mainly on the period considered. What are thought to be fixed costs can often be changed over an extended period of time.

COST ESTIMATES FOR THE CLARE GARMENTS CASE[8]

The purpose of this section is to provide an example of cost estimating. This is

---

[7] *Manual of Industrial Project Analysis in Developing Countries* (Paris: Organization for Economic Co-operation and Development, 1972).

[8] The material in this section is adapted from instructional materials prepared by the Institute

conveniently done by using a case study for a small company producing garments. It is presumed that the market analysis and all necessary steps of the technical analysis have been completed except for the last step, and that the results of this work are available. Cost estimates for fixed investment, manufacturing costs, and start-up costs are to be obtained. However, the major effort is devoted to manufacturing cost estimation for the first year.

Clare Garments Manufacturing, located in Davao City, Philippines, proposes the manufacture of quality outer garments with product lines in ladies' blouses, ladies' and men's pants, and men's shirts. The company will be registered as a proprietorship. The proprietor has various business experience in addition to being a practicing accountant. The production and purchasing function will be handled by an individual who has had 2 years of experience in the management and production of garments. He is a college graduate with knowledge of production planning and control and equipment maintenance. He also has demonstrated capability in managing production personnel.

A marketing program has been established and a market analysis completed. It is planned that initially the entire output will be sold in Davao and nearby provinces—particularly Negros Occidental, Cotabato, and Visayan provinces. Sales efforts will be concentrated on highly populated areas where commercial centers are in existence. The market analysis indicates the following sales are attainable:

Product	Sales (dozens) Year 1
Ladies' blouses	825
Men's shirts	825
Ladies' pants	825
Men's pants	825
Sales	3300
Increase in inventory	300
Total production	3600

Also, as shown above, a safety stock in excess of 1 month's sales is required.

for Small Scale Industries, University of the Philippines, as used in the seminar on Project Evaluation, conducted by the Economic Development Laboratory, Georgia Institute of Technology and Institute for Small Scale Industries, University of the Philippines on June 23 to 27, 1975.

Thus the first year's production must provide 75 dozen of each product in addition to sales requirements.

Fixed Investment

The proposed plant will be housed in a building presently owned by the proprietor. Its value is estimated as follows.

Land (500 ft^2 @ $1.80/ft^2)	$ 900
Building	2200
Total	$3120

A process analysis has been completed and the following production equipment selected.

Item No.	Quantity	Description	Quoted Price
1	1	Electric cloth-cutting machine, 7 in.	$ 856
2	6	Lockstitch single-needle straightsewer @ $400 each	2400
3	2	Overlockstitch machine @ $610 each	1220
4	1	Buttonholing machine	1660
5	1	Feedoff arm machine—two-needle, double chainstitch	1035
6	1	A/B steam iron	212
7	2	Electric ceiling fan	
8	11	Work baskets	
9	1	Cutting table 16 × 48 × 36 in.	
10	4	Bins—for storage of cutwork	590
11	3	Small table for bundling	
12	15	Working chairs	
13		Materials and labor for machine installation	437
Total equipment and installation			$8410

Tools and spare parts will cost an additional $80. In addition to this investment in production equipment, it is estimated that the cost of office equipment will be $390.

The total fixed investment is summarized as follows.

Land	$ 900
Building	2,220
Equipment and installation	8,410
Tools and spare parts	80
Office equipment	390
Total	$12,000

Manufacturing Costs and Expenses (First Year)

Direct material consists of woven and knitted fabric in assorted colors of light and medium weight.

Product	Fabric	Cost/ Yard	Use per Garment	Yards Required	Total Cost
Ladies' blouses	Knitted fabric, 72 in. wide	$2.25	32 in.	9,600	$21,600
Men's shirts	35% cotton–65% polyester blend	0.65	63 in.	18,900	12,285
Ladies' pants	Light denim	0.75	63 in.	18,900	14,175
Men's pants	Light denim	0.75	63 in.	18,900	14,175
Total					$62,235

Direct labor consists of total outlay for wages paid to production workers. Assuming the following labor complement and 25 working days per month, annual labor cost will be:

Labor Requirements	Monthly	Annually
1 Designer–pattern maker–cutter	$ 44	$ 528
6 Straight-needle sewer @ $1.20/day	180	2160
2 Overlockstitch sewer @ $1.20/day	60	720
1 Buttonholer and chainstitch sewer @ $1.20/day	30	360
1 Overlockstitch with safety stitch sewer	30	360
1 Presser and packer	30	360
1 Button sewer and inspector and trimmer	30	360
First Year	$404	$4348

Factory overhead estimation requires a thorough understanding of the business operation. Perusal of published statements of several industries along with use of the checklist in the previous section will help to ensure·that no costs are omitted. In this case, the following are the usual overhead.

1. Indirect labor:

Production supervisor	$ 880/year
Stock clerk/utility man	440/year
Total	$1320/year

2. Factory supplies:

Polybags	$ 380.00
Boxes	630.00
Thread	140.00
Zippers	955.00
Buttons	385.00
	$2490.00

3. Depreciation of equipment: $ 566.00
   Depreciation is calculated on total equipment and installation plus the cost of tools and spare parts. The straight-line method is used with an estimated life of 15 years and no salvage value.

4. Maintenance cost: $ 56.60
   Maintenance of sewing machines and other equipment is estimated at 10% of depreciation.

5. Utilities:
   Computation of electricity cost is arrived at by considering the total kilowatt-hour requirement. To illustrate, the total energy requirement for this project is arrived at as follows.

Electricity Cost	Monthly	Annually
Demand charge:		
11 machines × 1.33 hp = 14.63 hp at $1.55/hp	$22.68	$ 272.16
Energy charge: (See Computation below)	68.04	816.48
11 industrial machines		
12 40-W fluorescent bulbs		
Total	$90.72	$1088.64

Energy use computation:

14.63 hp $\times$ 0.746 kW/hp = 10.91 kW $\times$ 10 hr =   109.1 kW-hr/day

$$\frac{12 \times 40\text{-W}}{1000} = 0.48 \text{ kW} \times 10 \text{ hr} =$$ 4.8 kW-hr/day

Total   113.9 kW-hr/day

113.9 kW-hr/day $\times$ 25 working days =   2847.5 kW-hr/month

Energy charge at Davao rate:
  1st 1000 kW-h $\times$ \$0.0298 =   \$29.80
  2nd 1847.5 kW-hr $\times$ \$0.0207 =   38.24

Total   \$68.04/month

6. Other factory overhead items:
   Aside from the overhead items mentioned, there are other items such as fringe benefits for the workers, factory insurance, factory rental (on rented premises), security services, and so on. Other factory overhead items for our illustrative case include the following.

	Monthly	Annually
Factory rental	\$29.50	\$354
Factory insurance (fire)	14.75	177

The total factory overhead is summarized as follows.

Indirect labor	\$1320.00
Factory supplies	2490.00
Depreciation of equipment	566.00
Maintenance cost	56.60
Utilities	1088.64
Factory rental	354.00
Factory insurance	177.00
	\$6052.24

Based on the preceding information, the projected statement of cost of goods manufactured and sold can now be prepared.

BIBLIOGRAPHY

Apple, James M. *Material Handling Systems Design*. New York: The Ronald Press, 1972.

Apple, James M. *Plant Layout and Materials Handling*. 2nd ed. New York: The Ronald Press, 1963.

Barish, Norman N. *Economic Analysis for Engineering and Managerial Decision-Making*. New York: McGraw-Hill, 1962.

Fisk, Margaret. *Encyclopedia of Associations*. 9th ed. Detroit: Gale Research Co., 1975.

Grant, Eugene L. and W. Grant Ireson. *Principles of Engineering Economy*. 5th ed. New York: The Ronald Press, 1970.

Greenhut, Melvin L. *Plant Location in Theory and in Practice*. Chapel Hill, N.C.: The University of North Carolina Press, 1956.

Organization for Economic Co-operation and Development. *Manual of Industrial Project Analysis in Developing Countries*. Paris, 1972.

United Nations. *Manual on Economic Development Projects*. New York, 1958.

Chapter Five

FINANCIAL ANALYSIS

The depth of the financial analysis depends, to a certain extent, on the project and the overall objectives of the feasibility analysis. The process of financial analysis is outlined by the major steps shown in Figure 5.1. In all instances, one stage of the financial analysis that must be completed is to assemble the market and technical data into the necessary pro forma statements. The information contained in the financial analysis can be used to determine if the project satisfies the investment criteria, that is, if it shows an acceptable level of commercial profitability.

If the objective of the feasibility analysis is to attract investors to a particular region by publishing a "manufacturing opportunity" report, the financial analysis may only require the presentation of financial statements for a "normal" operating year. This financial information is usually enough to interest potential investors who, once they have been identified, can be provided with more detailed financial data tailored to their needs. The Clare Garment Manufacturing case, discussed in the preceding chapter, is used to illustrate the process of preparing the financial statements. For an entrepreneur or a loan appraisal team from a lending institution, the objective of the feasibility analysis is also to indicate whether or not the project is worthwhile. However, the data generated in the initial stage of the financial analysis, which is often referred to as "conventional investment analysis," may not be satisfactory. The necessary pro forma statements may be required for a period

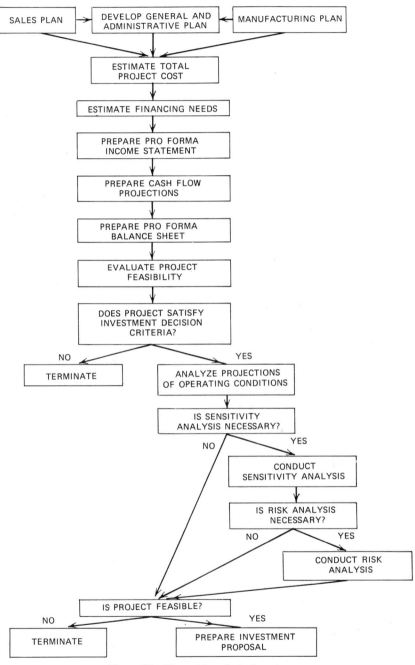

Figure 5.1 Financial analysis flow chart.

of 3 to 10 years, or even the entire lifetime of the project. More information on which to base an investment decision also can be obtained through a sensitivity analysis which identifies the variables that have a large impact on profitability. Finally, the risk involved in the project can be isolated and quantified, so that an indication of the likelihood or possibility of profitable outcomes can be evaluated.

SALES PLAN

The sales plan is an output of the market analysis and provides information necessary for constructing the financial statements. The sales plan includes an estimate of sales revenue, promotion and advertising costs, and selling and distribution expenses. Cost items that should be included are:

- Salespeople's salaries.
- Commissions.
- Advertising.
- Promotions.
- Clerical salaries.
- Credit checks.
- Transportation.
- Warehousing.
- Finished goods inventory charges.
- Shrinkage.

For Clare Garments, the sales revenue for the first year is shown in Table 5.1, broken down by product.

Table 5.1   Sales revenue for Clare Garments

	Quantity (dozens)	Price per Dozen ($)	Sales Revenue ($)
Ladies' blouses	825	34.00	28,050.00
Men's shirts	825	19.50	16,087.50
Ladies' pants	825	21.50	17,737.50
Men's pants	825	25.00	20,625.00
Total	3300		82,500.00

The marketing strategy for Clare Garments is to sell the finished garments in Davao Province initially and then to expand the market area to encompass the nearby islands. Clare Garments' strict quality specifications and competitive prices should provide the means to achieve the desired market penetration, since the primary source of competition is small garment traders.

Since the volume of sales is small, the only promotion planned is the presentation to customers of product samples which will then be returned to the plant. These presentations will be made by the owner and the salesman. During the first year of operation, newspaper advertising will be conducted once a month at a cost of $37 per space.

Sales and distribution expenses are also part of the sales plan. The salesman will be paid on a 2% gross sales commission basis. Delivery of the finished garments will be made by vehicle for Davao Province and by air to the surrounding islands. Local deliveries will be handled by a driver who has several other duties and his cost will be accounted for under general and administrative expenses. Freight out by air cargo is $0.14/kilo, with three garments constituting a kilo. The market analysis indicated that one-fourth of the sales will be to the islands and therefore transported by air. Table 5.2 summarizes the selling expenses for Clare Garments.

Table 5.2   Sales and Distribution Expenses for Clare Garments

Advertising	$444
Sales commission	1650
Air freight	462
Total	$2556

MANUFACTURING PLAN

The manufacturing plan results from the technical analysis and is composed of three elements: direct materials, direct labor, and manufacturing expense or overhead. These costs were determined for Clare Garments in the preceding chapter and are summarized in Table 5.3.

Table 5.3   Cost of Goods Manufactured for Clare Garments

Raw materials used	$62,235
Direct labor	4,848
Overhead	6,052
Total	$73,135

The computation for the finished goods inventory is shown in Table 5.4. The average costs per dozen for material, labor, and overhead are calculated by dividing the respective figures for cost of goods manufactured, shown in Table 5.3, by the production level of 3600 dozen. The cost of the finished goods

Table 5.4   Cost of Finished Goods Inventory for Clare Garments

Production (dozens)	3600	
Average material cost (per dozen)		$17.288
Average labor cost (per dozen)		$ 1.346
Average manufacturing overhead (cost per dozen)		$ 1.681
Total cost (per dozen)		$20.315
Finished goods inventory (dozens)	300	
Cost of inventory		$6094.500

inventory is simply a matter of multiplying the total cost per dozen by the inventory level of 300 dozen.

DEVELOP GENERAL AND ADMINISTRATIVE PLAN

Until now the focus has been on expenses directly connected with selling, distribution, and manufacturing processes. General and administrative expenses, then, are all expenses other than selling, distribution, and manufacturing incurred in operating the plant. These expenses, which have not been determined to this point in the project feasibility study, are related to providing the required administrative, legal, secretarial, financial, and other services. General and administrative expenses include the following:

- Management salaries.
- General office.
- Health.
- Publications.
- Postage.
- Telephone.
- Travel and entertainment.
- Maintenance of grounds.
- Company automobile.
- Office supplies.

- Research and development.
- Donations.
- Product design.
- Taxes and insurance.

The staff of Clare Garments consists of the owner–general manager, a secretary-bookkeeper, and a driver. Table 5.5 provides a display of these

Table 5.5   General and Administrative Expenses for Clare Garments

Salaries and wages	$2300
Travel expense	1236
Venture initiation expense	442
Office rental	265
Telephone and telegraph	90
Stationery and supplies	90
Gas and oil	168
Social Security and Medicare contribution	398
Sales tax	1419
Depreciation—office equipment	78
Total	$6486

expenses, which are, for the most part, self-explanatory. The majority of these expenses are constant and are set by the management. For Clare Garments the travel expense, gas and oil expense, and sales tax require some explanation. Travel expense is $103 a month, which covers the driver. Gas and oil expense has been estimated at $14 per month. Depreciation was calculated on office equipment valued at $390 using the straight-line method and an estimated life of 5 years. Sales tax is calculated as 7% of gross sales minus the cost of raw materials.

ESTIMATE
TOTAL PROJECT COST

The estimate of total project cost is basically a summary statement of information from the sales plan, manufacturing plan, and general and administrative plan, and it answers the question, "How much will it cost to start this venture?" The total project capital expenditures consist of the fixed investment, working capital, and venture initiation costs.

Fixed Investment

The fixed investment, or fixed assets, of the project is the cost of land and improvements, buildings and site facilities, and machinery and equipment required by the enterprise. These costs are frequently underestimated through omission of necessary nonproduction facilities (e.g., social facilities, a canteen, and an infirmary) and failure to include installation and debugging costs in capital equipment costs. The technical analysis contains a list of fixed costs for Clare Garments.

Working Capital

For the purpose of estimating total investment, it is recommended that gross working capital be used, as opposed to net working capital. Gross working capital is defined as current assets required. Net working capital is current assets less current liabilities. Current assets required for a new enterprise include the following.

- Cash.
- Materials inventories.
- In-process inventories.
- Finished goods inventories.
- Accounts receivable.
- Expendable supplies.
- Prepaid expenses.

>   Fuel and gas.
>   Power.
>   Water.
>   Sales expense.
>   Insurance.
>   Repairs and maintenance parts.
>   General office expenses and supplies.
>   Fees (legal, consulting, etc.).
>   Rents.

It is important to realize that extra cash is needed at the beginning of the new venture in order to meet expenses, such as payroll, utilities, telephone, and interest, which must be paid before cash inflow from sales is received. The most common source of error in project cost estimation and a common cause of business failure is inadequate working capital. Table 5.6 contains the estimated working capital for Clare Garments.

Table 5.6 Project Cost Summary for Clare Garments

A.	Fixed investment		
	Land		$900.00
	Building		2,220.00
	Machinery, equipment, and installation		8,410.00
	Tools and spare parts		80.00
	Office equipment		390.00
	Total fixed assets		$12,000.00
B.	Working capital		
	Cash		$1,737.64
	Direct labor ($404/month × 2)	808.00	
	Indirect labor ($110/month × 2)	220.00	
	Factory supplies ($207.50/month × 2)	415.00	
	Maintenance ($56.60/month × 2)	113.20	
	Utilities ($90.72/month × 2)	181.44	
	Raw material supplies ($5,186.25/month × 2)		10,372.50
	Finished goods inventory ($6094.50/month × $\frac{1}{2}$)		3,047.25
	Work-in-process inventory ($6,094.50/month × $\frac{1}{4}$)		1,523.63
	Prepaid factory insurance ($14.75/month × 2)		29.50
	Prepaid factory rental ($29.50/month × 2)		59.00
	Total working capital		$16,769.52
C.	Venture initiation cost		442.48
	Total project cost		$29,212.00

Venture Initiation Costs

Venture initiation costs are incurred in making initial investigations and forming the company. It is likely that these will be considered capital costs and amortized over some time period. They must not be omitted from the project cost estimate.

- Costs of forming the company.
- Initial investigations.
- Marketing study.
- Legal fees.
- Research and technical studies.
- Consultants' fees.
- Expenses of obtaining financing.
- Patents.

Project Cost Summary

Since the project cost summary is the basis for the financial plan and loan request, it is extremely important. Perhaps most important is that the entrepreneur not *underestimate* the project cost. Lenders tend to be displeased with entrepreneurs who are forced to return and say, "I underestimated my capital needs, and if I cannot obtain an additional loan my business will fail." The Clare Garment project cost summary is shown in Table 5.6.

ESTIMATE FINANCING NEEDS

Once the total investment has been determined, attention is given to an initial estimate of the magnitude of financing needs. Later, when cash flow projections have been made, it may be necessary to revise the original estimate. The usual case is that the entrepreneur cannot supply all the funds and that at least some external financing is necessary.

The matter of how much external money is needed is not the only question facing the entrepreneur. Other questions are as follows.

- What form of financing should be used?
- What are the sources of funds?

For Clare Garments the sources of financing and its magnitude are shown in Table 5.7.

Table 5.7   Sources and Magnitude of Financing for Clare Garments

Owner's investment (land, building, and part of working capital)	$11,212
External financing (at estimated 10% interest, 10 years, payable semiannually)	18,000
Total	$29,212

PREPARE PRO FORMA INCOME STATEMENT

The most important financial forecast related to the project is the income projections. This is the estimate that shows whether the project will be profitable at the volume of production likely to be salable. It shows how much margin can be counted on for repayment of debt, for plowing back into the business for expansion, and for payment of dividends to the owners. This is the all-important test which shows how safe the project is for the prospective lender and how attractive it is to the investor.

The pro forma income statement attempts to forecast business operations over a specific time interval by means of the profit equation:

$$\text{Aftertax net profit} =$$

gross sales — returns and allowances

— cost of goods sold

– operating expenses

+ other revenue

— interest expenses

— income taxes

In making the income statement projections for a new venture, it is highly desirable to provide monthly or quarterly forecasts for the first year of operation and annual projections for at least four additional years. The major entries on the income statement are sales, cost of goods sold, operating expenses, other revenue and expenses, and net profit after taxes.

Sales

The market analysis provides necessary data for this section of the statement. Estimates of returns, allowances, and discounts may be obtained from those experienced in the industry. For Clare Garments they were estimated at 1% of gross sales.

Cost of Goods Sold

The purpose of this section is to obtain an estimate of the cost of goods that produced the sales revenues. These costs are obtained by adjusting the cost of goods manufactured to reflect finished goods inventory changes. For Clare Garments the computation for the finished goods inventory is shown in Table 5.4. Net sales less cost of goods sold on the income statement provide an estimate of gross margin (gross profit) for the period.

Operating Expenses

Estimates of selling expenses and general and administrative expenses were provided by the technical analysis. Subtracting operating expenses from gross margin produces an estimate of operating profit for the period.

Other Revenue and Expense

It is likely that the proposed new venture will have no revenue other than product sales. If so, "other revenue earned" is omitted and the interest expense on borrowed funds is subtracted from operating profit to obtain an estimate of before-tax profit.

Net Profit after Taxes

This figure is the all-important "bottom line." As stated earlier, it provides an estimate of funds that will be available to repay lenders, expand the business, and reward the entrepreneur. Projections over a 5-year horizon are useful to indicate growth and healthy development of the new firm.

Clare Garments Income Statement

Table 5.8 illustrates an income statement for 1 year for Clare Garments. The references next to each item indicate the table from which they were derived.

Table 5.8   Clare Garments Pro Forma Income Statement for the Year Ended 1975

Gross sales (Table 5.1)		$82,500
Less: sales returns and allowances		825
Net sales		$81,675
Cost of goods sold		
Finished goods, beginning inventory	0	
Cost of goods manufactured (Table 5.3)	$73,135	
Goods available	$73,135	
Less: finished goods, ending inventory (Table 5.4)	6,095	
Total cost of goods sold		67,040
Gross margin		$14,635
Operating expenses		
Selling expenses (Table 5.2)	2,556	
General and administrative expenses (Table 5.5)	6,486	
Total operating expenses		9,042
Operating profit		$5,593
Other revenue and expense		
Other revenue earned	0	
Less: interest expense (Table 5.7)	1,800	1,800
Profit before income taxes		$3,793
Income taxes		1,896
Net profit after taxes		$1,897

**PREPARE
CASH FLOW PROJECTIONS**

The purpose of the cash flow statement is to show the movement of cash into and out of the business. In the financial analysis of a project feasibility study, cash flow projections are particularly important. The would-be entrepreneur wants to know, "Will my cash account always have sufficient money to meet my bills and debt service?" And potential lenders want to know, "Will cash be available to meet interest and principal payments on my loan?" The cash-flow statement format that is of interest here, then, does not include noncash items such as depreciation and provisions for bad debts. It is in fact a cash flow budget which is useful to (a) determine the amount of cash needed to start the enterprise, (b) plan for timing of loan funds, and (c) ensure that, if projected cash flows are met, cash will be available to meet payments as they come due. Thus cash flow projections are used for financial planning, project evaluation, and control (if the project is implemented).

Cash flow projections should be made for monthly periods during the pre-operating period (i.e., from time of first expenditures to plant operation) and the first year of operation. Projections for subsequent years may be on a quarterly or annual basis.

Cash Receipts

The cash receipts section of the cash flow projections lists all sources of cash. Collections of receivables may be estimated as follows.

> Collection of receivables =
> estimated balance (beginning)
> + net sales
> − estimated balance (ending)

The estimated receivables balance at the end of a period is based on billing practices and terms given to purchasers. For example, if customers are billed at the time of shipment and given 30-day terms, receivables will consist of 30 days' sales. Other cash items listed below are self-explanatory.

- Collection of receivables.
- Cash sales.
- Sale of temporary investments.
- Sale of equity.

- Short-term borrowings.
- Long-term borrowings.
- Investments.

Cash Disbursements

The disbursements section lists all uses of cash. Since raw materials are usually purchased in anticipation of production requirements, payments during a given month depend on production schedules, lead time, and purchase terms.

In practice, there is always a certain amount of unpaid labor, since workers are paid at the end of a work period. However, for the purposes of cash flow projections, it is convenient to assume that labor is paid in the same month the cost is incurred. Typical cash disbursements are listed below:

- Payments for raw materials purchases.
- Payments for labor.
- Manufacturing overhead and expense.*
- Selling expense.*
- General and administrative expense.*
- Payments for fixed assets.
- Interest payments.
- Loan repayments.
- Payments on real estate mortgage.
- Payments on income taxes.
- Other taxes and assessments.

Cash Flow Statement for Clare Garments

The preparation of the cash flow projections for Clare Garments proceeds in the following manner. Cash receipts are limited to accounts receivable and the owner's initial cash investment of $5000. The terms of sale can be either in cash or on credit, and in this case it is assumed that all sales will be on credit for 30 days. Net sales of $81,675 divided by 12 months yields uncollected accounts at the end of the year of $6806. Since there are no accounts receivable outstanding for the previous year, total collections for the initial year are equal to $74,866.

The next step in the preparation of the cash flow statement is to account for cash disbursements. In order to arrive at the cash needed for raw materials and supplies, the inventory levels and terms of payments must be known. It is

---

* Cash outlays only.

assumed that a 1-month inventory of raw materials and supplies is required and that the terms of payment are 30 days. Table 5.9 illustrates the procedure

Table 5.9   Clare Garments Cash Disbursements for Raw Materials

Raw materials used (Table 5.3)	$62,235
Factory supplies used (from technical analysis)	2,490
Total production needs	$64,725
Plus: desired inventory ending (assumed at 1 month's production needs, $64,725/12 months)	5,394
Less: inventory beginning	0
Total purchases	$70,119
Plus: accounts payable beginning (prior year's payable)	0
Less: accounts payable ending (equivalent to 1 month, $59,331/12 months)	4,944
Total cash payments	$65,175

for calculating the payments for raw materials and supplies. Table 5.10 shows the payments for all other expenses and costs programmed for payment whether they are on account or cash. A loan amortization table should be prepared for Clare Garments, which shows the amortization for the $18,000 loan at 10% interest on the declining balance. For the first year, payment of interest amounts to $1800 with no payment on the principal.

Table 5.10   Clare Garments Cash Disbursements for Other Expenses and Costs

Direct labor	$4,848
Manufacturing overhead (less depreciation, factory supplies)	2,996
Operating expenses (less depreciation, organization costs)	8,522
Total cash outlay	$16,366

In the actual cash flow statement, the preoperating period, that is, the period from conception until actual operation, should be shown separately from the operating periods. The preoperating period includes expenditures associated with the preparation of the project feasibility study, registration with government agencies, construction of facilities, purchases of machinery and

equipment, and others. Table 5.11 shows the cash flow statement for Clare
Garments.

Table 5.11   Clare Garments Projected Cash Flow Statement

	Preoperating Period	Year 1
Estimated cash inflow		
Owner's investment	$5,000	
Loan	18,000	
Sales		$74,869
Total estimated receipts	$23,000	$74,869
Estimated disbursements		
Purchase of machinery	$8,490	
Purchase of land	900	
Construction of building	2,220	
Purchase of office equipment	390	
Organization cost	442	
Purchase of raw materials (Table 5.9)		$65,175
Payment of loan		1,800
Payment for		
Direct labor		4,848
Manufacturing overhead		2,996
Operating expenses		8,522
Total estimated disbursement	$12,442	$83,341
Net inflow (deficit)	10,558	(8,472)
Plus: cash balancing beginning		10,558
Cash balance ending	$10,558	$2,086

PREPARE PRO FORMA
BALANCE SHEET

In an ongoing business, the balance sheet tells "where we are" at a particular
point in time. The pro forma balance sheet for a proposed venture represents
an effort to project "where we will be" after a specific period of operation. It is
dependent on the income statement and cash flow statement as indicated in
Figure 5.1. In essence, the balance sheet is a listing of all the resources of the
business, together with interests of creditors and owners in these resources. It
represents the financial position of the firm at a given date.

In order to assess properly the profitability of the proposed firm, it is necessary to make balance sheet projections for at least the first 5 years of operation. It may be desirable to make monthly projections for the first year. The following discussion covers the major categories of the balance sheet.

Assets

The assets (resources) of the business are grouped into several categories according to liquidity. Current assets consist of cash and other resources which, under normal operations, are converted to cash within the operating cycle. In most cases the operating cycle is a year or less. Current assets frequently consist of the following items:

- Cash.
- Accounts receivable.
- Inventories.
- Prepaid expenses.

The cash portion of current assets represents only that which is on hand and on deposit, that is, available for general business purposes. Cash held for a special purpose (e.g., bond retirement) is not included in current assets. The amount estimated for the cash account in the pro forma balance sheet should be based on the pro forma cash flow projections.

Receivables are an important element of current assets, since they represent money that otherwise might be available as cash. It is not unusual for a firm to extend credit to virtually all its customers and to have 1 to 2 months' sales tied up in receivables.

Inventories consist of finished goods available for immediate sales, goods in various stages of manufacture, and materials to be used in the creation of products. In addition, expendable supplies used in production are also a resource and are included here. Estimates of inventories are available from the technical analysis.

Prepaid expenses are payments for services that will be received in the near future. These include such items as insurance premiums, rent, and interest. Although these items are not converted to cash in the normal course of business operation, they are expenses which, if not prepaid, would have resulted in additional cash. They would, however, have had to be paid eventually.

The total value of current assets is a measure of funds available to the business in normal operation. The use of this measure in evaluating project feasibility is discussed later.

Liabilities and Owners' Equity

The liabilities and owners' equity section of the balance sheet lists all the claims against the assets of the firm. Current liabilities represent claims arising from normal current operations of the business and which will require, within approximately 1 year, cash or replacement by another current liability. Current liabilities frequently consist of the following items:

- Accounts payable.
- Notes payable.
- Accrued wages and other expenses.
- Estimated income taxes payable.

Accounts payable include only amounts owed for materials and supplies purchased on credit. An estimate of accounts payable is obtained by estimating the value of materials purchases required to support the projected production schedule and assuming reasonable "terms" for payment of these billings (e.g., payment in 30 days).

Notes payable can be projected by means of the cash flow statement under the assumption that temporary cash shortage will be met with short-term loans. Estimates for accrued wages and other expenses should be based on the projected production schedule and payroll practices. An estimate of income taxes payable should be based on the pro forma income statement.

A long-term liability is an obligation that normally will not be paid within 1 year from the date of the balance sheet. These may include mortgage notes payable and term loans.

The preceding liabilities to "outside parties" must be sharply distinguished from the owner's equity, which is represented by the difference between total assets and liabilities to others. Liabilities represent priority claims to the assets of the business, and the residue belongs to the owner.

The foregoing is a brief and incomplete discussion of the balance sheet. No effort has been made to deal with special questions such as, "How do we handle estimated major repairs and renewals which we know must be made in 5 years?" Such matters are beyond the scope of this book, and the reader is referred to the texts listed in the bibliography.

Balance Sheet for Clare Garments

The pro forma balance sheet for Clare Garments can be prepared easily with the data from the completed statements on total project cost, income, and cash flow. Table 5.12 illustrates the Clare Garments balance sheet.

Table 5.12 Clare Garments Pro Forma Balance Sheet

Assets	
Current	
Cash (Table 5.11)	$2,086
Accounts receivable	6,806
Raw material inventory (Table 5.9)	5,394
Finished goods inventory (Table 5.4)	6,095
Total current assets	$20,381
Fixed assets (Table 5.6)	
Land	$900
Office equipment	390
Building	2,220
Machinery and equipment	8,490
Less: accumulated depreciation	(644)
Total fixed assets	$11,356
Total assets	$31,737
Liabilities and capital	
Accounts payable (Table 5.9)	$4,944
Loan payable	18,000
Total liabilities	$22,944
Capital	
Entrepreneur, capital beginning	$5,000
Net (loss) income (Table 5.8)	3,793
Entrepreneur, capital ending	$8,793
Total liabilities and capital	$31,737

EVALUATE PROJECT FEASIBILITY

The assembly of the market and technical data provides the necessary financial information to evaluate the project. There are three basic areas of decision making for any project: investment, operations, and financing. The proposed project must be analyzed to decide if the investment should be made. An analysis of the projections of operating conditions for the project also can be conducted. Finally, if possible under the constraints of budget, time, and available personnel, it is sometimes desirable to conduct a sensitivity analysis.

This is a way to examine the effects of assumed changes in the key variables, such as revenues and operating costs, on the final result, that is, the measure of profitability. Another technique that can provide the decision maker with better information is risk analysis. Ranges of possible outcomes and the probability distributions for these ranges are assigned to key variables, so the project's final results are presented as a series of outcomes with the probability of their occurrence. For instance, a statement may be made that the likelihood or probability is 70% that the rate of return for the project will be 10% or better; or the chances are 6 out of 10 that the project will meet the minimum standard rate of return of 12%.

DOES PROJECT SATISFY
INVESTMENT DECISION
CRITERIA?

The use of investment criteria is a means of evaluating whether or not the project should be undertaken. Extensive literature exists on this capital budgeting decision and some available texts are listed in the bibliography. To this point in the project feasibility analysis, the project alone has been considered. However, to evaluate the project properly, it is extremely important to consider the project in the context of other possible alternatives even if one of these alternatives is to do nothing. For example, consider the situation where the project is to establish a new plant to manufacture a product and where the investment decision criteria used indicate positive results. An alternative, however, may be to expand an existing plant to manufacture the product; this could yield even better results according to the same criteria. Without identification of the appropriate alternatives, that is, adequate definition of the problem, decision making is impaired.

The analyst may obtain profitability measures for the project or projects being studied in several ways. Common nontime value approaches to measuring profitability are the payback period and financial statement (accounting) rates of return. Financial statement rates of return are based on some net income figure divided by some investment base. Frequently used profitability measures of this type are net income to assets, first-year earnings to initial investment, average net income to initial investment, and average net income to average investment.

Profitability measures which consider the time value of money, that is, discounted cash flow methods, are net present value, internal rate of return, and the discounted benefit/cost ratio. The Appendix contains discussion, examples, and evaluations of both nontime value and time value profitability measures.

When profitability measures other than financial statement rates of return are used as the investment decision criteria, the analyst needs estimates of the following: the net investment, which is gross capital less any capital recovered from the sale or trade of existing assets; the operating cash flows, which are the after-tax cash flow resulting from the investment; the economic life of the project, defined as the time period during which benefits can be obtained from the project; and the appropriate discount rate. The discount rate is usually set by management based on the "cost of capital," which is the weighted average of the compensation for all long-term funds provided by the company, or on an "opportunity rate," which is an estimate of the future rates of return at which funds can be invested in the business (in the case of new companies, the "opportunity rate" can be the rate of return of an alternative investment such as bonds, assuming risk-free investment).

Caution should be exercised in the application of discounted cash-flow methods. The following discussion should clarify the conventions that should be followed in the construction of the cash flow. Consider the case where the project under study is whether or not to construct a new plant. To simplify the analysis, assume that plant start-up is instantaneous so that the revenues and operating expenses will be the same throughout the life of the project. The cash flow used in the analysis is composed of the following elements:

1. Initial investment taken in year t_0, considered to be outlays for fixed investment, working capital and venture initiation costs.
2. After tax cash flow taken for years t_1 to t_n. The after tax cash flow is computed as after tax income plus depreciation. Annual depreciation can be calculated for the fixed investment based on the estimated life of buildings and equipment. The after tax cash flow can be computed using the following equation:

$$\text{After Tax Cash Flow} = (1 - t) \times (S - E - D) + D$$

Where t = tax rate
S = sales (less discounts and allowances)
E = cash operating expenses other than interest
D = annual depreciation charges

The above after tax cash flow computation does not include cash disbursed for interest payments. Interest charges are omitted from the computation because in the net present value method the discount rate is the interest analogous to the interest expense and to also include the cash disbursed for interest would result in double counting. The effects of interest payments on income taxes is also excluded from the computation. This is brought into the analysis when computing the effective rate of interest of debt sources of capital, which is used in the determination of the after tax cost of capital.

3. Annual replacement investment, equal to annual current depreciation taken for years t_1 to t_n.

4. Salvage value of investment taken in year t_n. Salvage value is usually defined as the liquidation value of the fixed investment plus net working capital.

With the relevant cash flows computed for the project or projects, the next step is to decide which investment decision criterion to use for the acceptance or rejection of projects, as well as their ranking. Theoretically, the net present value criterion is the best measure of profitability. The Appendix presents the investment decision criteria.

Research into current practices with respect to capital budgeting in existing companies indicates that more than 74% use more than one investment criterion in the capital budgeting process.[1] The primary reasons given for the use of more than one investment criterion were multiple criteria; for example, the project had to satisfy a minimum payback and a minimum internal rate of return (20%), different types of projects (20%), different types of products (15.6%), and different project lives (12%).

Of the investment decision criteria used to evaluate new product lines, the internal rate of return appears most often as the technique believed to be of prime importance.[2] The accounting return on investment approach is the second most favored technique among those ranked first. Evidence indicates that the payback period is used primarily as a supplementary technique and that it far outdistances any other technique ranked second or third in importance.

As indicated, a company employs different investment criteria for different types of projects. According to Reul, "A company may use 'rate of return' to evaluate new project investments, switch to 'payout' for cost-reducing investments, and justify replacement investments with MAPI (Machine and Allied Products Institute formula), in order to show each investment in the most favorable light."[3] This type of investment evaluation process makes the comparison of alternative projects impossible and therefore defeats its purpose.

[1] Glenn H. Petry, "Effective Use of Capital Budgeting Pools," *Business Horizons*, **19**, No. 5 (Oct. 1975), pp. 57–65.

[2] J. William Petty and Monroe M. Bird, "The Capital Expenditure Decison-Making Process of Large Corporations," *The Engineering Economist*, **20**, No. 3 (Spring 1975), pp. 159–172.

[3] Ray I. Reul, "Profitability Index for Investments," *Capital Investment Series* Reprints from *Harvard Business Review*, July–Aug. 1957, pp. 43–59.

Since all types of projects are to be evaluated using the same investment criteria, care should be exercised in estimating the cash flows for projects. The following classification of investment proposals helps to identify the type of project that might require additional scrutiny.[4]

1. Profit-maintaining.
   - Replacement of existing facilities that no longer function.
   - Improvement of existing facilities to circumvent competition.
   - Provision of new facilities which were accidentally or intentionally omitted when the original facilities were installed but which have become essential to the continuation of existing activities.
2. Profit-adding.
   - Provision of new facilities that will increase profit by providing new business or by expanding existing operations.
   - Provision of facilities that will improve product quality and permit higher prices and profit margins.
   - Provision of facilities that will reduce the cost of production and result in increased profit through larger profit margins or an increased volume of sales.

Of particular concern are projects essential to the continuation of existing operations, that is, "profit-maintaining" projects. If, for example, the proposed project involves the replacement of a critical piece of equipment without which the plant must be shut down, to evaluate the project in the appropriate context, all other investments anticipated to keep the plant operational during the years for which the continued profit is predicted must be included.

For a profit-maintaining project such as replacement of a piece of machinery essential to the continuance of a division or plant, Donaldson argues that, despite unacceptable low profitability, such investments should be viewed as "tactical" investments which have to be made until the decision to withdraw completely is made, because one cannot be half in and half out of a business.[5] He argues that not to lower the profitability required endangers the net cash flow of the whole division or company. As Merrett and Sykes have pointed out, the problem is that the "net cash flows being attributed to the particular investment, and giving the apparently inadequate return, do not comprise all of the net cash flows involved."[6] This emphasizes the need to include all the

[4] *Ibid.*, p. 46.
[5] Gordon Donaldson, "Strategic Hurdle Rates for Capital Investment," *Harvard Business Review*, March–April 1972.
[6] A. J. Merrett and Allen Sykes, *The Finance and Analysis of Capital Projects* (2nd ed.; A Halsted Press Book; New York: Wiley, 1973), p. 84.

net cash flows dependent on the investment before applying the investment criteria for selection or rejection.

Finally, the investment criteria discussed thus far have relied on single estimates for important variables such as sales price and cash flows. The decision maker may consider this information sufficient. However, often a more sophisticated analysis involving the sensitivity of key variables or the risk associated with them may be in order. In such an instance, the project evaluation resulting from the above conventional investment criteria will not necessarily yield the same decision as to the acceptance or rejection and ranking of projects.

ANALYZE PROJECTIONS OF OPERATING CONDITIONS

The basic decision as to whether or not the project is an appropriate investment has been made. In reality, the pro forma financial statements represent a plan which can be analyzed to obtain insight into the operational aspects of the project. Such an analysis is especially useful for projects involving the establishment of a plant to manufacture a new product. The questions to be answered are, "How good is the plan?" and "Is the new venture competitive when compared with similar enterprises?" Certainly, the pro forma income statements, balance sheets, and cash flow statements provide information which goes a long way toward answering these questions.

Financial Ratios

Ratios show the relationship between various items or groups of items on the

---

Disclaimer Statement: RMA cannot emphasize too strongly that their composite figures for each industry may *not* be representative of that entire industry (except by coincidence), for the following reasons: (1) The only companies with a chance of being included in their study in the first place are those for whom their submitting banks have recent figures. (2) Even from this restricted group of potentially includable companies, those which are chosen, and the total number chosen, are not determined in any random or otherwise statistically reliable manner. (3) Many companies in their study have *varied* product lines; they are "mini-conglomerates," if you will. All they can do in these cases is categorize them by their *primary* product line, and be willing to tolerate any "impurity" thereby introduced.

In a word, don't automatically consider their figures as representative norms and don't attach any more or less significance to them than is indicated by the unique aspects of the data collection.

Table 5.13 Financial Statements and Ratios for Manufacturers of Metal Stamping

85 STATEMENTS
ENDED ON OR ABOUT JUNE 30, 1974
77 STATEMENTS
ENDED ON OR ABOUT DECEMBER 31, 1974

ASSET SIZE	UNDER $250M	$250M & LESS THAN $1MM	$1MM & LESS THAN $10MM	$10MM & LESS THAN $50MM	ALL SIZES
NUMBER OF STATEMENTS	10	56	85	11	162
ASSETS	%	%	%	%	%
Cash	1.9	7.5		3.1	4.2
Marketable Securities	4.4	.6	1.0	.8	.9
Receivables Net	28.2	25.5	24.3	23.4	23.9
Inventory Net	30.2	28.7	29.0	32.9	30.9
All Other Current	2.2	1.0	.7	.8	.8
Total Current	67.0	63.4	60.1	61.0	60.8
Fixed Assets Net	27.5	30.6	29.4	35.5	32.4
All Other Non-Current	5.5	6.0	10.5	3.5	6.8
Total	100.0	100.0	100.0	100.0	100.0
LIABILITIES					
Due To Banks—Short Term	5.9	8.3	8.3	6.9	7.6
Due To Trade	26.0	17.8	15.4	12.1	14.0
Income Taxes	.9	1.8	2.1	1.6	1.8
Current Maturities LT Debt	4.9	3.6	2.5	2.1	2.4
All Other Current	15.6	14.2	7.9	7.1	7.9
Total Current Debt	53.4	45.7	36.2	29.9	33.7
Non-Current Debt, Unsub.	15.3	14.2	9.5	17.5	13.6
Total Unsubordinated Debt	68.6	59.9	45.7	47.3	47.4
Subordinated Debt	.0	1.6	1.8	.6	1.2
Tangible Net Worth	31.4	38.5	52.5	52.1	51.4
Total	100.0	100.0	100.0	100.0	100.0
INCOME DATA					
Net Sales	100.0	100.0*	100.0*	100.0	100.0*
Cost Of Sales	79.4	79.1	81.3	81.6	81.3
Gross Profit	20.6	20.9	18.7	18.4	18.7
All Other Expense Net	22.4	16.9	12.1	12.2	12.5
Profit Before Taxes	-1.8	4.0	6.6	6.2	6.2
RATIOS					
Quick	1.1	1.1	1.1	1.1	1.1
	.5	.8	.8	.8	.8
	.4	.5	.6	.7	.6
Current	1.5	2.1	2.6	2.3	2.2
	1.3	1.6	1.7	2.0	1.6
	1.0	1.2	1.2	1.6	1.1
Fixed/Worth	.3	.4	.4	.5	.4
	1.1	.8	.5	.6	.6
	1.5	1.4	1.0	.9	1.1
Debt/Worth	.7	.8	.5	.6	.6
	3.3	1.5	.9	.8	1.1
	4.9	2.9	1.8	1.2	2.4
Unsub. Debt/Capital Funds	.7	.7	.5	.6	.6
	3.3	1.4	.8	.8	1.0
	4.9	2.7	1.5	1.1	2.2
Sales/Receivables	33 10.8	29 12.3	32 11.3	42 8.6	32 11.4
	39 9.2	40 9.1	41 8.7	46 7.8	40 8.9
	51 7.0	50 7.2	49 7.4	59 6.1	50 7.2
Cost Sales/Inventory	37 9.8	32 11.4	46 7.8	61 5.9	42 8.5
	44 8.2	55 6.6	58 6.2	75 4.8	56 6.4
	61 5.9	77 4.7	80 4.5	103 3.5	78 4.6
Sales/Working Capital	16.0	15.5	14.2	7.7	14.9
	12.2	8.1	6.9	5.4	7.2
	-49.3	4.2	4.3	5.0	4.4
Sales/Worth	19.3	10.9	5.8	4.2	7.4
	7.5	5.3	4.1	3.6	4.6
	1.7	3.7	3.3	2.5	3.3
% Profit Bef. Taxes/Worth		44.5	38.8	27.8	39.5
		30.0	24.7	21.2	24.7
		9.6	14.5	12.1	13.4
% Profit Bef. Taxes/Tot. Assets	8.5	17.1	20.0	14.2	18.8
	-2.0	10.1	12.0	11.3	11.0
	-23.9	4.4	5.9	5.8	5.0
Net Sales ($)	4286M	77487M	548129M	486247M	1116149M
Total Assets ($)	1518M	32381M	255749M	269098M	558746M

Source. Robert Morris Associates, *Annual Statement Studies, 1975 Edition, Revised* (Philadelphia: November 1975), p. 88.

balance sheet and income statement. Financial ratios are primarily used to analyze the operations of an existing company. However, they also can be useful tools for analyzing a new project. A ratio based on estimates for a new project, when compared with the same ratio for a similar business already in operation, may furnish a means to decide whether the proposed project will be financially competitive.

Financial data on existing companies is provided by industry groups in publications such as Robert Morris Associates, *Annual Statement Studies, 1975 Edition, Revised*.[7] Table 5.13 shows such a display for the manufacturers of metal stampings. The statement provides the balance sheet, income statement, and financial ratios by different asset sizes. There are three figures for each financial ratio, representing the upper-quartile, median, and lower-quartile figures. These figures give the analyst some idea of the spread or range of ratio values for an industry. For two of the ratios, sales or revenues/receivables and cost of sales/inventory, there are figures to the left of the main column. These figures show receivables turnover and inventory turnover, respectively, calculated in days. The following definitions provided by Robert Morris Associates are helpful.

QUICK RATIO

Method of Computation. The total of cash, short-term marketable securities, and net receivables for the industry composite is divided by the total current liabilities.

Result. The ratio measures short-term liquidity available to meet current debt.

Principle. Also known as the "acid test" or liquidity ratio, it is of particular benefit to short-term creditors, as it expresses the extent to which cash and those assets most readily convertible to cash can meet the demands of current liabilities. Any value of less than 1 : 1 implies a reciprocal dependency on inventory or other current assets to liquidate short-term debts.

CURRENT RATIO

Method of Computation. The total current assets for the industry composite is divided by the total current liabilities.

Result. The ratio is one measure of the ability of the industry to meet its current debt.

---

[7] See also ratios published by Dun & Bradstreet, Inc.

Principle. In comparing an individual company to the industry, a higher current ratio indicates that more current assets are free from debt claims of creditors and that prompter payment can be expected.

FIXED/WORTH

Method of Computation. The net fixed assets (plant and equipment less reserve for depreciation) for the industry is divided by the tangible net worth.

Result. The ratio expresses the proportion between investment in capital assets (plant and equipment) and the owners' capital.

Principle. The higher the ratio, the less owners' capital is available for working capital. The lower this ratio, the more liquid the net worth and the more effective the owners' capital as a liquidating protection to creditors. The presence of substantial leased fixed assets—off the balance sheet—may deceptively lower the ratio.

DEBT/WORTH

Method of Computation. The total debt for the industry composite is divided by the tangible net worth.

Result. The ratio expresses the relationship between capital contributed by creditors to owners' capital—"What is owed is what is owned."

Principle. Total assets or resources represent the entire capital at the disposal of a given company and consist of new worth or owners' capital and creditor capital—that provided by those outside the business for temporary use. The proportion existing between debt and worth—or leverage—records the debt pressure. The lower the ratio, the less the pressure and the greater the protection for creditors.

SALES/RECEIVABLES

Method of Computation. The net annual sales for the industry are divided by the total of trade accounts and bills receivables.

Result. The ratio expresses the relationship of the volume of business to the outstanding receivables.

Principle. A higher ratio—a higher turnover of receivables as it is sometimes called—indicates a more rapid collection of sales during the period and greater liquidity of the receivables.

COST OF SALES/INVENTORY

Method of Computation. Cost of sales for the industry is divided by the total inventory.

Result. The ratio expresses the proportion between the cost of sales and the inventory at the end of the fiscal period.

Principle. The physical turnover measures merchandising capacity. The higher the ratio, the greater this capacity and the more probable the freshness, salability and liquidating value of the inventory. Since profit has been eliminated, the cost of sales/inventory ratio gives a more accurate measure of physical turnover than the sales/inventory ratio. Other measures of physical turnover use monthly inventory or an average of the inventories at the beginning and end of the period.

SALES/WORKING CAPITAL

Method of Computation. The net annual sales for the industry composite are divided by the net working capital or excess of total current assets over current liabilities.

Result. The ratio expresses the turnover or annual activity of the portion of net capital not devoted to fixed or other noncurrent assets.

Principle. Net working capital represents the basic support for assets undergoing conversion cycles (as inventory-receivables-cash) during the selling year. Relating sales to working capital suggests the number of turns in working capital per annum. A low ratio may indicate unprofitable use of working capital, while a very high ratio often signifies overtrading —a vulnerable condition for creditors.

SALES/NET WORTH

Method of Computation. The net annual sales are divided by the tangible net worth.

Result. The ratio reflects the activity of the owners' capital during the year.

Principle. Capital is invested in an enterprise in the hope of a substantial return. The probability of such a return is largely dependent on reasonable activity of the investment. This ratio is one measure of this activity. When the relation increases from year to year, it indicates that the owners' capital is being used more frequently during the year. A very high ratio may indicate undercapitalization (lack of sufficient ownership capital) or overtrading.

PROFITS BEFORE TAXES/WORTH

Method of Computation. The amount of net profit before taxes is divided by the tangible net worth.

Result. The ratio expresses the relationship between the owners' share of operations before taxes for the year and the capital already contributed by the owners.

Principle. Capital is usually invested in a company in anticipation of a return on that investment—in the form of a profit. This hope for a profit is the attraction for original and new capital. The higher the profit before taxes/worth ratio, the greater the probability of making appreciable addition to the owners' capital after payment of dividends and taxes.

PROFITS BEFORE TAXES/TOTAL ASSETS

Method of Computation. The amount of net profit before taxes of the industry is divided by the total assets for the industry.

Result. The ratio expresses the owners' share of the year's operations before taxes as related to the resources contributed by both owners and creditors.

Principle. The relationship indicates the net profitability of the use of all the resources of the business.

CASH FLOW/CURRENT MATURITIES LONG-TERM DEBT

Method of Computation. The net profits plus depreciation and amortization are divided by the current portion of long-term liabilities.

Result. The ratio expresses the ability to retire term debt each year from cash generated by operations.

Principle. Cash flow or "throw off" is the primary source of regular repayment of long-term debt, and this ratio measures the coverage of such debt service. Often much, if not all, the depreciation is needed for fixed-asset replacements and expenditures, but similarly some part of the net profits may be committed to dividends. Although it is misleading to think that all cash flow is available for debt service, the ratio is a valid measure of the optimum coverage and a very useful calculation in all considerations of term lending.

Analyze Cash Flows

The cash flow projection, as previously stated, is a schedule over time of cash inflows and outflows and is an attempt to pinpoint cash surpluses and shortages so that arrangements can be made to cover the maturing obligations of the firm. Analysis of the cash flow projections consists of ascertaining that a minimum cash balance is not penetrated at any time. For example, the entrepreneur may decide that a minimum cash balance of $1000 should be maintained. Therefore it is not sufficient to examine only the ending balances. If disbursements for the period exceed the beginning cash balance, it is necessary to consider the timing of receipts and disbursements within the period.

If the projection indicates a cash problem, consideration can be given to one or more of the following:

- Receivables financing.
- Inventory financing.
- Faster receivables collection.
- Inventory turnover improvement.
- Gross profit improvement.
- Extended terms from suppliers.
- Additional borrowings.

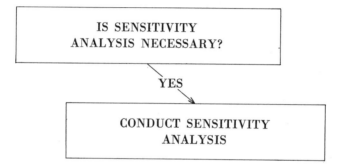

Recognizing that the project's profitability forecast hinges on future developments whose occurrence cannot be predicted with certainty, the decision maker may want to probe further. Questions for which answers are sought are of the "what if" type, such as, "What if the sales price is lower than expected?" or, "What if the project life is shorter than initially thought?"

Sensitivity analysis and risk analysis, discussed in the next section, are techniques that allow the analyst to deal with such questions. In the conventional approach to project analysis discussed so far, the investment decision was based on best-estimate data. The analyst may want to determine the impact of changes in variables such as product price, raw materials costs, and operating costs on the overall results. Sensitivity analysis involves specifying the possible range for a variable, such as price, and calculating the effect of changes in this variable on the project's profitability. With such a calculation for the variables the analyst can then determine the relative importance of each of the variables to profitability. The purpose of sensitivity analysis, then, is to identify the variables that most affect the outcome of a project. Sensitivity analysis is useful for determining *consequences* of a stated percentage change in a variable such as product price. However, only risk analysis can provide any indication of the *likelihood* that such events will actually occur.

Break-Even Analysis

Break-even analysis can be viewed as a form of sensitivity analysis in that it enables the analyst to examine how changes in cost, production volume, and price affect the profits. In general, break-even analysis is useful because it allows the analyst to determine the minimum conditions under which the company can be kept operational. The break-even analysis is a preliminary step to ascertain how the prospective return from a project is affected by important variables. Data required to conduct a break-even analysis for a product are estimates of fixed costs, variable costs per unit, volume of production, and price per unit. Fixed costs are those that do not vary with the level of production. At times it is difficult to separate costs into fixed or variable categories, because some items defy such classification.

The different aspects of break-even analysis can be illustrated with an example. Suppose the analysis involves the construction of a plant with a production capacity of 15,000 units of a product for which the market analysis indicates a selling price of $40 per unit. The fixed costs and the variable costs are obtained from the technical analysis and are estimated at $15,000 and $25 per unit, respectively. The break-even point is defined as the point where total revenue equals the variable costs plus the fixed costs.

$$PX = F + VX$$

where P = price per unit
X = volume of production in units
F = fixed costs
V = variable costs per unit.

Therefore

$$(40)X = 150,000 + 25X$$
$$X = 10,000 \text{ units}$$

Figure 5.2 shows a graphical representation of the break-even concept. As can be seen, at a selling price of $40 per unit the break-even point, 10,000 units, is defined by the intersection of the lines for total revenues and total costs. The break-even condition represents a point where there is no profit and no loss.

The analyst may be interested in the sensitivity of profits to changes in volume, price, or other variables. Profits are defined as operating profits before taxes, excluding interest and other income and expenses.

The relationship between profits and volume of production is illustrated in Figure 5.2. Table 5.14 presents the relationship between profits and volume for a series of 10% increments above and below the break-even point, which is the minimum volume of production at which operations can continue without a loss. As can be seen from the table, changes in the volume of production close to the break-even point result in large variations in profits or losses, while changes in the volume of production well above or below the break-even point cause smaller variations.

In a manner similar to the calculation of the break-even volume, the analyst can compute the minimum sales price. If the selling price falls for the production of 15,000 units, the company will continue to show a profit until such time as the price declines to the value determined by the equation

$$PX = F + VX$$
$$P(15,000) = 150,000 + 25(15,000)$$
$$P = 35$$

Analysis of the market revealed a demand for 15,000 units. The safety margin for the company, if there is a change in demand (and all other factors such as price remain the same), is 33.3%. This is computed by subtracting the market demand, 15,000, from the break-even point, 10,000, and dividing the result by the market demand.

The safety margin for price changes also can be computed by subtracting from the unit selling price, $40, the minimum selling price, $35, and dividing by the unit selling price to obtain a safety margin of 12.5%.

The analyst can determine how variables other than production volume, such as changes in price, fixed costs, and variable costs, affect profits. For example, the effect of lowering the price per unit to $38, a 5% reduction, results in an increase in the break-even volume to 11,538, a rise of 15.4%. If 15,000 units are being sold, a 5% reduction in price will result in a 40% decrease in profits.

Limitations of break-even analysis are that the cost, volume, and price changes are analyzed separately, although in reality these variables are inter-

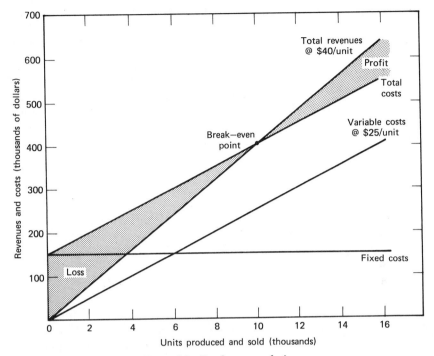

Figure 5.2 Break-even analysis.

related. For instance, a reduction in price often leads to an increase in production. Another simplifying assumption in break-even analysis is that the variable cost per unit remains the same over a large range of production, and this is seldom true.

Table 5.14 Sensitivity of Profits to Changes in the Production Volume

Volume	Percent Change	Profit (or loss) ($)	Percent Change
6,561	10	(51,585)	27
7,290	10	(40,650)	43
8,100	10	(28,500)	90
9,000	10	(15,000)	
10,000		0	
11,000	10	15,000	
12,100	10	31,500	110
13,310	10	49,650	58
14,641	10	69,615	40
16,105	10	91,575	31

Sensitivity Analysis Using a Simple Model

Probably the simplest type of sensitivity analysis, other than break-even analysis, is to construct a single-equation model which relates the variables that determine profitability.[8] Such a sensitivity analysis, however, can become more complex if several equations are used to specify a profitability model. For example, in the following equation where pretax profit P is related to other variables, the analyst may also want to include an equation that relates sales price to sales level.

$$P = S\,(p - rc - vc) - FC$$

where P = pretax profit
        S = sales level
        p = sales price
        rc = raw materials cost
        vc = other variable costs
        FC = fixed costs for the period.

A sensitivity analysis is conducted by replacing the input variables that determine profitability with their expected values, identified in the feasibility analysis, in order to determine the numerical value of profitability. The input variables are then assigned a like percentage change in order to calculate the resultant change in profitability.

Table 5.15   Sensitivity Analysis using a Simple Model

Variable	Best Estimate Value	Increasing Variables by 5%	Results in Profits of ($)	Percentage Change in Profits	Rank Order of Variable
Sales (units)	15,000	15,750	82,500	10	3
Price ($/unit)	40	42	105,000	40	1
Variable costs ($/unit)					
Raw material	5	5.25	71,250	—5	4
Other variable costs	20	21	60,000	−20	2
Fixed costs ($)	150,000	157,500	67,500	−10	3

The best estimates, that is, the expected values, of the variables are shown in Table 5.15. By using these values and substituting them into the equation, the profitability of the project can be calculated as $75,000. Table 5.15 shows the

[8] L. Daniel Maxim and Frank X. Cook, Jr., *Financial Risk Analysis* (New York: American Management Association, Inc., 1972).

effect on profitability of a 5% change in the variables. With equal percentage changes in the variables, profit is most sensitive to changes in price, followed by changes in other variable costs, the effects of changes in sales and fixed costs are the same, and changes in raw materials ranks last. Although this simple analysis has identified the most sensitive variables, when all variables have the same percentage change no insight is provided into the likelihood or probability of these changes taking place. For instance, the chances of a 5% increase in raw materials cost may be very high, while the chances of a 5% increase in product price may be low. The section on risk analysis integrates the likelihood of events into the project analysis.

Sensitivity Analysis Using Discounted Cash Flow Models

The analyst may have used a particular investment decision model such as net present value, which is based on a discounted cash flow method, to evaluate the profitability of the project. If so, he will want to use it to measure the effect of changes in relevant variables on net present value. Under circumstances of no risk, the net present value represents the increase in wealth resulting from implementing the project. It is equivalent to capital gain, yet unrealized. The net present value of a project is:

$$NPV = \sum_{i=1}^{n} \frac{F_t}{(1+r)^t} - F_0$$

where r = required rate of return, that is, the discount rate
F_t = net cash flow for period t
n = project's expected life
F_o = initial investment.

Suppose the feasibility analysis yields the following estimates for the project under study.

- Projected expected life $n = 10$.
- Net cash flow $F_t = \$20,000$ annually.
- Required rate of return $r = 10\%$.
- Initial investment $F_0 = \$122,892$.

For this project the sensitivity of the net present value to changes in the required rate of return can be shown in a graphical representation as in Figure 5.3. Similar presentations of the net present value for the project can be shown for variations in the project's life, initial investment, and net cash flows. More complex presentations of sensitivity data are possible within the limits of two-dimensional graphical presentations, for example, the effect of joint errors in estimated cash flow and project life on present value.[9] The presentation of

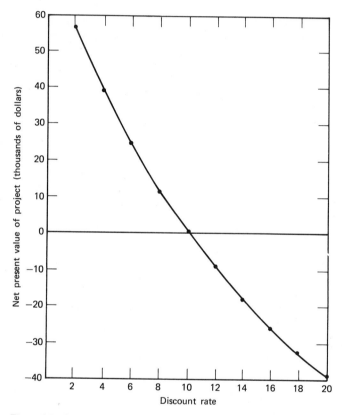

Figure 5.3   Sensitivity of net present value of project to the discount rate.

sensitivity data can be overdone, however, and the analyst will be wise to avoid the extensive use of graphs and tables which might overwhelm the decision maker.

[9] Ronald J. Huefner, "Analyzing and Reporting Sensitivity Data," *The Accounting Review*, **46**, No. 4 (Oct. 1971), pp. 717–732.

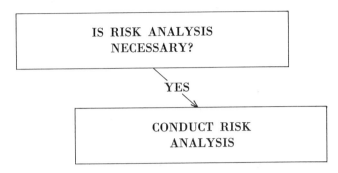

Risk analysis is concerned with identifying the risks associated with a project and incorporating them, in a quantitative manner, into the measure of a project's results. The decision whether or not to conduct a risk analysis depends to a large extent on the magnitude and type of project. For instance, a precise estimate of future returns can be calculated for a project that involves cost saving where the operation is to continue even if the project is not implemented. In this case, the demand for the project product or service is relatively risk-free, and there is only a small risk that the estimates of other variables, such as project cost and cost saving, are in error.

Contrasted with this type of project, where the variability in expected returns is small, consider the project that involves the introduction of a new product. This is the type of project involving the most risk, because of the lack of knowledge of competitor's reactions, consumer acceptance, the production process, and other factors, which makes it difficult to determine future returns. These examples of project types illustrate that the type of project dictates, to a large extent, whether or not a risk analysis should be undertaken and, if so, the extensiveness of such an analysis.

It should be noted that risk analysis differs from sensitivity analysis in that risk analysis provides an indication of the *likelihood* that an event, such as a change in product price, will take place, whereas, with sensitivity analysis, only the *consequences* of such an event can be specified. However, variables isolated by the sensitivity analysis as being essential to the performance of the project are the same variables that need to be considered in the risk analysis.

In investment decisions, risk arises from many possible sources. Some sources of risk are due to a lack of previous experience with similar investments, misinterpretation of data, bias in the data and their assessment, errors in analysis, and changes in the external economic environment which invalidate much of the usefulness of past experience.[10]

[10] Merrett and Sykes, p. 144.

Risk Analysis for Projects

Risk analysis takes into account the recognized fact that variables, such as product price, that are used to determine profitability depend on future events whose occurrence cannot be predicted with certainty. Investment decision situations can be characterized with respect to certainty, risk, and uncertainty. Since, in the real world, certainty seldom exists for future returns on investments, only risk and uncertainty are of interest here. Uncertainty is used to refer to an event, such as a technological breakthrough resulting in obsolescence, that is expected to take place although the probability of its occurrence cannot be forecasted during the project's lifetime. Although uncertainties can be treated in a descriptive manner, the data are insufficient to incorporate them into the analysis in a quantitative manner.

Risk refers to the situation in which a probability distribution of future returns can be established for the project. The riskiness of a project can be defined as the variability or dispersion of its future returns. Likewise, for a variable such as sales from which future returns are derived, sales risk can be defined as the variability of future sales. For instance, instead of using the best estimate of sales, a probability distribution of possible sales levels can be constructed. Information may indicate that there is a 10% confidence that sales of 15,000 units will be achieved or exceeded, 70% confidence for sales of 10,000 units, and 90% confidence for sales of 6000 units.

However, if the only risk associated with the project were a sales risk, there would be no need for a complex risk analysis. The aggregate risk associated with the project is limited only to the sales risk. Therefore the investment decision criteria can relate profitability to sales. For example, the required rate of return of 20% depends on achieving a sales level of 15,000. Whether or not the project is feasible, then, depends on an evaluation of the likelihood that future sales will be at least 15,000 units, which, in this case, compels rejection of the project.

In practice, during project feasibility analysis, there are usually several variables, possibly identified during the sensitivity analysis, for which doubts exist as to their best estimates. With several variables and the respective ranges of values for each, the complexity of project evaluation is greater because of the numerous possible combinations of variables, some yielding positive results and others yielding negative results. The aggregate risk of a project, then, cannot be determined easily as in the case above, because it is composed of numerous risks. The purpose of risk analysis is to isolate the risks and to provide a means by which the various project outcomes can be reduced to a format from which a decision can be made. The final result of a risk analysis is a judgment regarding the possible range of future returns, as well as the likelihood of each value within this range.

The likelihood of risk, in this text, is oriented toward determining the riskiness of a particular project. Another approach is to examine overall risk, referred to as portfolio risk. The entrepreneur's or company's portfolio risk can be analyzed by considering the relationship between the proposed project and existing investments. While this type of risk analysis is not covered here, it should be noted that a project that may have been rejected when evaluated alone could be acceptable, under certain circumstances, if evaluated with present investments because the overall risk would be reduced. Similarly, a project accepted when considered in isolation could be rejected because it would increase overall risk.

Current Industry Practice toward Risk

Current industry practice in the treatment of risk gives an indication as to the frequency with which particular techniques are employed. Petry indicates that 71% of the industrial and retail corporations he surveyed accounted for risk explicitly in project analysis. The risk adjustment techniques used were changing the discount rate or rate of return (30%), adjusting cash flows on a probability basis (26%), adjusting cash flows on a subjective basis (21%), changing the payback periods (14%), and other methods (9%).[11] Some of these methods of risk analysis—the risk-adjusted discount rate, the certainty equivalent adjustment, simulation models, and decision trees—are examined in the following discussion.

Risk Analysis Using Discounted Cash Flow Models

When the risk analysis is being conducted using discounted cash flow models such as the internal rate of return or net present value, several methods such as the risk-adjusted discount rate and the certainty equivalent adjustment are commonly used.

In addition to these methods for treating risk, an informal approach is sometimes employed. The net present value of possible projects may be the only information developed; in this case, the decision maker, based on his own subjective judgment, can then incorporate the risk he perceives for each

[11] Petry, p. 64.

project to arrive at a decision. With such an approach, however, the decision maker has no objective measure of risk. To provide more information, the expected value and standard deviation of either the net present value or the rate of return for the project can be calculated. The risk associated with the possible cash flows for a project depends on the variability of the cash flows and their associated probability of occurrence. To illustrate, suppose the project involves the introduction of a new product with an estimated life of 3 years entailing an initial investment of $9000. The analyst then obtains information on the expected cash flows and their probabilities from the decision maker or other informed individuals. In this instance, assume that the following discrete probability distribution of expected cash flows obtained for the first year remains the same throughout the project's life.

Annual Cash Flows	Probability
$5500	.10
4000	.60
2500	.30

The annual cash flows and their probability can be based on how the decision maker perceives the reaction of his competitors, if they are a primary factor, or possibly, on the state of the economy, if it is an important consideration. His best estimate of cash flow of $4000, used in the feasibility analysis, can be based on his belief that competitors will cause a slight reduction in his price. To this cash flow he assigns a 60% likelihood of occurrence. Similarly, the cash flow of $5500 can be based on no reaction from competitors, which is thought to have only a 10% chance of occurring, while the cash flow of $2500 is based on a possible strong response from competitors and is assigned a 30% probability. The expected value of the annual cash flows $\bar{F}_t$ can be calculated as follows.

$$\bar{F}_t = \sum_{x=1}^{n} F_{xt} P_{xt}$$
$$\bar{F}_t = .10(5500) + .60(4000) + .30(2500)$$
$$\bar{F}_t = 3700.$$

where F_{xt} = cash flow for the xth possibility in period t
P_{xt} = probability of occurrence of that cash flow in period t

The expected value of the cash flows is $3700, as opposed to the best estimate of $4000 from the feasibility analysis. The decision maker now has a better perception of the risk involved, that is, the expected value of the project is $3700 with a range of probable outcomes from $2500 to $5500. Since this project's risk is associated with the variability or dispersion of cash flows, he has some conception of the risk. However, a more formalized measure of risk, which can be used to measure the dispersion of the probability distribution of expected cash flows, is the standard deviation. The smaller the standard deviation – the lower the risk of the project. For the above project, the standard deviation can be calculated as follows.

$$\sigma = \sqrt{\sum_{x=1}^{n} (F_{xt} - \bar{F}_t)^2 \ P_{xt}}$$

$$\sigma = \left[.10(5500 - 3700)^2 + .60(4000 - 3700)^2 + .30(2500 - 3700)^2\right]^{\frac{1}{2}}$$

$$\sigma = 900$$

To summarize, for this project, the expected value of the cash flows is $3700 and the standard deviation is $900. If the choice were between two mutually exclusive projects, the project above and a second project which also had an expected value of $3700 but a standard deviation of $2000, the first project would be preferred because it has a smaller standard deviation, hence less risk. It should be noted that, if it is assumed that the cash flows are related from one future period to another, the above formula cannot be used. The bibliography at the end of this chapter lists several publications that suggest ways to incorporate the dependence of cash flows over time into the risk analysis.

Although the expected value and standard deviation for the net present value provide the decision maker with more information, the acceptance or rejection decision still must be based on a subjective evaluation of these measures. The risk-adjusted discount rate method and the certainty equivalent adjustment methods, however, do provide the criteria for the acceptance or rejection of the project.

Risk-Adjusted Discount Rate Method

With the risk-adjusted discount rate method, the treatment for a riskier project involves either increasing the applied discount rate in order to ascertain the net present value, or increasing the cutoff, or "hurdle," rate, using the rate-of-return procedure. The risk premium, that is, the increase in the riskless discount rate, can be determined in several ways: The variability (standard deviation) of the probability distribution of the cash flows can be examined with the larger the variability the higher the discount rate; different categories of projects can be assigned different discount rates based on past experience (in such a case a market expansion project is assigned the highest discount rate); and frequently, the selection of the discount rate is arbitrary. If the project initially costs $19,000, after which the expected cash flows are $5500 per year for 5 years, the net present value using a 10% discount rate will be $1849 and the project will be accepted. However, if information indicates a degree of risk associated with the project, a risk premium of 4% can be added, which will increase the discount rate to 14% and result in a net present value of −$118 and rejection.

Although easy to apply, the risk-adjusted discount rate has its disadvantages. The raised discount rate is applied to all revenues and costs that comprise the cash flows, even if some can be estimated with near certainty. For example, the revenue generated by the project is known with near certainty in a case where the product has been sold in advance through a long-term sales contract. Another drawback to this treatment of risk is that it tends to hide the riskier items in the calculations, so that the entrepreneur or decision maker may not be aware of them. Other criticisms have also been made.[12]

Certainty Equivalent Adjustment Method

An alternative method which takes risk into account involves the adjustment of the cash flows emanating from the project. After the cash flows have been adjusted to reflect the risk, either the net present value or the internal rate of return investment criteria can be used.

The analyst elicits information from the entrepreneur or decision maker as to how he perceives the risk associated with the cash flow for each future year. If the cash flow for the first year is estimated at $10,000 with a probability of 50%, its expected value will be $5000. The decision maker is then offered a choice between this risky sum of $10,000 with 50% probability and various certain sums until he indicates an indifference between two alternatives. Assume that he finds the risky cash flow ($F_1 = \$5000$) and a certain cash flow ($F_1^* = \$1000$) equally desirable. The certainty equivalent coefficient for the first year (α_1) can be computed as follows.

[12] See Harold Bierman, Jr. and Seymour Smidt, *The Capital Budgeting Decision* (2nd ed; New York: Macmillan, 1966), pp. 322–326, and Harold Biermen, Jr. and Jerome E. Haas, "Are High Cut-off Rates a Fallacy?" *Financial Executive*, **41**, No. 5 (June 1973), pp. 88–91.

$$\alpha_t = \frac{F_t^*}{F_t} = \frac{\text{certain cash flow}}{\text{risky cash flow}}$$

$$\alpha_1 = \frac{1000}{5000} = 0.20$$

Therefore the certainty equivalent of the first year's cash flow of $5000 is
$1000. The net present value of certainty equivalent cash flows can be deter-
mined with the riskless discount rate r using the following equation.

$$NPV = \sum_{t=1}^{n} \frac{\alpha_t F_t}{(1 + r)^t} - F_0$$

The certainty equivalent coefficient α_t assumes values between 0 and 1, and
the larger the degree of risk the closer α_t is to 0.

In the above discussion, cash flows have been isolated as the risky variable,
with consideration given only to the variability of these cash flows. Other
variables, such as project life, which may require a probability distribution of
their possible values, have not been taken into account. The decision maker
may have no perception of the probable net cash flows for a project. However,
he may be able to estimate the possible values for sales revenue, fixed costs,
variable costs, tax rate, and depreciation, that is, the variables that make up
the net cash flow. Whenever several variables have been isolated as being
important in the evaluation of the project's risk, a simulation model can be
used.

Risk Analysis Using Simulation Models

Another technique that can be used to evaluate a project's risk is simulation.
The use of a computer allows the consideration of many variables and their
probability distributions, which provides a large amount of information on
which to base an investment decision. Based on the inputs, simulation analysis
can provide probability distributions for cash flows, rate of return, and net
present value. Firm statements can be made such as, "The likelihood is 70%
that the rate of return will equal or achieve 10%," or "There is a 10% chance
that the project will result in a $100,000 loss."

Model Specification.   The initial step in simulation analysis is to specify the
relationship between the investment decision criteria used to measure profitability and the variables that determine profitability. The model can be a simple

equation similar to the one discussed in the sensitivity analysis, or it can be complex like the one used by Hertz. His model contains the following input variables and allows for dependency between some variables.[13]

1. Market analysis.
   - Market size.
   - Selling price.
   - Market growth rate.
   - Share of market (which results in physical sales volume).
2. Investment cost analysis.
   - Investment required.
   - Residual value of investment.
3. Operating and fixed costs.
   - Operating costs.
   - Fixed costs.
   - Useful life of facilities.

Probability Analysis.   Only variables that have been isolated as being important in determining profitability need be considered in the probability analysis. At this point the question is, "How accurate is the estimate of a variable such as sales?" Additional information is necessary concerning the possible range of sales around the best estimate, as well as a judgment on the probability of each value for sales within this range. These judgments take the form of probability distributions.

Next, the analyst needs to collect information that will allow the construction of probability distributions for the sensitive variables. Subjective judgments on the likelihood of possible values for sales, for example, are elicited in a systematic manner using carefully phrased questions. The likelihood of a possible value of sales resulting from this process is referred to as the subjective probability. Chesley reviews several techniques for the elicitation of subjective probabilities and various problems associated with these techniques.[14] Before covering the procedures used, it should be emphasized that the analyst's role is to elicit the probabilities from the entrepreneur, sales manager, or other informed individuals.

The derivation of a probability distribution for sales can proceed in a manner

---

[13] David B. Hertz, "Risk Analysis in Capital Investment," *Capital Investment Series* reprints from *Harvard Business Review*, Jan.–Feb. 1964, pp. 175–186, and Hertz, "Investment Policies That Pay Off," *Harvard Business Review*, **46**, No. 1 (Jan.–Feb. 1968), pp. 96–108.
[14] G. R. Chesley, "Elicitation of Subjective Probabilities: A Review," *The Accounting Review*, **50**, No. 2 (April 1975), pp. 325–337.

similar to that used by Pouliquen.[15] The sales manager is asked, "What are the lowest and highest values expected for sales?" The range he specifies (6000 to 15,000) is divided into two intervals: 6000 to 12,000 and 12,000 to 15,000. Using a trial-and-error approach, he is asked to assign a probability to each interval. The analyst suggests a 50%–50% split. The sales manager believes that this assigns too high a probability to the 12,000 to 15,000 interval, as does 60%–40%; however, 70%–30% seems, in his judgment, to be reasonable.

By using the same procedure, the 6000 to 12,000 interval is divided into 6000 to 9000 and 9000 to 12,000, and the analyst asks the sales manager to allocate the 70% probability between these intervals. In this case, the sales manager may assign a probability of 20% to the 6000 to 9000 interval and the remaining 50% to the 9000 to 12,000 interval. The 12,000 to 15,000 interval is further subdivided into 12,000 to 14,000 with a probability of 25%, and 14,000 to 15,000 with a probability of 5%. The subdivision of the 12,000 to 15,000 interval finally reaches a point where the sales manager is guessing when he says that the 7000 to 9000 interval, for example, is more probable than the 6000 to 7000 interval. With the subdivision complete, the analyst and sales manager compare the sales intervals and their associated probabilities with each other to identify any discrepancies. Adjustments can be made to the probabilities if the sales manager believes that some sales intervals are inconsistent with one another. Figure 5.4 shows the steps in obtaining the step-rectangular probability distribution. Such a visual display can assist in the estimation of the subjective probabilities during the questioning process.

An excellent example of another approach in eliciting a subjective probability distribution is provided by Raiffa in an example of a hypothetical dialogue between the analyst and a decision maker.[16]

The step-rectangular probability distribution shown in Figure 5.4 represents one type of probability distribution. It is possible that the sales manager may not believe he can specify the likelihood for sales intervals as required to construct the step-rectangular distribution. He may only be able to estimate that future sales will be 11,000, but values of 6000 to 15,000 are also possible. Since probability distributions are, for the most part, triangular in shape, the analyst can use a triangular distribution as shown in Figure 5.5. These two examples illustrate that the information available for determining a probability distribution for a variable varies.

The primary consideration in choosing a probability distribution for a

---

[15] Louis Y. Pouliquen, *Risk Analysis in Project Appraisal* (World Bank Staff Occasional Papers No. 11; Baltimore: Johns Hopkins, 1972).

[16] Howard Raiffa, *Decision Analysis* (Reading, Mass.: Addison-Wesley, 1968), pp. 161–168.

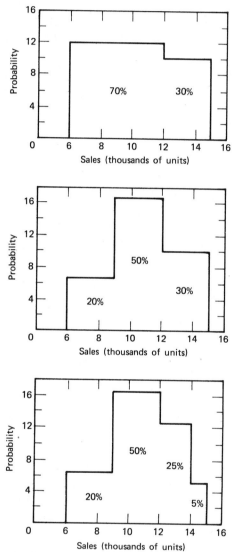

Figure 5.4 Steps in establishing the probability distribution of sales.

168

variable, then, is to utilize all the information available while not requiring more information than can actually be provided. Pouliquen provides a dis-

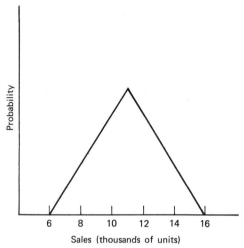

Figure 5.5   Triangular probability distribution.

cussion on the advantages and disadvantages of the following probability distributions useful for risk analysis.

- Step-rectangular distribution.
- Discrete distribution.
- Uniform distribution.
- Beta distribution.
- Trapezoidal distribution.
- Triangular distribution.
- Normal distribution.[17]

Simulation Process.   With the probability distributions specified for the pertinent variables and using constant values for the low-sensitivity variables, a computer can be used to generate random values for each variable and to compute the rate of return or the net present value. The simulation process can be illustrated using the previous determined probability distribution for sales, which is as follows.

---

[17] Pouliquen, Chap. 7.

Sales	Probability
6,000– 9,000	.20
9,000–12,000	.50
12,000–14,000	.25
14,000–15,000	.05

A random value for sales can be generated from the sales probability distribution using random chips. These 100 chips, numbered from 00 to 99, of similar size, shape, and composition, are placed in a container and mixed thoroughly. Each chip has a probability of 1/100 of being selected in any draw. Therefore if chips numbered 00 to 19 are assigned to the sales interval 6000 to 9000, the probability will be 20% that this sales interval will be selected. Similarly, chips are assigned to the remaining sales intervals as follows: 9000 to 12,000, chips numbered 20 to 69; 12,000 to 14,000, chips numbered 70 to 94; and 14,000 to 15,000, chips numbered 95 to 99. For each simulation trial, a chip is selected, tbe sales interval identified, and the chip replaced and mixed again. This procedure continues until a sufficient number of sales values has been generated.

In like fashion, a computer can be used to generate a random value for each of the variables and to calculate a rate of return. This process continues until the number of rates of return generated is sufficient to construct a probability distribution of their values. The number of simulation trials can be determined using statistical procedures.

Decision Criteria.   The probability distribution of the rate of return for the project summarizes the risk. This result of the simulation, however, does not provide any indication as to whether or not the project is suitable. Once the analyst has divided the probability distributions, he needs to use one of the previously mentioned decision criteria for selecting projects.

Risk Analysis Using Decision Trees

Today's project acceptance or rejection decision has implications for future investment decisions. Consideration, then, should be given to possible future events and decisions which may directly affect the present investment decision. The relationship between the investment decision that must be made now and decisions that may have to be made in the future is complex. Emanating from the investment decision are alternative scenarios which depend on the chances that various future events may occur and the consequences that will result if certain events do occur. Decision trees for the proposed project offer a systematic framework for analyzing a sequence of interrelated decisions which may have to be made over time.

The following example illustrates the decision tree approach.[18] Suppose a product with an expected life of 9 years has been developed. No manufacturing facilities exist at the present time, and a decision must be made as to what size plant to build. The market analysis indicated that the domestic market for the product seemed sufficient for a small plant, yet the magnitude of the export market, which would require a large plant, was difficult to ascertain. The immediate investment decision, then, is whether to build a large or small plant. If the initial demand, both domestic and export, for the product is high, a second decision will have to be made as to whether or not to expand the plant. At this point, the decision tree in Figure 5.6 can be laid out without the accompanying probability and cost data. The main elements of the decision tree are the squares, which represent decision points, and the nodes, which represent chance events and in this case are the levels of demand. For instance, if a small plant is built, there is a 70% chance that the initial demand will be high.

Data Collection.   After the alternatives have been identified and the decision process specified, the probabilities, cash flows, and costs associated with various outcomes must be computed and illustrated. Although probability estimates for only high and low estimates of demand are provided, this need not be the case. A continuous demand level can be specified, and simulation procedures used so that, instead of expected net present value, the result will provide a probability distribution of net present value.

Probability estimates for the demand levels are obtained in the following manner. Input data obtained from marketing indicate that a chance of a high demand in the long term is 60%, while the chance is 40% that the long-term demand will be low. Further demand information, broken down into two stages corresponding to the decision points, is required: the initial 3-year period and the subsequent 6-year period in the product's life. The following subjective probability estimates of demand were obtained from marketing for these "compound events," such as high demand in the first stage and subsequent low demand.

---

[18] See John F. Magee, "Decision Trees for Decision Making," *Harvard Business Review*, **42**, No. 4 (July–Aug. 1964), pp. 126–130, and Magee, "How to Use Decision Trees in Capital Investment," *Harvard Business Review*, **42**, No. 5 (Sept.–Oct. 1964), pp. 79–96.

172

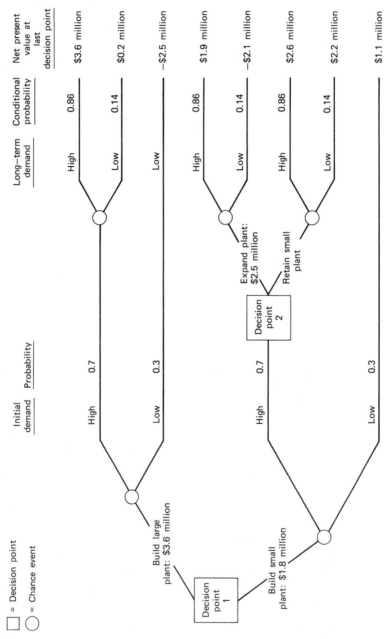

Figure 5.6 Decision tree.

□ = Decision point
○ = Chance event

Initial demand	Probability
High	0.7
Low	0.3

Build large plant: $3.6 million

Decision point 1

Build small plant: $1.8 million

| High | 0.7 |
| Low | 0.3 |

Decision point 2

Expand plant: $2.5 million

Retain small plant

Long—term demand	Conditional probability	Net present value at last decision point
High	0.86	$3.6 million
Low	0.14	$0.2 million
Low		—$2.5 million
High	0.86	$1.9 million
Low	0.14	—$2.1 million
High	0.86	$2.6 million
Low	0.14	$2.2 million
		$1.1 million

High initial demand, high long-term demand	60%
High initial demand, low long-term demand	10%
Low initial demand, low long-term demand	30%
Low initial demand, high long-term demand	0%

From this information the initial demand probabilities can be calculated and placed on the decision tree. The chances that demand will be initially high are 70%, while the chances that initial demand will be low are 30%. The remaining probabilities required for the decision tree are conditional. The conditional probability that a long-term high demand will occur in the last stage, given that the initial demand was high, can be computed as 86% by dividing the probability of long-term high demand (60%) by the probability of initial high demand (70%).

The remaining data needed for the decision tree can be obtained with inputs on investment costs, annual net cash flows, and the discount rate. The estimates on plant cost can be entered directly on the decision tree: large plant, $4 million; small plant, $3 million; and small-plant expansion, $3 million. The cash flow estimates for the different plants for various levels of demand are shown in Table 5.16.

Table 5.16 Projections of Net Annual Cash Flows

	Demand Level	Annual Net Cash Flow (thousands of dollars)
Large plant	High	1250
Large plant	Low	200
Small plant	High	600
Small plant	Low	500
Small plant expanded	High	1000
Small plant expanded	Low	100

Evaluation. The initial step in the process to determine the optimal sequence of decisions is to calculate the net present values for each of the alternatives, starting at the last chronological decision on the tree. At decision point 2, for example, the initial investment is $2.5 million if the plant is to be expanded and, with a high level of demand, the annual cash flow is $1 million for 6 years, which gives a net present value of $1.9 million. At decision point 2, the decision on whether or not to expand the plant must be made. The decision criterion used to choose between the two alternatives is to maximize expected net present

value. For the alternative to expand the plant, the expected net present value
is:

$$NPV = .86(1.9) + .14(-2.1) = \$1.3 \text{ million}$$

For the alternative to retain the small plant, the expected net present value is
\$2.5 million. Therefore, if decision point 2 is reached, the optimal decision will
be to maintain the small plant. All the alternatives stemming from decision
point 2 can be eliminated and replaced by the expected net present value, \$2.5
million.

The subsequent step is to determine what the optimal decision is at decision
point 1. The expected net present value for the small-plant alternative is:

$$NPV = .7(2.5) + .3(1.1) = \$2.1 \text{ million}$$

Similarly, for the large-plant alternative, the expected net present value is:

$$NPV = .7(3.1) + (.3)(-2.5) = \$1.4 \text{ million}$$

Therefore the optimal decision at point 1 is to build the small plant, because its
expected net present value exceeds that of the large plant. If the standard
deviations of the probability distributions of possible net present values are
calculated, that for the small plant is \$0.6 million compared with \$2.6 million
for the large plant. When the initial investments for two alternatives are not
the same, the coefficient of variation can be calculated to determine which
involves the greater risk. The coefficient of variation, defined as the standard
deviation divided by the expected value, is .29 for the small plant's net present
value, while for the large plant it is 1.86. The decision to build the large plant,
then, involves the greater risk.

Risk Reduction

Up to this point in the risk analysis, the concern has been to isolate and quantify
the risks associated with the project and to incorporate them into some investment decision criteria. A definite benefit of conducting a risk analysis is the
identification of sources of risk, but it also offers an opportunity to redesign the
project. If the risks associated with the project are found to be too large,
possible methods to reduce the risk can be examined. Even if the project is
found suitable with respect to risk, risk reduction means can improve its possible
net present value. Some ways in which risks can be reduced have been listed by
Kennedy. Although none of these methods are free of costs, the costs incurred
in reducing risks are usually less than the risks themselves.

1. If the perceived risk is founded on uncertainty rather than true risk, it can be reduced by investing in more information through further market, technical, or cost research.
2. If the risk is one commonly faced by businesses, it may be covered by straightforward commercial insurance. In many other cases virtual insurance can be achieved through (a) the inclusion of suitable penalty clauses in contracts, (b) the inclusion of suitable escalation clauses in sales contracts, and (c) operations in future markets for foreign currency, raw materials, or finished products.
3. If capital costs are the risky part of an otherwise promising venture, it may be possible to have facilities erected on a fixed-cost basis by an outside contractor.
4. If the risk lies in future sales volumes, it may be possible to mitigate this risk by forward vertical integration or long-term bulk sales contracts.
5. If material costs are sensitive, backward vertical integration or long-term bulk purchase contracts may be able to reduce this risk.
6. If technological difficulties render productivity very uncertain, it may be possible to subcontract critical steps in the process or even to subcontract virtually the entirety of production (perhaps via a royalty agreement).
7. If the risk springs from an inherent organizational weakness, it may be possible to reduce or eliminate this by modifying the policies or staff of the firm.[19]

IS PROJECT FEASIBLE?

To say that a project is feasible implies that it meets the following criteria:

- The market either exists or can be developed.
- The necessary technology either exists or can be developed.
- The financial returns and risk are satisfactory to all those who will invest funds in the project.

The first two requirements have been ensured by analyses described in previous chapters of this text. The question raised by the last criterion must be answered by the individuals who provide funds for the venture. The answer depends on the comparative attractiveness of this and other investment alternatives.

[19] Miles Kennedy, "Risk in Capital Budgeting: An Interactive Sensitivity Approach," Industrial Management Review, **9**, No. 3 Spring 1968, pp. 121–138.

Even if the project is not feasible, a report must be prepared in order to present the data collected during the market, technical, and financial analysis, as well as to present the conclusions. The next chapter includes an example of an economic feasibility study which illustrates the form of presentation.

BIBLIOGRAPHY

Beenhakker, H. L. *Capital Investment Planning for Management and Engineering*. Rotterdam: Rotterdam University Press, 1975.

Belew, Richard C. *How to Win Profits and Influence Bankers*. New York: Van Nostrand Reinhold C., 1973.

Bierman, Harold, Jr., and Jerome E. Haas. "Are High Cut-off Rates a Fallacy?" *Financial Executive*, **61**, No. 5 (June 1973).

Bierman, Harold, Jr. "Capital Budgeting under Uncertainty: A Reformulation," *The Journal of Finance*, **28**, No. 2 (May 1973).

Bierman, Harold, Jr., and Seymour Smidt. *The Capital Budgeting Decision*. 2nd ed. New York: Macmillan, 1966.

Bower, Richard S., and Donald R. Lessard. "An Operational Approach to Risk-Screening,' *The Journal of Finance*, **28**, No. 2 (May 1973).

Chesley, G. R. "Elicitation of Subjective Probabilities: A Review," *The Accounting Review*, **50**, No. 2 (April 1975).

Davey, Patrick J. *Capital Investments: Appraisals and Limits*. New York: The Conference Board, 1974.

Donaldson, Gordon. "Strategic Hurdle Rates for Capital Investment," *Harvard Business Review*, March–April 1972.

Goodman, Sam R. *Techniques of Profitability Analysis*. New York: Wiley, 1970.

Graham, Benjamin, and Charles McGolrick. *The Interpretation of Financial Statements*. 3rd rev. New York: Harper & Row, 1975.

Helfert, Erich A. *Techniques of Financial Analysis*. 2nd printing. Homewood, Ill.: Dow Jones-Irwin, 1973.

Hertz, David B. "Investment Policies That Pay Off," *Harvard Business Review*, **46**, No. 1 (Jan.–Feb. 1968).

Hertz, David B. "Risk Analysis in Capital Investments," *Capital Investment Series Reprints* from *Harvard Business Review*, Jan.–Feb. 1964.

Hillier, Frederick S. "The Derivation of Probabilistic Information for the Evaluation of Risk Investments," *Management Science*, No. 9 (April 1963).

House, William C., Jr. *Sensitivity Analysis in Making Capital Investment Decisions*. Research Monograph 3. New York: National Association of Accountants, 1963.

Huefner, Ronald J. "Analysis and Reporting Sensitivity Data," *The Accounting Review*, **60**, No. 4 (Oct. 1971).

Huefner, Ronald J. "Sensitivity Analysis and Risk Evaluaion," *Decision Sciences*, **3**, No. 3 (July 1972).

Jones, Reginald L., and H. George Trentin. *Budgeting: Key to Planning and Control*. Rev. ed. New York: American Management Association, Inc., 1971.

Joy, Maurice O., and Jerry O. Bradley. "A Note on Sensitivity Analysis of Rates of Return," *The Journal of Finance*, **28**, No. 5 (Dec. 1973).

Kennedy, Miles. "Risk in Capital Budgeting: An Interactive Sensitivity Approach," *Industrial Management Review*, Spring 1968.

Magee, John F. "Decision Trees for Decision Making," *Harvard Business Review*, **42**, No. 4 (July–Aug. 1964).

Magee, John F. "How to Use Decision Trees in Capital Investment," *Harvard Business Review*, **42**, No. 5 (Sept.–Oct. 1964).

Maxim, L. Daniel, and Frank X. Cook, Jr. *Financial Risk Analysis*. An ANA Management Briefing. New York: American Management Association, Inc., 1972.

Merrett, A. J., and Allen Sykes. *The Finance and Analysis of Capital Projects*. 2nd ed. A Halsted Press Book. New York: Wiley, 1973.

Petry, Glenn H. "Effective Use of Capital Budgeting Tools," *Business Horizons*, **14**, No. 5 (October 1975).

Petty, J. William, and Monroe M. Bird. "The Capital Expenditure Decision-Making Process of Large Corporations," *The Engineering Economist*, **20**, No. 3 (Spring 1975).

Pouliquen, Louis Y. *Risk Analysis in Project Appraisal*. World Bank Staff Occasional Papers No. 11. Baltimore: Johns Hopkins Press, 1972.

Quirin, G. David. *Capital Expenditure Decision*. Homewood, Ill.: Richard D. Irwin, 1967.

Raiffa, Howard. *Decision Analysis*. Reading, Mass.: Addison-Wesley, 1968.

Rudisill, Edward L. "Analyzing Investment Risk," *Financial Executive*, **40**, No. 9 (Sept. 1972).

Schlaifer, Robert. *Analysis of Decisions under Uncertainty*. New York: McGraw-Hill, 1969.

Schlaifer, Robert. *Probability and Statistics for Business Decisions*. New York: McGraw-Hill, 1959.

Shook, Robert C., Joseph Harold Highland, and Esther H. Highland. *Probability Models with Business Applications*. Homewood, Ill.: Richard D. Irwin, 1969.

Solomon, Martin B., Jr. "Uncertainty and its Effect on Capital Investment Analysis," *Management Science*, **12**, No. 8 (April 1966).

Van Horne, James C. "The Analysis of Uncertainty Resolution in Capital Budgeting for New Products," *Management Science*, **15**, No. 8 (April 1969).

Van Horne, James C. *Financial Management and Policy*. 3rd ed. Englewood Cliffs, N.J.: Prentice-Hall, 1974.

Weston, J. Fred, and Eugene F. Brigham. *Managerial Finance*. 4th ed. New York: Holt, Rinehart and Winston, 1972.

Chapter Six

THE THERMOMECHANICAL
PULP MILL CASE

In the preceding chapters techniques for project feasibility analysis required to develop the necessary information were discussed in detail. The presentation of the material in this manner, however, has obscured the overall feasibility study and its continuity. Therefore, in an effort to tie together the previous discussions, this chapter illustrates a feasibility study with the presentation of an actual case.

This feasibility study originated with a request by the Southeastern Lumber Manufacturers Association (SLMA) that the Economic Development Laboratory, Engineering Experiment Station, Georgia Institute of Technology, investigate the possibility of converting surplus wood chips and other forms of wood residues from sawmill operations into marketable pump and paper products.[1]

To members of the Southeastern Lumber Manufacturers Association the significance of this study resides in two factors: Under today's economic conditions, most sawmills will not survive without the income from wood chips and, because of the necessarily stringent pollution regulations, the disposal of wood residues from sawmill operations has become a problem.

This study of the feasibility of establishing pulp mills or pulp and paper mills based on surplus wood chips and wood residues was funded by the Coastal

[1] Tze I. Chiang and Frank Kingsland, "The Feasibility of Establishing Thermo-Mechanical Market Pulp Mills in the Coastal Plains Region of the United States," Atlanta: Economic Development Laboratory, March 1976.

178

Plains Regions Commission because of the above factors. Other considerations were indications that there will be a worldwide wood fiber shortage by 1978 and the hope of developing a new pulping technology which can overcome previous obstacles of high capital costs and pollution.

The objectives of the study were to determine the type and size of pulp mill or pulp and paper mill to be constructed, to recommend a plant location, to analyze wood waste supply conditions in a 150-mile radius of the potential plant location, to investigate investment requirements, to project production costs and returns, to investigate market conditions, and to outline a marketing strategy for the proposed production.

The results of this feasibility study are organized into six major parts. Part one describes the raw material supply conditions, based on a detailed survey of sawmills in a seven-state area. The attitudes of responding sawmill owners concerning a proposed pulp mill and the timber supply outlook in the Coastal Plains region are also included.

Part two presents trends in pulping technology and production practices, constraints in making a choice, and the final choice of a thermomechanical pulping (TMP) system.

Part three involves potential plant locations. Although extensive locational data were presented in the original feasibility study, only an extract of the considerations is included here.

The fourth part involves markets and marketing. In-depth analyses are given of economic trends, markets for wood pulp, marketing methods and strategies, prices, and the results of a worldwide market survey. An analysis of world fiber capacities is also included in this section.

Part five presents the design and engineering of a proposed TMP mill. Detailed descriptions and designs for the whole plant and for each major component system are given. The discussion includes design criteria and an overview, a chip station, TMP refining, pulp screening and cleaning, pulp baling, the electrical distribution system, the water supply system, the effluent control system, steam generation, optional second-stage bleaching, and the infrastructure of the proposed mill.

The sixth part gives a detailed economic analysis and financial projections on capital costs, production costs, and financial evaluations. All capital costs, including land, buildings, equipment, infrastructure, construction overhead, and engineering and working capital, are itemized. Construction schedules and costs are presented. Detailed production costs in terms of both variable and fixed costs are given. Also included in this section are different financial evaluations in the forms of a pro forma profit and loss statement, cash flow projection, and balance sheet. Most of these projections cover a 10-year period. Finally, a financial sensitivity analysis is given.

RAW MATERIAL SUPPLY CONDITIONS

Residues as a Source of Wood Raw Materials for the Pulp and Paper Industry

Residues, often thought of as merely salvageable waste material, are currently providing one-fourth of the fiber used by the U.S. pulp and paper industry. Wood pulp manufacture depends on two main sources of raw material inputs —roundwood and residues. In recent years, a significant quantity of wood fiber reaching U.S. pulp mills has been in the form of chips. However, not all these wood chips qualify as residuals. Some have been manufactured from regular roundwood at chipping plants.

The American Paper Institute classifies wood residues in two categories:

1. *Forest residues* comprise chips, particles, and fibers arising as by-products of logging operations, including culled material, slash, limbs, saplings, and so on. Also included are other secondary forest material usually defined as logging residues, such as tops, branches, standing saplings, and cull trees.
2. *Manufacturing residues* comprise chips, particles, and fibers arising from primary and secondary manufacturing, such as sawmills, plywood and veneer mills, flooring and furniture factories. They include slabs, cores, edgings, shavings, sawdust, and so on, but not bark.

The wood raw materials considered in this study come entirely from sawmills and other woodworking plants and should be classified as manufacturing residues. Manufacturing residues are important to the U.S. pulpwood consumption. On an industrywide basis, manufacturing residues provided 31% of the pulpwood consumed in 1973. In the South Atlantic region and in the South Central region, manufacturing residues provided 19 and 25%, respectively, during the same year.

The consumption of wood residues as pulpwood has been increasing persistently. Wood residues provided about 17% of the pulpwood consumed in the United States in 1960. They increased to 35% in 1973 and are expected to reach 37% in 1975. The trend of increase is:

1960—17%	1962—21%
1961—20%	1963—24%

1964—25%	1970—29%
1965—25%	1971—32%
1966—27%	1972—35%
1967—30%	1973—35%
1968—30%	1974—37%
1969—30%	1975—37%

The potential supply of wood residues for the U.S. pulp and paper industry depends on two considerations—physical availability and economic availability. In terms of physical availability, the U.S. Forest Service estimated the quantity of unused manufacturing residues in 1970 at approximately 1 billion cubic feet, the equivalent of 12 million cords. In that year, the U.S. pulp industry consumed approximately 20 million cord equivalents of pulpwood in the form of residuals, which in turn represented 29% of the total pulpwood consumed in the manufacture of 42.2 million short tons of wood. In recent years, unused manufacturing wood residues no doubt have been increasing, especially since the adoption of chip-and-saw technology.

Disposing of unused manufacturing wood residues has been a problem for the woodworking industry. Environmental standards virtually forbid their burning except as boiler fuel. High fuel costs in recent years have permitted wood residues such as trims, edgings, sawdust, shavings, and barks to be used economically as boiler fuel. However, wood chips that are the processed products from other wood residues are too expensive to be burned as boiler fuel. Outlets with higher value must be found for these chips. The export of wood chips to wood-short areas such as Europe and Japan is a fact of life today. However, exporting wood pulp and paper products would be a more profitable method of disposal than exporting chips. In addition, wood chip exports can absorb only a small fraction of the large volume of manufacturing residues available in the South and in the United States as a whole.

A Survey of Sawmills

Between February and March 1975, a survey was conducted to determine the amount of surplus wood raw materials available and the number of sawmill owners willing to participate in the proposed pulp mills. The Economic Development Laboratory (EDL) cooperated with the SLMA in carrying out a survey in the seven-state area that is the territory of SLMA. Cover letters and questionnaires were sent to 227 SLMA members in Alabama, Florida, Georgia, Mississippi, North Carolina, South Carolina, and Virginia. Ninety-six sawmills responded to the survey.

Survey of SLMA Members For Feasibility Study on Proposed Pulp Mill

1. Lumber Production Record
   (List separately for each plant location)

   Monthly information requested to determine if seasonal variations exist.

Month	Pine--MBF	Hardwood--MBF
January		
February		
March		
April		
May		
June		
July		
August		
September		
October		
November		
December		
TOTAL		

2. Equipment in Your Mill
   (Check each type of equipment in your operation)

Chip-N-Saw	_____	Chipping Edger	_____
Circular Saw	_____	Circular Gang	_____
Band Saw	_____	Circular Edger	_____
Resaw	_____	Trim Saw	_____
Sash Gang	_____		

3. 1974 Wood Chip Production
   (In green tons)

   Monthly information requested to determine if seasonal variations exist.

Month	Pine	Hardwood
January		
February		
March		
April		
May		
June		
July		
August		
September		
October		
November		
December		
TOTAL		

Attachment 6.1   Raw Material Questionnaire

4. <u>1974 Wood Residue Record</u>
   (In <u>tons</u>)

   Monthly information requested to determine if seasonal variations exist.

Month	Shavings*	Pine Sawdust	Bark	Hardwood Shavings	Sawdust	Bark
January						
February						
March						
April						
May						
June						
July						
August						
September						
October						
November						
December						
TOTAL						

   *Please indicate a percentage of your shavings from kiln dried lumber:
   _____percent

5. <u>Timber Supplies</u>

   Please indicate your source of raw material:
   A. Company owns _____ acres of timberland.
   B. Company has cutting rights on _____ acres of timberland.
   C. Logs are purchased from loggers. _____percent
   D. Standing timber is purchased from local landowners. _____percent.
   E. Logs and standing timber are purchased from other sources. _____
      Please specify and list percentage. _____.

6. <u>Transportation</u>
   Please indicate whether you are transporting these items by truck or rail:

          Chips _____   Sawdust _____
          Shavings _____   Bark _____

7. If this pulp and paper mill is feasible and the price for your raw materials
   is economical, would you be willing to:

   A. Financially participate in the construction and ownership of this mill?
      _____

   B. Obligate the raw materials from your mill to supply the needs of such a
      plant? _____

   Please indicate if the information furnished is for more than one mill. ____
   If yes, give locations: _____

                    Name _____

                    Company _____

                    Date _____

Attachment 6.1 (Continued)

Besides the two main objectives mentioned, other questions concerning lumber production, timber supplies, transportation means, equipment installed, and seasonal variation in production were included in the survey. (See Attachment 6.1.)

The distribution of SLMA's members, survey respondents, and willing participants in the seven states is given in Table 6.1. Among 96 responding sawmills, 40 of them were willing to participate financially, 39 were undecided, and 17 responded negatively. Among the responding sawmills, 70 were willing to commit their wood chips and wood residues for the proposed pulp mills, 22 were undecided, and only 4 gave a negative answer. It is assumed that the sawmills that expressed willingness to obligate their raw materials would commit their reported volumes of wood chips and residues to the proposed pulp mills if prices paid for these wood materials were attractive to them. Certainly a contract would be drawn between a proposed pulp mill and participating sawmills to ensure long-term supplies.

The tabulation of data obtained through the survey emphasized the 70 sawmills willing to commit their wood chips and residues for the proposed pulp mills. However, those who were undecided were tabulated separately, and those with negative answers were dropped from the tabulation. The distribution of the 70 sawmills willing to commit their wood raw materials and the 22 undecided sawmills is presented in Map 1.

Wood Raw Materials Obligated

Raw materials committed by the participating sawmills in the seven states are quantified in Table 6.2, which presents data on number of sawmills, volume of wood chips in pine and hardwood, and wood residue volume in the form of shavings, sawdust, and bark. Of 1,012,570 tons of pinewood chips committed annually, Georgia would supply 442,037 tons and North Carolina 278,300 tons. These two states account for 71% of the total pinewood chips committed. Of 192,199 tons of hardwood chips committed, Georgia and North Carolina account for 58%. Wood chips would be intended solely for pulpmaking purposes under this program. Obviously, pinewood chips would be the main source of raw materials supplies for any pulp mill to be considered under this study program.

Committed pinewood residues totaled 269,933 tons, while hardwood residues totaled 438,381 tons in the seven-state area (Table 6.2). Sawdust is the dominant source of available wood residues. All residues are intended for boiler fuel. Detailed statistics on wood residues are given in the table. However, it

Table 6.1 The Distribution of SLMA Members, Survey Respondents and Participating Sawmills in Seven Southeastern States, 1975

State	Number of Sawmills and Questionnaires Sent	Number of Survey Respondents	Willingness to Participate Financially			Willingness to Commit Wood Chips and Residue		
			Yes	No	Undecided	Yes	No	Undecided
Alabama	30	17	7	1	9	13	0	4
Florida	9	3	1	1	1	1	1	1
Georgia	55	24	14	3	7	20	0	4
Mississippi	12	5	0	5	0	3	2	0
North Carolina	72	27	10	5	12	20	1	6
South Carolina	33	13	5	2	6	10	0	3
Virginia	16	7	3	0	4	3	0	4
Total	227	96	40	17	39	70	4	22

Table 6.2 Sawmills willing to Commit Raw Materials: Number of Mills, Volume, and Kind of Raw Materials (Wood materials on annual basis and in green tons)

State	Number of Sawmills	Wood Chips		Pinewood Residues			Hardwood Residues		
		Pine	Hardwood	Shavings	Sawdust	Bark	Shavings	Sawdust	Bark
Alabama	13	146,350	28,345	15,636	7,718	4,741	156	470	282
Florida	1	29,071	1,530	152	999	—	—	—	—
Georgia	20	442,037	51,696	42,439	69,030	56,011	13	408,463	11,013
Mississippi	3	7,872	10,080	7,200	2,880	2,400	—	—	—
North Carolina	20	278,300	60,715	10,466	26,320	10,740	1,519	7,017	76
South Carolina	10	90,920	17,565	3,902	4,472	2,362	1,288	2,464	1,848
Virginia	3	18,020	22,268	—	2,465	—	—	3,772	—
Total	70	1,012,570	192,199	79,795	113,884	76,254	2,976	422,186	13,219

should be noted that not all reporting sawmills gave their residue volume. Many of them simply did not know their volume.

Among the seven states, Georgia and North Carolina stand out in all categories either in number of sawmills responding and participating or in the volume of wood materials committed. Of the 70 sawmills that expressed willingness to obligate their wood raw materials, 40 are located in these two states. (See details in Table 6.1.)

Wood Raw Materials Not Yet Obligated

Twenty sawmill owners indicated that they had not made up their minds to obligate their wood raw materials to the proposed pulp mills. These 20 sawmills generate 310,899 tons of pinewood chips and 31,954 tons of hardwood chips annually. Four sawmills in Georgia generate 57% of the pine chip total, while five sawmills in North Carolina generate 15% of the total. These two states stand out again in most of the wood raw materials generated, although these materials have not yet been committed to the proposed pulp mills. These wood materials may increase the committed volume by 20 to 30% if the proposed pulp mills prove to be feasible and prices paid for these raw materials are attractive.

Details of not yet committed wood materials and their distribution in the seven southeastern states are given in Table 6.3. All sawmills gave their wood chip volume; however, wood residue volume is incomplete, because many sawmills did not report residue volume.

Slight Seasonal Variation

Wood chip production corresponds generally with lumber production. The ratio of wood chips generated and lumber produced depends on wood species and equipment installed in a sawmill. Sawmills were requested to give their monthly lumber production together with monthly wood chip production.

About 52 sawmills reported their monthly lumber production, and 46 sawmills reported their monthly wood chip production. Few sawmills kept records on monthly wood residues generated.

The number of participating sawmills and their monthly production volume of wood chips are presented in Table 6.4, while lumber production is given in Table 6.5. Each month has a total representing the aggregate volume of all sawmills willing to participate. It is apparent from these two tables that there is little seasonal variation in the production of either wood chips or lumber,

188

Table 6.3 Sawmills Undecided to Commit Raw Materials: Number of Mills, Volume, and Kind of Raw Materials (Wood materials on annual basis and in green tons)

State	Number of Sawmills	Wood Chips Pine	Wood Chips Hardwood	Pinewood Residues Shavings	Pinewood Residues Sawdust	Pinewood Residues Bark	Hardwood Residues Shavings	Hardwood Residues Sawdust	Hardwood Residues Bark
Alabama	3	21,892	6,875	4,363	7,340	5,800	—	—	—
Florida	1	25,000	—	4,100	6,500	—	—	—	25,000
Georgia	4	178,679	3,770	12,327	6,384	3,404	4,680	—	—
Mississippi	1	7,485	—	—	—	—	—	—	—
North Carolina	5	45,799	5,917	6,805	5,202	—	360	1,544	—
South Carolina	2	16,395	—	1,602	5,087	2,656	—	—	—
Virginia	4	15,639	15,392	1,022	11,933	—	25	4,099	2,365
Total	20	310,899	31,954	30,219	42,446	11,860	5,065	5,643	27,365

Table 6.4 Monthly Pinewood Chip Production by Participating Sawmills, 1974–1975 (in thousands of green tons)

State	No. of Mills	January	February	March	April	May	June	July	August	September	October	November	December
Alabama	10	9,158	10,111	11,777	10,082	12,256	11,602	9,785	12,139	10,244	11,145	11,206	8,072
Florida	1	2,748	2,772	3,017	2,668	4,095	3,887	1,777	2,022	2,394	1,680	1,774	1,707
Georgia	16	34,137	33,625	36,408	35,176	33,176	37,377	30,609	35,389	32,249	34,341	32,116	27,215
Mississippi	2	656	656	656	656	656	656	656	656	656	656	656	656
North Carolina	15	13,206	13,058	15,129	14,696	17,578	16,466	12,616	15,074	16,195	16,606	16,269	12,572
South Carolina	7	5,496	7,185	6,980	7,013	8,022	6,797	4,792	7,736	6,046	6,347	6,347	5,115
Virginia	1	950	639	914	539	1,096	865	826	579	348	344	99	521
Total	52	66,351	68,046	74,881	70,830	76,879	77,650	61,061	73,595	68,432	71,164	68,467	55,858

Table 6.5 Monthly Pine Lumber Production by Participating Sawmills, 1974–1975 (thousands of broad feet)

State	No. of Mills	January	February	March	April	May	June	July	August	September	October	November	December
Alabama	10	6,495	5,577	6,924	4,834	7,051	6,218	6,015	6,373	5,798	6,321	5,131	4,157
Florida	1	438	838	844	824	915	1,006	616	528	564	623	494	660
Georgia	15	9,742	9,565	9,076	9,286	10,616	10,177	9,456	8,956	9,145	10,232	8,270	8,396
Mississippi	2	1,337	917	1,118	1,290	1,606	1,148	1,450	1,119	1,120	1,332	1,012	816
North Carolina	12	4,484	4,200	4,986	5,314	6,350	5,648	4,906	5,373	5,352	4,912	4,331	3,496
South Carolina	5	2,219	2,420	3,092	3,055	3,392	2,927	2,814	2,917	2,308	3,027	2,449	1,695
Virginia	1	670	466	596	206	839	546	545	267	363	489	138	259
Total	46	25,385	23,983	26,636	24,809	30,769	27,670	25,802	25,533	24,650	26,936	21,825	19,479

Table 6.6 Major Equipment Units Installed in the Participating Sawmills, 1974–1975

State	Chip-N-Saw	Circular Saw	Band Saw	Resaw	Slash Saw	Chipping Edger	Circular Gang	Circular Edger	Trim Saw
Alabama	0	14	3	6	3	1	7	16	12
Florida	0	1	1	1	0	1	2	2	2
Georgia	1	23	5	14	4	4	13	18	23
Mississippi	0	2	1	0	0	0	0	1	2
North Carolina	1	19	8	10	6	1	7	19	22
South Carolina	0	8	5	3	2	0	4	10	9
Virginia	0	5	3	3	0	0	2	5	6
Total	2	72	26	37	15	7	35	71	76

except in December. There was a 23% decline in wood chip production in December compared with the peak in May, and there was a 27% drop in lumber production in the same month. The principal reason for the slackened production in December was the holiday season.

Major Equipment Installed

Major equipment installed in the participating sawmills is given in Table 6.6. Of course, the type of equipment used affects the production of lumber and wood chips and the rate of wood residues generated. Chip-N-Saw is the most modern facility designed to process small-diameter logs into studs at high speed with wood chips as by-products. There are only two participating sawmills with Chip-N-Saw units. One is in Georgia and the other is in North Carolina. Conventional sawmills with traditional saws, such as circular saw, band saw, and so on, are also tabulated.

It appears that the circular saw, trim saw, and circular edger are most commonly installed in conventional sawmills. Other units, such as the band saw, resaw, circular gang, slash saw, and chipping edger, are less frequently installed.

Sources of Timber Supplies

The sources of timber supplies of the participating sawmills are of concern and interest to this study program. There are three main sources of timber supplies —from owned timberland, from cutting rights, and from purchases. Sawmills supplied mainly from their own timberland are few today. Sawmills with cutting rights on leased timberland are not prevalent either. The majority of the timber used by sawmills today comes from purchases. Sawmills may purchase from independent or contract loggers, directly from local timberland owners, or from other sources such as pulp mills or other sawmills.

The participating sawmills that reported their sources of timber supply are tabulated by state in Table 6.7. Twenty sawmills were supplied from their own timberland, 19 used cutting rights, 50 purchased from loggers, 62 purchased from local landowners, and 25 purchased from other sources. The table shows total acres of owned land and leased land and average percentage supplied by purchases. For purchased supplies, local landowners are the most important source, followed by loggers, and then by other sources.

It should be noted that each source is not exclusive. One sawmill may use several sources of supply at the same time. The average percentages of purchased timber are not weighted by timber volume and do not add up to 100%. They should be viewed as an indicator of relative importance among methods used to acquire timber.

Timber Supply Outlook

Since the proposed pulp mills would depend entirely on wood chips and wood residues generated by participating sawmills, it is important to ascertain whether adequate timber supplies will continue to be available to keep these sawmills running. Several noticeable trends in timber supplies in the region are worthy of mention here. Southern yellow pine, which represents over 90% of softwood, has increasingly become the dominant species in the region because of large-scale efforts in planting and management. The total volume of growth greatly exceeds cut volume; as a result, a larger amount of pine timber will be available for cutting in the future. However, the quantity of large-diameter sawtimber, especially over 18 inches, is declining and, in some areas, large-diameter sawtimber is in tight supply. Because of this, the design of modern sawmills emphasizes efficient use of timber and small-diameter logs.

The timber supply outlook in Georgia is presented in this section. Similar projections were made in the study for North Carolina and South Carolina but are not included.

The Georgia outlook is based on two projections made by the U.S. Forest Service. The first projection was based on the continuation of current trends, while the second projection was based on the potential supply under conditions of maximum output and sound forestry management.

The first projection was for 30 years and was intended to establish a realistic measure of available cut based on a continuation of recent trends in forest area and the current level of timber culture activity. The results of this project, shown in Table 6.8, indicate a prospective available cut of 1733 million cubic feet annually by the year 2001. This is 70% greater than the volume of removals determined for 1971. The projection also allows for a further buildup in the inventory from 25.3 billion to 32.5 billion cubic feet. The prospective available cut of sawtimber is estimated to increase from 3706 million to 6370 million board feet over the same period.

Several basic assumptions were involved in this projection. The primary control was an assumption that growth and removals will be in balance by the year 2001. The area of commercial forest land was assumed to continue to decline at the rate of 50,000 acres each year. This is very near the average rate of real change which occurred between 1961 and 1972.

Table 6.7 Sources of Timber Supply of Participating Sawmills

State	Own Timberland		Cutting Rights		Purchases					
					From Loggers		From Landowners		From Other Sources	
	No. Mills	Acres	No. Mills	Acres	No. Mills	%	No. Mills	%	No. Mills	%
Alabama	4	9,330	4	8,242	10	25	10	57	5	28
Florida	0	0	0	0	1	15	1	40	1	45
Georgia	5	12,521	5	29,200	16	37	17	71	4	25
Mississippi	0	0	2	5,750	1	30	2	68	2	18
North Carolina	6	8,734	7	21,000	14	32	20	70	6	24
South Carolina	3	4,900	1	5,000	6	36	9	58	6	27
Virginia	2	7,000	1	2,000	2	60	3	58	1	5
Total/average	20	42,485	20	71,192	50	34	62	60	25	25

The 1971 growth rates were gradually reduced by 10% in anticipation of overstocked conditions developing in many of the unmanaged stands, and to compensate somewhat for the fact that the 1972 survey reflects a rate of ingrowth not likely to be sustained. The 1971 mortality rates were applied throughout the projection.

Separate projections were made for softwoods and hardwoods (Figure 6.1). Under the assumptions used, the results indicate that softwoods will provide two-thirds of the prospective increase in the available cut of total growing stock and 80% of the prospective increase in available sawtimber. Considerably

Table 6.8   Projection of Net Annual Growth, Available Cut and Inventory of Sawtimber and Growing Stock on Commercial Forest Land, by Softwood and Hardwood, Georgia, 1971–2001

		Projected to		
Species Group	1971	1981	1991	2001
Growing stock (thousands of cubic feet)				
Softwood				
Cut	783,800	1,012,500	1,168,200	1,260,200
Growth	1,153,100	1,282,800	1,307,700	1,260,200
Inventory[a]	14,768,900	17,667,100	19,273,300	19,537,300
Hardwood				
Cut	234,000	319,400	404,300	473,100
Growth	424,100	465,900	484,000	473,100
Inventory[a]	10,563,300	12,030,400	12,880,000	13,000,800
Total				
Cut	1,017,800	1,331,900	1,572,500	1,733,300
Growth	1,577,200	1,748,700	1,791,700	1,733,300
Inventory[a]	25,332,200	29,697,500	32,153,300	32,538,100
Sawtimber (thousands of board feet)				
Softwood				
Cut	2,918,300	3,780,300	4,577,000	5,061,700
Growth	4,008,100	4,867,000	5,175,900	5,061,700
Inventory[a]	45,654,900	56,885,400	63,932,200	65,486,200
Hardwood				
Cut	788,200	981,800	1,171,800	1,308,900
Growth	1,234,600	1,331,600	1,357,100	1,308,900
Inventory[a]	26,543,800	30,096,700	32,058,200	32,286,000
Total				
Cut	3,706,500	4,762,100	5,748,800	6,370,600
Growth	5,242,700	6,198,600	6,533,000	6,370,600
Inventory[a]	72,198,700	86,982,100	95,990,400	97,772,200

[a] Inventory as of January 1 of the following year.

Source. Georgia's Timber, 1972, U.S. Forest Service, Resource Bulletin SE-27, May 1974.

more effort has gone into the regeneration and management of pine than has gone into hardwood management.

The second projection also was for 30 years and was intended to establish a realistic measure of the maximum level of available cut that could be reached and sustained through accelerated timber management. Results of this projection indicate a potential available cut of 2045 million cubic feet by 2001, or about double the amount of removals in 1971. In this projection, the potential available cut of sawtimber climbed to 7586 million board feet (Figure 6.1). These estimates of potential available cut reflect the inherent capacity of the forest lands expected to be available for timber production when fully stocked.

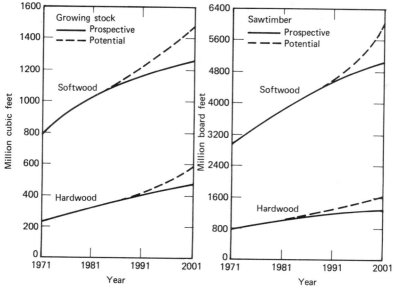

Figure 6.1 Prospective and potential available cut in Georgia, 1971–2001. *Source: Georgia's Timber, 1972*, U.S. Forest Service, Resource Bulletin SE-27, May 1974.

CHOICES OF PROCESSING METHOD, SCALE OF OPERATION, AND END PRODUCTS

Constraints in Choice

There are several constraints in the choices of processing method, scale of operation, and end products for the proposed pulp mills under this research program. These constraints are described below.

1. *Wood species.* Southern yellow pine is the dominant species available for the project—about 90% of the committed raw materials. Other species are soft hardwoods, such as oak and hickory. Southern yellow pine, which is preferred by only a few pulping processes, should be regarded as the main source of raw material supplies.

2. *Raw material volume.* The volume of wood raw material available affects the choice of pulping process and the size of the pulp mill to be built. The economic distance for hauling wood raw material to a potential pulp mill site depends on the wood cost and freight rate involved; however, 150 miles is a reasonable limit in hauling distance for any pulp mill. The volume of pine chips available within 150 miles of the selected potential pulp mill sites ranges from 285,000 tons to 622,000 tons a year.

3. *Capital outlay.* Pulp- and papermaking is a capital-intensive industry. The high cost of capital and the large sums involved have prevented many conceived pulp and paper plants from being realized. One of the purposes of this project is to minimize capital outlay so that a proposed mill will have a better chance of being established, either by sawmill owners themselves or by other potential investors.

4. *Minimum pollution.* It is clear from the events of recent years that both the public and private sectors desire to end industrial pollution. Stringent government regulations on pollution have put many pulp and paper mills with obsolete processing methods out of business. Contacts with environmental protection agencies reveal that it would be impossible to obtain an operating permit from governmental regulating agencies for any new pulp mill that did not meet their established pollution standards. The level of pollution and costs involved in containing it are of major concern to the proposed pulp mills.

With these constraints in mind, a review of the current pulp and paper technology and the trends of pulp and paper production is presented below to help in making a final choice of the pulping process to be adopted and end products to be produced.

Trends in Technology and Production Practice

The pulp and paper industry has been confronting three major problems in recent years: (*a*) competition for capital and its costs in relation to return on investment; (*b*) inflation and the high costs of raw materials, labor, and overhead; and (*c*) sociopolitical considerations in areas such as ecology and the environment. These problems are not likely to disappear soon and will affect the future development of pulp and paper technology and production practices.

Several noticeable trends in the development of pulping technology are expected to continue. (*a*) The technology for producing higher yield pulps will be emphasized so that wood raw material costs can be reduced and output be maximized. Screening and refining of higher yield pulps will be further developed, and a wide variety of papers and boards will be produced from higher-yield pulps. (*b*) Smaller production units will be emphasized, so that capital outlay can be reduced. (*c*) Processing methods that eliminate or lessen pollution will be further developed and emphasized.

There are only six major categories of pulping processes—mechanical or groundwood, waste paper, chemimechanical, semichemical, chemical, and dissolving. Table 6.9 shows each category and one or more typical processes for each. Fiber yield and preferred wood species under each category are also given in the table.

Table 6.9   Major Pulping Processes, Yield of Fiber, and Preferred Species

Pulping Process	Typical Process	Yield of Fiber (%)	Preferred Wood Species
Mechanical (or groundwood)	Stone groundwood Refiner mechanical Thermomechanical	90–95	Conifer
Waste paper	Deinking	65–90	Waste paper and kraft waste
Chemimechanical	Cold soda	80	Hardwood
Semichemical	Neutral Sulfite Semi-Chemical	60–85	Hardwood
Chemical	Sulfite Sulfate (kraft)	43–55	Almost any
Dissolving	Sulfite prehydro- lyzed sulfate Sivola	33–43	Almost any

Mechanical processes have the highest yields, with 90 to 95% of wood fiber input, while dissolving and chemical processes have the lowest yields, with 30 to 50% of fiber input. Southern yellow pine, which is a conifer, is the preferred wood species for mechanical processes. Chemical and dissolving processes can use any wood species; however, certain wood species are preferred for some of the processes. For example, the kraft (or sulfate) process, which accounts for 67% of all pulps produced in the United States in 1973, uses predominantly southern yellow pine. However, southern yellow pine logs or chips generally are not used in deinking (waste paper), chemimechanical, semimechanical, and dissolving processes.

Sulfite and sulfate (or kraft) are the two major chemical pulping processes. Sulfite pulp used to be the major pulp for making all grades of paper other than paperboard, coarse paper, and newsprint. However, it has steadily been losing ground to bleached and semibleached kraft in these traditional end uses. Production declined from 2.8 million tons in 1966 to 2.3 million tons in 1973. Many sulfite mills were closed down because they were noncompetitive and were heavy polluters.

The sulfate (kraft) process was the major breakthrough in pulping technology in the 1900s. Production increased from 1 million tons in 1931 to 33 million tons in 1973. Three major developments were primarily responsible for this achievement. First, in contrast to sulfite pulping, chemical recovery, because of the cost of the chemicals utilized, is an economic necessity in this process. In the 1930s, successful recovery techniques were applied, and since have been vastly improved. Second, the process was found to be adaptable to nearly all wood species, and its application to southern yellow pine resulted in a rapid expansion of kraft pulping. Third, new developments in kraft bleaching techniques spurred another dramatic growth period just after World War II. Kraft bleached by new processes, which retained its superior strength, began to replace sulfite in many bleached papers. Kraft then made further inroads on traditional sulfite markets with the production of dissolving pulp and greaseproof and tissue papers. Today, a broad spectrum of printing and fine papers, tissue, food and milk containers, and boxes and containers of many other varieties is manufactured from bleached kraft pulp.

However, kraft already may have reached its peak. First, most kraft mills built today rely on sheer size for commercial success. The minimum economic size for a market kraft mill is now considered to be about 800 air-dry tons per day (ADT/D), which requires $150 million to $200 million for capital outlay and over 1 million tons of wood raw material a year. The high cost of obtaining such a huge amount of capital and the low yield of the kraft process are not compatible with current economic thinking. Second, kraft mills require extensive pollution-control facilities in order to dispose of wastes and to recycle chemicals. It is also difficult to obtain an operating permit in the study area. As far as the proposed pulp mills in this study are concerned, the kraft process is impractical in terms of either raw material volume needed or capital outlay required.

Pollution level, which is one of our criteria in the choice of a pulping process, can be expressed by raw waste load. Table 6.10 indicates average raw waste

loads by major pulping processes selected from 144 pulp and paper mills by the
U.S. Environmental Protection Agency in a recent study. Raw waste loads are
expressed in flow volume, biochemical oxygen demand (BOD), and total
suspended solids (TSS). From the table, it is apparent that groundwood mills
have the smallest raw waste loads. Thermomechanical, one of the groundwood
processes, has the lowest flow volume and TSS and the second lowest BOD. The
thermomechanical process is discussed more intensively in later sections of
this chapter.

Table 6.10   Raw Waste Load by Pulping Processes

Pulping Process	Flow		BOD		TSS	
	kl/kkg	(kgal/ton)	kg/kkg	(lb/ton)	kg/kkg	(lb/ton)
BK-dissolving	241.9	(58.0)	55.0	(110)	150.0	(300)
BK-market	177.9	(42.5)	41.0	(82.0)	70.0	(140)
BK-fine	108.4	(26.0)	30.0	(60.0)	84.0	(168)
BK-BCT	152.2	(36.5)	33.5	(67.0)	51.5	(103)
Sulfite-papergrade	208.5	(50.0)	115.5	(231)	82.0	(164)
Sulfite-dissolving	271.9	(65.2)	132.0	(264)	92.5	(185)
Soda	123.0	(29.5)	42.5	(85.0)	105.0	(210)
GW-chemimechanical	83.4	(20.0)	50.5	(101)	28.0	(56.0)
GW-thermomechanical	62.5	(15.0)	28.0	(56.0)	25.0	(50.0)
GW-fine	90.9	(21.8)	17.0	(34.0)	52.0	(104)
GW-CMN	99.2	(23.8)	17.5	(35.0)	70.0	(140)
Deink	94.2	(22.6)	68.5	(137)	204.0	(408)

kl = kiloliter.
kkg = 1000 kilograms.
BOD = biochemical oxygen demand.
TSS = total suspended solids
BK-dissolving = bleached kraft for dissolving pulp.
BK-market = bleached kraft for market pulp.
BK-fine = bleached kraft for fine paper.
BK-BCT = bleached kraft for paperboard, coarse papers, and tissue papers.
Sulfite-papergrade = bleached sulfite pulp for paper products.
Sulfite-dissolving = Highly bleached and purified sulfite pulp for rayon and other products.
Soda = bleached pulp for printing and writing papers.
GW-chemimechanical = groundwood: chemimechanical pulp for fine paper, newsprint, and
    molded-fiber products.
GW-thermomechanical = groundwood: thermomechanical pulp for fine papers, newsprint, and
    tissue products.
GW-fine = groundwood pulp for paper containing 8% or more clays and fillers.
GW-CMN = groundwood pulp for coarse papers, molded-fiber products, and newsprint.
Deink = pulp brightened from recycled waste papers.

Final Choice: A Thermomechanical Pulping System (TMP)

It is clear from the foregoing discussion of the six major pulping processes that only mechanical (or groundwood) is suitable for our consideration. None of the others—waste paper, chemimechanical, semichemical, chemical, and dissolving —is compatible with the restraints imposed on the proposed pulp mill. Of the three typical mechanical processes, thermomechanical stands out as the final choice.

TMP is one of the major technical innovations in the pulp and paper industry in the last few years. Among the three mechanical pulping processes (stone groundwood, refiner mechanical, and thermomechanical), TMP has the brightest outlook. Stone groundwood has been gradually replaced either by refiner mechanical or by TMP in recent years. In fact, TMP is the improved version of refiner mechanical. Approximately 35 TMP systems have been purchased throughout the world during the past $2\frac{1}{2}$ years. Most of them are now in operation.

The ready acceptance and rapid commercialization of the TMP system has been hailed as the most important development in the pulp and paper industry subsequent to the adoption and commercialization of the kraft pulping process four decades ago. Paper executives express their opinion that no significant technological developments are foreseen over the next 5 years except in the area of thermomechanical pulping.

The merits of the TMP system can be summarized as:

1. Small production units are feasible for commercial adoption, thus minimizing capital outlay.
2. Fiber yield is high at about 90 to 95% of input. High yield reduces the cost of wood material used.
3. The system generates relatively low waste flow, BOD, and TSS. Thus capital outlay for pollution control is small compared with other processes. TMP emits no polluting factor into the air.
4. Wood chips and residues from sawmills can be accepted as the only wood raw materials input. Thus costly pulpwood procurement systems and chipping operations can be eliminated.
5. Both water requirements and wastewater volume are low, making the selection of a mill site comparatively easier than for chemical processes.

TMP meets all the choice-constraint requirements mentioned in the previous section and is consistent with current technical trends. Pulps made with TMP are used in producing fine papers, newsprint, sanitary and tissue papers, and paperboard. They also are being used as extenders of chemical pulps in many other paper grades. The market price of chemical pulp is about double that of TMP pulp. Further refinements of TMP pulp qualities, especially in the areas of brightness and strength, could enable it to penetrate a large portion of the traditional markets now being served by chemical pulps. Researchers around the world have been attempting to improve these two characteristics.

End products for the proposed mills would be market pulps with varied characteristics to meet the needs of different end uses. Three grades of TMP pulp are proposed under this study program: magazine, newsprint, and sanitary-tissue grades. There are slight differences in investment and production requirements for these three types of TMP pulps. However, this study does not go into the papermaking end, which would double the capital outlay of a TMP pulp mill.

The size of a TMP mill depends primarily on wood raw materials available and the market potentials of end products. TMP pulps are new to many papermakers, who are still trying to familiarize themselves with the pulps. Most of the TMP mills built or ordered are not over 300 ADT/D. Under this study program, 300 ADT/D will be adopted as the daily nominal capacity for the proposed TMP mills.

POTENTIAL PLANT LOCATIONS AND PRODUCTION CONDITIONS

Criteria and Decision

Six main criteria were used in selecting potential plant locations for the proposed pulp mills in the Coastal Plains region. They are (1) accessibility to as many participating sawmills as possible, (2) accessibility to rail and highway transportation, (3) water availability and quality, (4) available outlet for wastewater disposal, (5) power accessibility and cost, and (6) plant site availability.

Accessibility to participating sawmills is essential for wood raw material supply. Chosen locations must be close to as many participating sawmills as possible in order to ensure adequate supplies of wood raw materials. Proximity to participating sawmills also means economy in transportation costs for wood raw materials.

Rail and highway connections are important to a proposed pulp mill. Both raw materials and finished goods depend on either railroads or highways for transportation. Groundwater would be used as the main source of water supply for the proposed pulp mill. The level of groundwater and its quality affect the costs in pumping and chemical treating before use. Since the wastewater from a pulp mill generally is discharged into a river after the water is treated, the flow volume and quality of water in a river affects treatment method and costs.

Power accessibility and cost are critical to a thermomechanical pulp mill, which requires a large amount of power in processing. Plant site availability in a given location is another important point for consideration. The locational data presented in the original feasibility study are not included here.

MARKETS AND MARKETING

Economic Trends and Outlook

The demand for paper and board products is so diverse in daily life, in commerce, in various manufacturing sectors, and so on, that the trend of paper and board production is closely related to the nation's economy. However, an analysis has indicated that the production of wood pulp is closely related to the production of paper and board.

Wood pulp, paper, and board products are international commodities which play a significant role in the import and export business. Millions of tons of wood pulp, paper, and board products are imported and exported each year. U.S. paper and board production, imports, exports, and consumption data since 1947 are given in Table 6.11. Per capita consumption, the thousands of tons of consumption generated by each billion dollars of gross national product (GNP), population, and production as a percent of apparent consumption also are shown. Between 1947 and 1974, production increased 189%; imports, 102%, exports, 713%; consumption volume, 164%, and per capita consumption, 80%. In the same period, each billion dollars of real GNP (1958 prices) generated, on the average, 79,000 to 80,000 tons of paper and board consumption or demand. The trend of production as a percentage of apparent consumption exhibited a steady increase, from 85% in 1947 to 93% in 1974. These trends reflect the dynamism of the pulp and paper industry and the U.S. economy as a whole. These trends also can be used in projecting the future state of the national pulp and paper industry.

Statistical series on U.S. wood pulp production, imports, exports, new supply, and consumption in paper and board since 1947 are presented in Table 6.12. Between 1947 and 1974, production increased 275%; imports, 76%; exports, 2053%; new supply, 226%; and consumption in paper and board, 164%. The tremendous growth of exports since 1947 reflects the favorable conditions for wood pulp production in the United States in terms of timber resources, capital, technology, and social surroundings.

The production and consumption of wood pulp, paper and board products, as mentioned previously, are closely related to the national economy. Every fluctuation in the economy, using the GNP as a measuring stick, affects the pulp and paper industry. For instance, the large increase in demand for pulp and paper in 1972–1973 was consistent with the rapid growth of the GNP (Table 6.11). During this period, the sudden rise in fuel and power costs due to the Arab nations' oil embargo, together with inflation which reached the two-

Table 6.11   United States Paper and Board Production, Imports, Exports, and Consumption Census Data, Totals for All Grades (tons of 2000 lb)

Year	Production	Imports[1]	Exports[1]	Apparent Consumption Tons	Lb./ Capita	Thousand Tons per Billion $ (real GNP)	Popula- tion (thou- sands)	GNP in 1958 Prices (real GNP) (billion $)	Production as a % of Apparent Consumption
1947	21,101,833	4,121,854	474,486	24,749,201	343.4	79.9	144,126	309.9	85
1948	21,897,301	4,582,298	397,019	26,082,580	355.9	80.6	146,631	323.7	84
1949	20,315,436	4,751,810	372,277	24,694,969	331.0	76.2	149,188	324.1	82
1950	24,375,468	5,008,222	371,546	29,012,144	381.1	81.7	152,271	355.3	84
1951	26,046,697	5,149,517	635,303	30,560,911	394.6	79.7	154,878	383.4	85
1952	24,418,383	5,190,859	592,388	29,016,854	868.3	73.4	157,533	395.1	84
1953	26,604,583	5,230,866	475,345	31,360,104	391.6	76.0	160,184	412.8	85
1954	26,876,242	5,189,880	687,098	31,379,024	385.0	77.1	163,026	407.0	86
1955	30,178,102	5,385,786	845,227	34,718,661	418.5	79.3	165,931	438.0	87
1956	31,441,192	5,836,309	781,762	36,495,739	432.2	81.8	168,903	446.1	86
1957	30,666,469	5,471,512	869,736	35,268,245	410.1	77.9	171,984	452.5	87
1958	30,823,251	5,148,634	853,010	35,118,875	401.6	78.5	174,882	447.3	88
1959	34,014,825	5,622,175	911,917	38,725,083	435.5	81.4	177,830	475.9	88
1960	34,444,317	5,721,133	1,026,962	39,138,488	433.3	80.3	180,667	487.7	88
1961	35,749,430	5,778,172	1,215,570	40,312,032	439.0	81.1	183,672	497.2	87
1962	37,540,902	5,867,973	1,192,816	42,216,059	452.7	79.7	186,504	529.8	89
1963	39,230,020	5,825,775	1,340 798	43,714,997	462.1	79.3	189,197	551.0	90
1964	41,703,408	6,385,795	1,704,933	46,384,270	483.6	79.8	191,833	581.1	90
1965	44,079,880	6,800,332	1,778,472	49,101,740	505.6	79.5	194,237	617.8	90
1966	47,113,498	7,519,781	1,953,755	52,679,519	536.2	80.0	196,485	658.1	89
1967	46,925,753	7,114,643	2,095,692	51,944,704	522.8	76.9	198,629	675.2	90
1968	51,245,160	7,058,456	2,639,175	55,664,441	554.9	78.8	200,619	706.6	92
1969	54,187,214	7,493,492	2,765,632	58,915,074	581.4	81.2	202,677	725.6	92
1970	53,516,171	7,267,188	2,843,193	57,940,166	565.6	80.2	204,879	722.5	92
1971	55,085,805	7,617,316	3,145,781	59,557,340	575.3	79.8	207,045	746.3	92
1972	59,457,076	8,032,651	3,103,738	64,385,989	616.6	81.2	208,482	792.5	92
1973	62,087,000	8,477,225	3,070,463	67,494,000	641.5	80.4	210,400	839.2	92
1974[2]	61,010,000	8,315,000	3,857,000	65,468,000	617.1	79.7	211,900	821.2	93

[1] Imports and exports include products.

[2] Preliminary.

Source: U. S. Department of Commerce, Bureau of the Census.

digit level, inflamed a skyrocketing rise in pulp and paper prices here and abroad. Users of pulp and paper products reacted with rush purchases to build up their inventories in hopes of avoiding further price increases. Market pulp prices doubled. Nearly every line of pulp and paper was in short supply. Coincidentally, an economic recession followed in 1974 and 1975. Slow orders and high inventories occurred at the same time. Inevitably, prices of pulps and papers softened, but they are still substantially higher than in the 1972–1973 period. Some clear signs of economic recovery appeared in January 1976—retail sales up, industrial production up, unemployment rate down, interest rates down, sales of automobiles up, construction activities picking up, and a bull stock market. Nevertheless, the recovery is slow. Economists predict that a full

Table 6.12   United States: Total Wood Pulp, All Grades, 1947–1974 (tons of 2000 lb, air-dry weight)

Year	Production	Imports	Exports	New Supply	Consumption in Paper & Board
1947	11,945,864	2,322,460	130,096	14,138,228	13,252,924
1948	12,872,292	2,176,111	93,727	14,954,676	14,374,586
1949	12,207,279	1,763,102	122,133	13,848,248	13,635,957
1950	14,848,951	2,385,181	95,673	17,138,459	16,508,905
1951	16,524,408	2,360,706	201,908	18,683,206	17,736,970
1952	16,472,979	1,941,259	211,924	18,202,314	17,286,030
1953	17,537,297	2,157,574	161,687	19,533,184	18,683,543
1954	18,302,273	2,051,798	443,870	19,910,201	18,989,159
1955	20,739,696	2,213,353	634,276	22,318,773	21,453,766
1956	22,130,949	2,334,253	534,494	23,930,708	22,998,380
1957	21,800,209	2,106,681	628,721	23,278,169	22,459,420
1958	21,795,652	2,101,787	515,859	23,381,580	22,483,118
1959	24,383,391	2,431,433	652,437	26,162,387	25,155,362
1960	25,315,589	2,381,487	1,141,534	26,555,542	25,700,031
1961	26,522,759	2,466,770	1,177,775	27,811,754	26,682,863
1962	27,908,330	2,788,281	1,186,213	29,510,398	28,598,333
1963	29,439,097	2,774,778	1,421,936	30,791,939	30,219,885
1964	31,911,056	2,942,303	1,580,154	33,273,205	32,087,548
1965	33,295,727	3,137,097	1,402,203	35,030,621	34,006,285
1966	35,636,268	3,358,183	1,547,379	37,447,072	36,922,186
1967	36,354,923	3,166,130	1,720,783	37,800,270	36,993,999
1968	39,196,454	3,532,020	1,915,604	40,812,870	41,302,856
1969	40,990,405	4,040,460	2,102,660	42,928,205	43,699,831
1970	42,216,056	3,512,872	3,095,390	42,633,538	43,191,642
1971	43,743,795	3,515,045	2,175,446	45,083,394	44,148,214
1972	46,604,395	3,727,776	2,252,778	48,079,393	47,347,254
1973	48,355,397	3,993,164	2,343,555	50,005,006	48,858,444
1974	44,839,433	4,123,000	2,802,000	46,160,433	48,300,000

Source: American Paper Institute, <u>Wood Pulp and Fiber Statistics</u>, 39th Edition, November 1975.

recovery will occur about 1977 or 1978 in the United States. As for the European countries, recovery may trail about 6 months behind that of the United States.

In planning a new pulp mill, one must project the future demand for pulp and paper products. This involves predicting general economic trends. Two questions must be examined: (1) How will the economy behave in the future? (2) Will the relationship between the GNP and paper and board demand hold at a normal level?

Forecasting or predicting is a precarious business; however, some basic assumptions must be made. It is assumed that the economy will be normal by 1978 with full employment (unemployment rate not over 5%), and the relationship between the GNP and paper and board demand will remain at a normal level of 79,000 to 80,000 tons per billion dollars of GNP. It is further predicted that the GNP will increase at an annual rate of 6% between 1976 and 1978 and at 3.75% after 1978. Based on these assumptions, the production of wood pulp, paper, and board, together with imports, exports, apparent consumption, and the GNP, are projected in Table 6.13. Projections in this section are partly based on trends, correlation analysis, and published materials concerning the pulp and paper industry.

Table 6.13 Production, Imports, Exports, and Consumption of Paper and Board, and Production of Wood Pulp in the United States, 1974 and Projected 1975 to 1985

| Year | Paper and Board (tons of 2000 lb) | | | | Wood Pulp Production (tons of 2000 lb dry weight) | GNP (billions of 1958 dollars) |
	Production	Imports	Exports	Apparent Consumption		
1974	61,010,000	8,315,000	3,857,000	65,468,000	44,839,000	821.2
1975	52,800,000	6,794,000	3,050,000	56,544,000	40,429,000	789.0
1976	61,000,000	7,600,000	3,100,000	65,500,000	46,708,000	840.0
1978	70,000,000	8,155,000	3,500,000	74,655,000	53,600,000	945.0
1980	76,000,000	7,700,000	3,700,000	80,000,000	58,193,000	1000.0
1985	90,000,000	9,000,000	4,000,000	95,000,000	68,913,000	1200.0

The production of wood pulp, paper, and board was expected to "bottom out" in 1975. Recovery was to begin in the latter part of 1975 and continue through 1977, with production returning to a normal level by 1978. It was projected that the GNP would reach $945 billion in 1978, $1 trillion in 1980, and $1.2 trillion in 1985. The production of paper and board would be 70 million tons in 1978, 76 million tons in 1980, and 90 million tons in 1985. Wood pulp production, which has averaged 76.6% of paper and pulp production in the last 10 years, would reach 53,600,000 tons in 1978, 58,193,000 tons in 1980, and 68,913,000 tons in 1985. Imports and exports of paper and board were projected based on the past trends.

World paper and board production was about 74 million metric tons in 1960 and 157 million metric tons in 1974. Production more than doubled between 1960 and 1974, and it is projected to double again by 1988 at an annual growth rate of 5%. However, whether or not raw materials, chemicals, capital, political conditions, and so on, will sustain this rate of growth is uncertain. The growth rate in developing nations is expected to be greater than in developed countries.

The Markets for Wood Pulp

A mill can produce wood pulp either for internal production of paper and board products or for sale as market pulp. The term "market pulp" is applied to pulp sold in the marketplace to producers of paper and paperboard for further conversion. Buyers of market pulp may not have any pulp-producing facilities of their own, or they may be producers of only part of their requirements. Many manufacturers of paper and board require a variety of pulp to obtain the necessary blends and may buy as many as 15 or 20 different types of pulp.

Market pulp is sold either in domestic markets or to foreign countries. This study includes U.S.-produced market pulp for both the domestic market and all export markets; market pulp produced by foreign companies and sold in their respective domestic markets is excluded. The U.S. production of market pulp as a percentage of total wood pulp production from 1950 to 1985 is given in Table 6.14. The production of U.S. market pulp increased from 1,646,788 tons in 1950 to 5,140,421 tons in 1974; however, output remained approximately 11.5% of total wood pulp production. Taking 1974 as an example, of the 5,140,421 tons produced, 2,802,429 tons, or 55%, were exported. The remaining 45% was sold in the domestic market. Chemical pulps constituted slightly over 95% of the market pulp, while groundwood or mechanical pulps constituted only 3% to 4% of the total market pulp in the United States. TMP, production of which is just barely starting in the United States, is not available as a market pulp in domestic commerce.

In 1974, the world production of pulp was estimated at 121,675,000 metric tons.[2] The United States produced 43,743,545 metric tons, or about 40% of the world total, in the same year. However, 94% of U.S. production was

[2] One metric ton is equal to 1.1023112 short tons.

consumed in domestic uses, and only about 6% was exported. The United States imported 3,740,515 metric tons of pulp, or about 20.5% of total world imports, and exported 2,542,316 metric tons, or about 13.3% of total world exports, in 1974. On balance, the United States has been a net importer of wood pulp for some time.

In 1974, a little over 19 million metric tons of wood pulp moved in the world market—about 15.6% of the total world production. The greater part of the world trade in market pulp is in the long-fibered grades based on coniferous trees. For this reason and the advanced state of pulping technology development, most of the market pulp is produced in the forested areas of the north temperate zone—northern Europe, Canada, and the United States.

World production, imports, and exports of wood pulp were analyzed. All net exporters of wood pulp in the world, that is, countries where the volume of exports exceeds the import volume, were identified. The reverse is true for net importers. Among the net exporters, Canada and the Scandinavian countries, Sweden, Finland, and Norway are dominant. Their pulp exports constitute a major portion of their total pulp production in terms of volume. Among the net importers, Western Europe (excluding Scandinavia), Japan, and the United States are the largest. Unlike the United States, the European countries and Japan have to rely heavily on imports as the major source of wood pulp supply. Major net importers of wood pulp in Western Europe are the United Kingdom, West Germany, France, Italy, the Netherlands, Belgium, Spain, and Switzerland. Other major importers of wood pulp are Japan, the United States, Australia, South Korea, and the People's Republic of China.

The United States, Canada, and the Scandinavian countries of Sweden, Finland, and Norway accounted for approximately 70% of the total pulp production and 83% of the total export volume of the world in 1974. The volumes of exports from these five major pulp-producing nations to various destinations showed that Europe received the bulk of the exports, followed by Asia and Oceania, Latin America, and Africa. The EEC countries of the United Kingdom, France, West Germany, Italy, and the Netherlands are major customers of all five, while Japan is the leading recipient of pulp from the United States and Canada.

It should be noted that timber resources in Sweden, Finland, and Norway, the three major pulp producers in Scandinavia, have reached their limits in supporting current production of pulp and paper products. The future development of the pulp and paper industry in this region will require that production be upgraded by exporting less wood pulp and producing more paper and board products in order to increase commodity values. As a result, the pulp supply

Table 6.14 U.S. Production of Market Pulp as a Percent of Total Wood Pulp Production, 1950–1985[a]

Year	Wood Pulp Production, All Grades (tons of 2000 lb, air-dry weight) Total	Market	Market Pulp as a Percent of Total Wood Pulp Production
1950	14,848,951	1,646,788	11.1
1951	16,524,408	1,906,764	11.5
1952	16,472,979	1,849,328	11.2
1953	17,537,297	1,783,921	10.2
1954	18,302,273	2,179,798	11.9
1955	20,739,696	2,707,420	13.1
1956	22,130,949	2,690,028	12.2
1957	21,800,209	2,586,104	11.9
1958	21,795,652	2,303,951	10.6
1959	24,383,391	2,580,850	10.6
1960	25,315,589	3,012,390	11.9
1961	26,522,759	2,973,650	11.2
1962	27,908,330	3,095,178	11.1
1963	29,439,097	3,394,479	11.5
1964	31,911,056	3,707,348	11.6
1965	33,295,727	3,846,643	11.6
1966	35,636,268	4,061,891	11.4
1967	36,354,923	4,023,446	11.1
1968	39,196,454	4,399,608	11.2
1969	40,990,405	4,854,926	11.8
1970	42,216,056	5,512,962	13.1
1971	43,743,795	4,976,632	11.4
1972	46,604,395	5,275,450	11.3
1973	48,355,397	5,062,211	10.5
1974	44,839,433	5,140,421	11.5
1975	40,429,000	4,618,540	11.4
1976	46,708,000	5,377,470	11.5
1978	53,600,000	6,210,490	11.6
1980	58,193,000	6,765,640	11.6
1985	68,913,000	8,061,350	11.7

[a] Linear correlation between total wood pulp production (X) and market pulp production (Y):

Estimating equation (thousands of tons): $Y = -268.04 + 0.12X$

Coefficient of correlation: $r = .96$

Standard error of estimate: $s = 236,470$ tons

Sources. 1950–1974: American Paper Institute, *Wood Pulp and Fiber Statistics*, 39th ed. 1975–1985: Projected by EDL.

for nonintegrated paper mills in the European Economic Community (EEC) countries will be tight in the latter part of the 1970s and will be even tighter in the 1980s. The United States and Canada are the only reliable alternative sources of supply for these pulp-consuming nations in Europe. Some developing nations in Latin America and Africa, where timber resources are available, also may play a role in increasing worldwide wood pulp supplies. However, constraints in capital and technology, as well as social surroundings suitable for investment purposes, in these countries are likely to hamper a desirable rate of growth in the pulp and paper sector.

The Marketing of Wood Pulp

The marketing of wood pulp can be accomplished in two basic ways:

1. Secure a market before becoming committed to the construction of a market pulp mill by:

   - Obtaining the financial participation of one or more major users who can guarantee the use of a substantial proportion of the mill's production in their paper- and paperboard-making operations.
   - Entering into long-term contracts with one or more major users for a substantial proportion of the mill's production.

2. Sell the proposed pulp output through one of the large, established pulp agents who operate in most of the pulp-consuming countries of the world. Many of these agents work on an international scale and maintain offices in many countries. Most of them handle a variety of pulps from a fairly substantial number of client mills. This multiclient arrangement may appear to create conflicts of interest among producers whose pulp an agent is handling, but the realities of the marketing situation and the integrity of the established agents make it a very satisfactory method.

   End users of pulp in the major pulp-consuming markets require a variety of grades and types (long-fibered, short-fibered, bleached, semibleached, unbleached, high-tear, high-burst factor, etc.) and usually find it advantageous to deal with an agent who can provide a range of pulps.

   Some of the large pulp producers maintain their own selling offices in certain large marketing areas, but most of these still use agents in the smaller consuming centers. Sales by pulp agents are usually made on the basis of set commissions which may vary in different areas or on the basis of volume of sales. The general commission rate is 3 to 5% of the c.i.f. price of the pulp.

Entrepreneurs should be cautioned that neither sales approach will provide an ironclad assurance of selling all mill production, and certainly the price that can be expected will only be equivalent to what is prevailing in the market for pulp of the quality being produced.

Captive buyers who have equity or contractual obligations with the producing mill no doubt give priority consideration to using pulp from the mill, but during periods of sustained economic stagnation in the paper and board markets, they cannot be expected to accept pulp they cannot use, because of constricted markets for their products. Pulp agents are in the same situation. They endeavor to do their best to dispose of their clients' pulp, but they cannot sell more than the market can absorb.

Pulp has a rather inelastic price curve. During an economic recession price cutting does not appreciably affect the quantities consumed in the market. It may enhance the competitive position of one producer for a given sale, but the longer-term effect is to reduce the de facto price for all producers who must maintain a competitive position on the basis of price. The practice of selling below the list price used to be quite prevalent in time of oversupply. However, pulp producers seem to have learned a lesson from the past; during the economic recession of 1974–1975, pulp prices sustained themselves quite well. Steep rises in production costs during the period also may have worked to prevent substantial price cutting. In addition, competition may take other forms, such as special freight allowances, quantity discounts, and special free services.

Nevertheless, a common marketing practice for a mill just entering the market is to offer start-up pulp at prices below the accepted level. This is economically justified during the period when a new mill is in its shakedown period and its operators are trying to attain the necessary quality standards on a consistent basis.

The entrepreneur of a new market pulp mill should provide himself with a strong team of expert pulp salespeople who understand both the mechanics of selling and the technical aspects of pulp production and use. The fact that he has a large captive market or that his selling is in the hands of a reputable agent should not cause him to default on his own basic responsibility—to market his pulp. The management of the new company should maintain liaison with its customers by periodic contact, even if those customers are located in distant areas, and should be fully conversant with the situation in the market. The end purpose of the enterprise is to sell, and this important function should not be passed on to others whose interests are not as deeply involved in the success of the venture.

The price of market pulp depends basically on the market conditions—demand and supply. In many ways, pulp inventory and mill operating rate reflect the demand and supply conditions. During a boom period, mill operating rates are generally high, while pulp inventories are low; consequently, pulp prices are high. The reverse is true during a recession period.

The prices of bleached softwood kraft pulp and groundwood pulp since 1946 in the United States are presented in Table 6.15. These prices are median list prices. Prices of chemical pulps are quoted on a delivered basis, while groundwood or mechanical pulp prices are f.o.b. mill. From the table it is apparent that pulp prices were relatively stable from 1951 to 1972. Between 1973 and 1975, pulp prices doubled. Bleached softwood kraft sold for $163 per ton in April 1973, and its price increased to $334 per ton in June 1975; some reported sales priced at $365 per ton during a peak period. These high prices were sustained even during the recession period of 1974–1975. The prices of groundwood pulp followed the same trend as bleached softwood kraft prices. The pulp sold for $87.50 per ton, f.o.b. mill, in May 1973, but increased to $200 per ton in April 1974. A high of $225 per ton was reported; however, the groundwood price has dropped to $170 per ton since January 1975. An extremely high pulp inventory being built up in the Scandinavian countries, which are the principal producers of mechanical pulp, has affected the world price.

TMP has never been offered as a market pulp in the United States. However, according to knowledgeable trade sources, the quality of bleached TMP should be between that of bleached softwood kraft and groundwood; consequently, its price should fall between that of these two pulps. TMP prices were estimated on the basis of its prices in the European market, where it has been sold for several years. There is only one market TMP unit presently in operation, at Rottneros in Sweden. Prices of TMP on October 29, 1975, Italy, are given in Table 6.16. The prices were given in Swedish kroner and converted to U.S. dollars, based on the exchange rate on that date. In order to derive a f.o.b. mill price at Dublin, Georgia, all transportation and marketing expenses were deducted according to established trade practices. Metric tons also were converted to short tons. The table shows TMP prices in two basic grades: (1) newsprint grade and (2) tissue and magazine grade.

Based on the Italian c.i.f. prices, TMP should be priced at $195.88 to $221.65 per ton, f.o.b., Dublin, Georgia. These prices were between the prices of bleached softwood kraft and groundwood in the U.S. market in October 1975, and they are still valid in today's market. It should be noted that the sales commission at 3%, c.i.f., and the cash discount at 1.5% have not been included. These expenses, together with pricing policy, are given in a later section concerning

Table 6.15 Bleached Softwood Kraft and Groundwood Prices, Domestic Pulps in the U.S. Market, 1946–1975 (dollars per ton of 2000 lb, air-dry weight)[a]

Year	Month	Bleached Softwood Kraft[b]	Ground-wood[c]	Year	Month	Bleached Softwood Kraft[b]	Ground-wood[c]
1946	May	94.0	58.0		Apr.	153.0	—
	Sept.	103.5	64.0				
	Nov.	107.5	—	1957	Oct.	158.0	—
	Dec.	—	75.0	1960	Nov.	147.0	—
1947	Jan.	—	77.5				
	Mar.	127.0	—	1961	Apr.	—	77.5
	Apr.	132.5	—	1962	Oct.	136.0	87.5
	June	—	82.5				
	Aug.	—	77.5	1963	Apr.	139.0	—
	Oct.	—	78.0		Oct.	146.0	—
1948	Jan.	178.0	82.5	1964	Oct.	150.0	—
	July	172.5	—	1967	June	147.0	—
	Oct.	162.0	—				
1949	Jan.	142.0	—	1968	June	—	87.5
	Apr.	138.0	—	1969	Dec.	147.0	—
	May	—	67.5	1970	Feb.	157.0	—
	June	—	62.5		July	165.0	—
	July	124.0	—	1971	Aug.	163.0	—
	Aug.	122.0	—				
	Dec.	—	66.5	1973	Apr.	163.0	100.0
1950	July	126.5	—		May	—	87.5
	Sept.	—	71.5		June	178.0	—
	Oct.	129.5	76.5		July	176.0	125.0
1951	Jan.	167.0	—		Aug.	188.0	—
	Feb.	—	102.5		Sept.	195.0	—
	Apr.	—	100.0		Dec.	205.0	115.0
	July	145.0	101.5	1974	Jan.	—	—
1952	July	146.0	96.0		Mar.	205.0	—
	Sept.	—	87.0		Apr.	257.0	200.0
	Nov.	—	85.0		June	262.5	—
1955	Jan.	—	77.5		July	326.5	185.0
	Apr.	148.0	—		Nov.	332.5	—
	Oct.	—	82.5	1975	Jan.	332.5	170.0
1956	Jan.	—	86.0		Feb.	334.0	—
					June	334.0	170.0

[a] Median list prices.
[b] Delivered.
[c] F.o.b. shipping point.
Source. American Paper Institute, *Wood Pulp and Fiber Statistics*, 39th ed., November 1975.

211

Table 6.16 TMP List Prices in Newsprint Grade and in Tissue-Magazine Grade, Italy, October 29, 1975, and Converted to F.O.B. Prices, Dublin, Georgia

	Newsprint Grade	Tissue and Magazine Grade
Swedish kroner, c.i.f. Italy	Kr 1325/metric ton	Kr 1450/metric ton
U.S. dollars, c.i.f. Italy	$303.69/metric ton	$332.34/metric ton
Trade discount[a]	$20.00/metric ton	$20.00/metric ton
C.i.f. sales price	$283.69/metric ton	$312.34/metric ton
Deduct:		
Insurance	$2.33/metric ton	$2.58/metric ton
Ocean freight	$50.00/metric ton	$50.00/metric ton
Free alongside ship price[b]	$231.36/metric ton	$259.76/metric ton
Convert to short tons	$209.88/short ton	$235.65/short ton
Deduct:		
Rail freight to Savannah, Georgia	$8.00/short ton	$8.00/short ton
Wharfage and warehouse	$6.00/short ton	$6.00/short ton
F.o.b. Dublin, Georgia	$195.88/short ton	$221.65/short ton

[a] Discount given during current economic recession.

[b] Free alongside ship at Savannah, Georgia.

costs and returns in this study. In addition, the price discount should be removed when the demand for pulp is strong.

Pulp prices in France and Germany are about $20 per ton lower than in Italy. However, the ocean freight rate to Italy is about $10 per ton lower than to France or Germany. The net difference is $10 per ton less on sales to northern countries in the EEC.

World Fiber Capacities

The American Paper Institute published a review of world fiber trends based on annual survey data published by the Food and Agriculture Organization (FAO). The FAO 1975 world survey reveals that paper and board manufacturing capacities outstripped pulp mill capacities by 35,353,000 metric tons in 1974 and are expected to exceed pulp capacities by 40,645,000 metric tons in 1977. Based on these trends, a forecast was made by the FAO that the pulp supplies in the world will be tight by 1977 or 1978. The detailed survey data are summarized in Table 6.17. In 1974, worldwide annual capacities were 167,059,000 metric tons for paper and board and 131,696,000 metric tons for pulp. The ratio of paper-grade pulp to paper and paperboard was 78.8%. By 1977, paper and board capacities are projected to increase to 187,891,000 metric tons and paper-grade pulp capacities to 147,246,000 metric tons, with the ratio of paper-grade

Table 6.17   Worldwide Annual Capacities in Pulp, Paper,
and Board, 1974 and 1977 (thousands of metric tons)

	1974	1977	1974–1977 Change
Paper and paperboard	167,059	187,891	+20,832
Paper-grade pulp[a]			
Wood	123,322	137,256	13,934
Other fiber	8,374	9,990	1,616
Total pulp	131,696	147,246	+15,550
Ratio of paper-grade pulp to paper and paperboard	78.8%	78.4%	−0.4%

[a] Excludes dissolving pulp.
Sources. FAO and the American Paper Institute.

pulp to paper and board decreasing slightly to 78.4%. The imbalance of paper pulp versus paper and board capacities can be remedied either by increasing the use of waste papers or by adding new pulpmaking capacities around the world.

The regional distribution of planned net additions in paper-paperboard and pulp annual capacities from 1974 to 1977 is given in Table 6.18. North America accounts for 25.8% of the paper and paperboard planned additions and 31.3% of those for paper pulp. Worldwide, additional paper and paperboard capacities will exceed paper pulp additions by 5,282,000 metric tons. Paper and board planned additions will exceed pulp in all regions except Latin America, with Western Europe (excluding Scandinavia) leading in excess capacities. This reflects the shortage of timber resources in the region in relation to its papermaking capacities. Western Europe, as mentioned previously, is heavily dependent on imports for its wood pulp requirements. New pulpmaking capacities will constitute only about 29% of the added paper and board manufacturing capacities in the region between 1974 and 1977, while worldwide paper pulp additional capacities will amount to about 75% of paper and paperboard. The predicted shortage of paper pulp in the future can become very real if steps are not taken to build additional pulp mills or to increase use of waste papers by adding deinking (or recycling) plants around the world. In North America, if the recent rate of increase in recycling waste papers continues, this could easily eliminate the shortage of wood pulp in the region. However, this cannot be done in Western Europe, where the shortage is too great. Imports of wood pulp are necessary to keep their paper and board mills running.

There are about 35 TMP mills in operation around the world. Twelve of

Table 6.18   Regional Location of Planned Net Additions in Paper/Paperboard and Paper Pulp Annual Capacities, 1974–1977

Region	(A) Paper and Paperboard		(B) Wood and Other Fiber Paper Pulp		(A − B) Excess Paper and Paperboard Capacities over Pulp Capacities (thousands of metric tons)	(B/A) Ratio of Pulp to Paper and Board (%)
	Capacity (thousands of metric tons)	% of Total	Capacity (thousands of metric tons)	% of Total		
North America	5,377	25.8	4,865	31.3	512	90
Scandinavia	1,835	8.8	1,410	9.1	425	77
Latin America	2,067	9.9	2,569	16.5	−502	124
Western Europe[a]	4,560	21.9	1,340	8.6	3,220	29
Eastern Europe[b]	2,520	12.1	2,055	13.2	465	82
Africa and the Middle East	585	2.8	310	2.0	275	53
Asia and the Far East[c]	3,888	18.7	3,001	19.3	887	77
Total	20,832	100.0	15,550	100.0	5,282	75

[a] Excludes Scandinavia.
[b] Includes USSR.
[c] Includes Japan and Oceania.
Sources.   FAO and the American Paper Institute.

them are located in the United States, 8 in Canada, 11 in Europe, 3 in Asia, and 1 in Newfoundland. Of the 12 TMP mills in the United States, three use southern yellow pine as raw materials. All three mills are integrated with paper mills producing either newsprint or magazine paper. A TMP mill in Everett, Washington (Weyerhaeuser Company), with 300 ADT/D capacity, produces market pulp. However, the bulk of its production is shipped to Japan to fulfill its long-term sales contract with a major paper company there. The Everett Mill produces bleached pulp for sanitary and tissue papers. This new breed of high-bleached mechanical pulps may well take a good share of the market for disposable sanitary products now held by chemical pulps, and its use in tissue is bound to grow.

A Market Survey

For the purpose of testing the marketability of TMP in the world market, a survey was conducted between September and November 1975. A cover letter was drafted presenting the characteristics of four grades of TMP for the potential production of a proposed market pulp mill in the Southeast. The four pulp grades presented were board, tissue, newsprint, and magazine. Pulp characteristics such as freeness, brightness, shives content, breaking length, and burst and tear factors were given for each grade. An accompanying questionnaire was designed to find out the respondent's interest in purchasing from the mill, including grade, volume, sales arrangement, end product to be produced, and any comments. The questionnaire and cover letter (see Attachment 6.2) were sent to 273 nonintegrated paper mills selected from the *1975–1976 International Pulp and Paper Directory*. The selection emphasized large to medium-sized mills because small paper mills are too numerous. The selected mills turned out to be highly concentrated in the United States, Western Europe, and Japan.

The geographic distribution of selected paper mills, survey respondents, and responding classifications is given in Table 6.19. Of the 273 questionnaires sent, 121 went to mills in the United States, 126 to Europe, and 26 to Japan, Latin America, and the Middle East. The responding rate was 46%, or 125 mills. Of the 125 responding mills, 22 gave an affirmative answer with the specific grade and volume of pulp, 9 expressed interest but no volume was given, 3 were undecided and indicated neither an affirmative nor a negative answer, and 91 said they were not interested in purchasing. Details of these responses are given in Table 6.19.

The pulp volumes that the 22 affirmatively responding paper mills would consider purchasing annually are presented for each grade in Table 6.20. All volumes are in short tons; the metric tons used by responding paper mills outside North America were converted to short tons. It is clear from the results of the survey that tissue-grade and magazine-grade pulps are more marketable than either board-grade or newsprint-grade pulp. These results also indicate that producers of tissue and magazine papers rely more on market pulp than do producers of newsprint and paperboard products, which are generally integrated with pulp mills. Respondent volumes were 101,795 tons for tissue grade, 60,659 tons for magazine grade, 21,983 tons for board grade, and 19,188 tons for newsprint grade. The total respondent volume was 203,625 tons, of which 135,584 tons came from Europe, 48,200 tons from the United States, and 19,841 tons from Asia and the Middle East. The survey reveals again that Western Europe (excluding Scandinavia) relies more on imports of market pulp than any other region in the world.

It should be noted that the survey was not intended to be an exhaustive one. Many small to medium-sized paper mills, as well as integrated mills that

September 19, 1975

Dear Sir:

   The Industrial Services Division is conducting a feasibility study for
a group of potential investors who are planning a thermo-mechanical pulp (TMP)
mill in the Southeast of the United States. The proposed mill would use southern yellow pine chips as the basic raw material, and the pulp produced would
be sold either under contract or on spot markets to potential users throughout
the world. The proposed TMP mill could produce four basic grades of pulp: board,
tissue, newsprint, and magazine. The purpose of this survey is to find out the
market potentials for the proposed production.

   As you are aware, tight supplies of market pulp in the world have been
projected by many pulp and paper marketing authorities. The supplies by 1977
and onward could be worse than 1973-74. Thermo-mechanical pulps have been used
not only in the four outlets mentioned, but increasingly as an extension of chemical pulps which are much more expensive. Your response will help us in designing
a new TMP mill and may bring you a new source of pulp supplies by 1978.

   A typical analysis of TMP on four grades is given below:

	BOARD	TISSUE	NEWSPRINT	MAGAZINE
Decker Freeness, csf	395	140	70-75	45-50
Brightness, ge	51	58-69	58-61	65-69
%Somerville Shives	1.01	0.18	0.02	0.01
Fiber Fraction +30%	50	34	17	20
30-200%	32	47	49	44
+200%	18	19	34	36
Breaking Length, meters	1450	2740	2050	3150
Burst Factor	6	12	14	18
Tear Factor	42	55	56	74
Bulk, cm^3/g	3.8	3.1	2.9	2.7
Refining Stage	1 stage	2 stage	2 stage	3 stage
Bleaching	No	Semi or full	Semi	Full

   Actually our plant design can be geared to your needs if a certain
volume can be reached. Please advise if you have any opinion concerning
pulp characteristics.

   Enclosed is a questionnaire with a few simple questions. Please
answer them and return the questionnaire in the self-addressed envelope.
We would appreciate your prompt reply in order to meet our time limit on
this study. All of your answers, according to our established policy, will
be kept in strict confidence.

                           Very truly yours,

                           Tze I. Chiang
                           Project Director

Attachment 6.2   Cover Letter and Questionnaire for a Market Survey.

216

QUESTIONNAIRE

1. Do you have an interest in the proposed production? Yes (   ) No (   )

2. If yes, what grade(s) of pulp would you be interested in?

    Board (   )   Tissue (   )   Newsprint (   )   Magazine (   )

3. What volume of each grade would you consider purchasing annually? In

    metric ton (   ) or short ton (   )?

    Board _____   Newsprint _____

    Tissue _____   Magazine _____

4. What kind of sale arrangement would you prefer?

    Contract _____   Spot market _____   Others _____

5. What end products do you intend to make? _____

    _____

    _____

6. Comments or suggestions, if any: _____

    _____

    _____

    _____

    _____

                                        Name _____

                                        Position _____

                                        Date _____

Attachment 6.2 (Continued)

purchase a portion of their pulp supplies, were excluded from the survey. In
addition, the survey selection emphasized paper mills located in the United
States and Western Europe; thus many mills in Asia and Latin America were
skipped. It also should be noted that the survey was conducted during a recession period when the outlook for economic recovery was still ominous.
However, the survey results are encouraging enough. The respondent tissue-
grade total volume, 101,795 tons, is sufficiently large to keep a 300 ADT/D

TMP mill in full operation for a year. The reader should be cautioned, however, that survey respondents were not asked for purchasing commitments; they were merely asked to express their purchasing intentions.

Table 6.19 The Distribution of Selected Paper Mills, Survey Respondents, and Responding Classifications, 1975

Region	Question-naires Sent	Responses	Yes[b]	Interested[c]	Undecided	No
United States	121	58	9	5	2	42
Western Europe	126	64	12	4	1	47
Others[a]	26	3	1	0	0	2
Total	273	125	22	9	3	91

[a] Includes Japan, Latin America, and the Middle East.
[b] Respondents giving affirmative answer and specific pulp grade and volume.
[c] Respondents giving affirmative answer without giving specific pulp volume or grade.

Table 6.20 Demand for TMP Market Pulp among Survey Respondents, by Grade and by Area, 1975 (tons of 2000 lb, air-dry weight)

Region	No. of Companies	Board	Tissue	Newsprint	Magazine	Total Tonnage
United States	9	6,000	32,350	1,000	8,850	48,200
Western Europe	12	14,330	69,445	0	51,809	135,584
Other	1	1,653	0	18,188	0	19,841
Total	22	21,983	101,795	19,188	60,659	203,625

The nine companies that expressed interest without giving specific volumes may turn out to have the greatest market potential for the TMP mill proposed under this study program. Several of these mills are among the largest papermakers in the world. Responsible personnel of these companies responded to the survey with letters outlining their needs and expressed opinions concerning the proposed production. They suggested that the brightness of the proposed TMP be increased to 75 ge through a second-stage bleaching. With this level of brightness attained, the proposed TMP could penetrate many traditional markets held by chemical pulps. They suggested that the principals of the venture meet with them after the specifics of the proposed TMP mill are determined. Nearly all affirmative respondents preferred a contract arrangement on sales over a spot market.

Markets and Marketing Strategy

Based on the information presented in the previous sections, it is now time to devise practical approaches or strategies in several important areas concerning the proposed TMP mill. These areas are type of pulp to be produced, marketing method, scale or volume, market distribution, prices, and follow-up activities.

1. *Type of pulp to be produced.* TMP is generally used for the production of paperboard products, tissue and sanitary papers, newsprint, and coated magazine and writing papers. The pulp characteristics required vary according to end use, and the production requirements of pulp also depend on the type of pulp to be produced. It is preferable to produce only one main type of pulp in order to save on engineering, equipment, and labor costs involved in a switchover. However, a two-line operation can be set up to produce two main types of pulp without involving a switchover or lost time.

   The type of pulp to be produced depends primarily on market outlets. Based on the survey results mentioned in the previous section, tissue-grade pulp is clearly the choice. An additional line of production can be set up to produce magazine-grade pulp, if desired. Board-grade and newsprint-grade pulps should be avoided unless a captive market can be found for them.

2. *Marketing method.* Vigorous efforts should be expended to secure a market before a commitment is made to build a market pulp mill. It would be most desirable to have the financial participation of one or more major users who can guarantee the purchase of a substantial portion of the proposed production. During the past year, several overtures were made in this direction, which revealed that the opportunities exist. The Wood Fibre Marketing Corporation, a new organization representing SLMA's members in exporting surplus wood chips to Europe, has cooperated with research personnel in taking preliminary steps. Meaningful dialogue should be maintained, and the Wood Fibre Marketing Corporation should have more financial backing from its members to carry out steps necessary in securing a market, such as sending wood chips for testing and sending pulp samples to prospective users for evaluation. The chip testing and pulp sample making can be done by major TMP system manufacturers at cost.

   Also, EDL personnel cooperated with a leading market pulp agent, who has offices or representatives in Europe and Japan, to explore the possibility of long-term contracts with potential users abroad. Pulp samples, provided by a major TMP system manufacturer, were sent to potential users for evaluation. Contacts in this direction should be widened and maintained. However, when the time comes for serious negotiation, the contacting party should be in a position to reach an agreement. This means that the proposed TMP mill should have solid backing; otherwise, all efforts will be in vain.

3. *Scale or volume.* In reviewing the raw material supply conditions, market potentials, and engineering considerations, a 300 ADT/D TMP mill should be considered. It would have two production lines, with each line representing 150 ADT/D. Annual output of the mill, based on 345 working days, would be 103,500 to 114,000 tons, depending on the type of pulp produced and production conditions.

4. *Market distribution.* Western Europe (excluding Scandinavia) and the United States should become the major markets for the proposed production if the survey results are reliable guides. However, other areas, especially Japan should not be overlooked.

5. *Prices.* Pricing of TMP should follow established market prices and practices, which in turn are determined by the forces of demand and supply. However, because of the uncertainty of pulp quality during the start-up period, some price concessions should be made in order to break into the market. It is suggested that a 5 to 10% reduction from established market prices be offered on the first-year output. Details are given in a later section.

6. *Follow-up activities.* Much follow-up work must be done before the proposed TMP mill can become a reality. Securing long-term contracts for the proposed production may be the key to a successful venture. In order to secure long-term contracts, pulp samples must be prepared and potential users must be contacted. Also, a party with authority to negotiate must be on hand in dealing with potential buyers or investors. The completion of this study also would expedite the process of establishing a TMP mill in the Coastal Plains region.

DESIGN AND ENGINEERING OF A TMP MILL

Design Criteria and Overview

The engineering design of a TMP mill involves putting together major component units to become a viable working system. These major units are a chip station, a TMP refining system, a screening and cleaning system, a drying system, a bleaching system, an electrical distribution system, a water supply system, an effluent control system, and a steam-generating unit (boiler house). Although the TMP refining system is only a portion of the complete plant design, it is central to the design, and the other components should be planned around it. The major criteria for designing the TMP mill proposed in this study are as follows:

1. Output of 300 short tons of air-dry pulp per day.
2. Two-line operation.
3. Flexible design so that, with minor changes, three major grades of pulp can be produced—sanitary tissue, newsprint, and magazine.
4. Southern pinewood chips as the major material for pulp production.
5. Wood residues such as bark and sawdust for boiler fuel.
6. Only semibleaching planned. If intensive bleaching is needed, a separate bleaching facility should be added.
7. Power to be purchased.

Based on the above criteria, the machinery and equipment needed for each component system were chosen from leading manufacturers. Extensive contacts were made in order to make a final selection, especially for the TMP refining system. Four companies submitted proposals with detailed price quotations on the TMP refining system; after exhaustive consultations and with the consent of SLMA's personnel, a decision was made to adopt one engineering system with single-disc refiners. However, components and machinery for other parts of the mill are mixed selections from many contending manufacturers.

A TMP process flow diagram is presented in Figure 6.2. Wood chips unloaded by railcar or truck at a chip station are stored in a chip yard and then blown to a chip storage bin ready for screening and washing. Washed chips are preheated with semibleached chemicals. Steamed chips are then fed to the first-stage refiners through twin screws. The production rate is determined by the speed of these twin screws.

After pasaage through the refining discs, pulp is blown to two cyclones for steam removal. First-stage refined pulp is diluted with white water at the bottom of the cyclones and conveyed to two second-stage refiners. Refined pulp is stored in a chest at 3% consistency for latency removal. Next are one-stage screening and three-stage centrifugal cleaning. The rejects from the screen and cleaners are dewatered on a vacuum filter and pumped to the second-stage refiner for reprocessing.

Finished pulp is dewatered and goes through the fluffer and flash dryer. Dried pulp is then pressed, baled, unit-tied, and transported to the warehouse.

The quality of TMP is affected by temperature, refining consistency, horsepower applied, the power split between stages, and the quality of raw material. By adjusting the refiner temperature, refining horsepower, and refiner cycle time, adding a third-stage flow-through refiner, and controlling various other parameters of the TMP process, the characteristics of the pulp can be varied

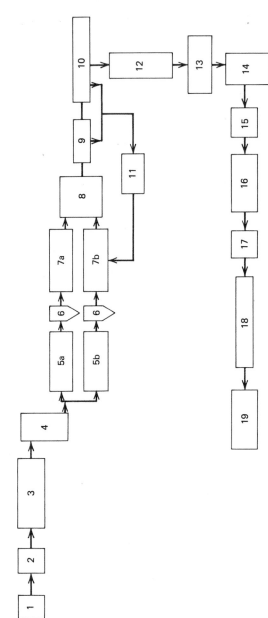

Figure 6.2 TMP process flow diagram. DT = daily tonnage; C = consistency. (1) Railcar and truck unloading of southern pine chips, T-648 green. (2) Screening and rechipping of chips. (3) Chip washer; DT = 324 C = 50. (4) Chemical impregnator and preheater. (5) First-stage pressurized refining; DT = 314, C = 27. (6) Cyclones. (7) Second-stage open-discharge refining; DT = 310 + 70 (rejects), C = 23. (8) Latency retention chest. (9) Pressure screening. (10) Centrifugal cleaning; DT = 331, C = 0.7. (11) Reject press. (12) Decker; DT = 300, C = 0.67. (13) Optional flow-through refining (optional for newsprint grade; required for magazine grade). (14) Roll press; DT = 300, C = 48. (15) Fluffer. (66) Flash-dryer. (17) Bale press. (18) Baling line. (19) Warehouse; DT = 300, C = 90.

to produce different grades of market pulp. Typical characteristics of these grades are given in Table 6.21.

A plant layout for major TMP equipment is presented in Figure 6.3. A typical TMP site layout is given in Figure 6.4. The site layout includes all major facilities and installations required for the proposed TMP mill on a 40-acre site along a river. The site layout includes office and plant buildings, an outdoor flash dryer, a warehouse, chemical storage, a maintenance building, an electric substation, a boiler house, a chip pile and chip unloading areas, a water tower, two water wells, a freshwater reservoir, an effluent system bar screen, a clarifier, an aeration lagoon, an effluent settling tank, an optional coagulation tank, a river outflow, sludge piping, effluent piping, a chip conveyor, a bark conveyor, and an employee parking area.

Table 6.21   Typical Characteristics of TMP in Tissue, Newsprint, Magazine Grades

	Tissue	Newsprint	Magazine
Decker freeness (csf)	140	70–75	45–50
Brightness (ge)	59–75[a]	59	59–75[a]
Percent Somerville shives	0.18	0.02	0.01
Fiber fraction			
+30%	34	17	20
30–200%	47	49	44
+200%	19	34	36
Breaking length (m)	2740	2050	3150
Burst factor	12	14	18
Tear factor	55	56	74
Bulk (cm^3/g)	3.1	2.9	2.7
Refining hpADT	80	95	120
TMP process	Two-stage	Two-stage	Three-stage
Bleaching	Semi or full	Semibleach	full bleach

[a] Brightness can be increased up to 75 ge by adding a bleaching tower and using a larger amount of chemicals as given in this section.

The major components of the pulp process are described in this chapter for a hypothetical mill. Also discussed are infrastructure requirements, such as plant site, roads, rail connections, and sewers, for the proposed TMP mill.

Chip Station

About 599 to 623 tons of green southern yellow pine chips are consumed daily in the plant's operation to produce 300 ADT/D of market pulp, depending on what grades of pulp are produced. The paved area for chip processing is approximately 298 × 570 feet, with a 170-foot conveyor running from the chip pile to the TMP mill. The raw material arrives at the plant site in both railroad hopper cars and tractor-trailers. Sufficient rail siding storage for five loaded chip cars and fine unloaded cars is provided. A secondary Caterpillar 920

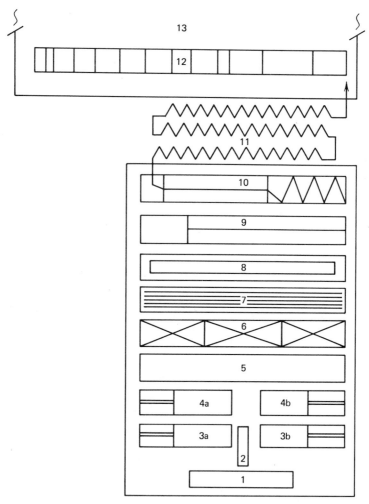

Figure 6.3 Major TMP equipment layout. (1) Chip washer. (2) Impregnator-preheater. (3) First-stage refining. (4) Second-stage refining. (5) Latency chest. (6) Screening. (7) Cleaning. (8) Decker. (9) Roll press. (10) Fluffer. (11) Outside flash-dryer. (12) Baling line. (13) Warehouse area.

loader moves the railcars along the siding for unloading and is a standby in case the primary chip dozer, Caterpillar D4, is down for repairs. Railcars are unloaded over an open pit, whereas trucks are upended and dumped into a recovery pit below. From the two pit areas, the chips are conveyed to a screening and rechipping area.

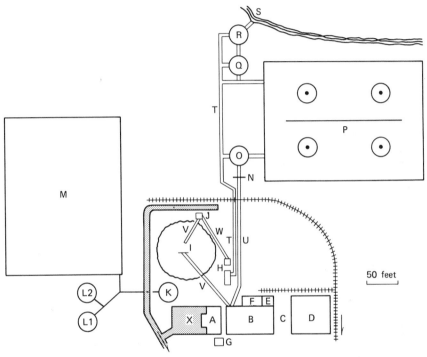

Figure 6.4 Typical TMP site layout. (A) Office building. (B) TMP plant. (C) Outdoor flash-dryer. (D) Warehouse. (E) Chemical storage. (F) Maintenance building. (G) Electric substation. (H) Boiler-house area. (I) Chip pile. (J) Chip unloading area. (K) Water tower. (L) Water wells 1 and 2. (M) 4-Acre freshwater reservoir. (N) Effluent system bar screen. (O) Clarifier. (P) 4-Acre aeration lagoon. (Q) Effluent settling tank. (R) Optional coagulation tank. (S) River outflow. (T) Sludge piping. (U) Effluent piping. (V) Chip conveyor. (W) Bark conveyor. (X) Employee parking area.

Chips $\frac{3}{4}$ to 1 inch in size are accepted and blown to a chip pile. A Caterpillar D4 bulldozer moves the chips to a recovery pit, where they are blown to a 500-cubic-foot chip bin for temporary process storage. The recovery pit is activated by an automatic signal from sensors in the chip bin indicating a low chip supply.

The chips are screw-conveyed into a chip washer with a capacity of 6000 cubic feet per hour, where sand, dirt, and metal are washed off. Washed chips are then screw-conveyed to the impregnator. Television cameras monitor the conveyor flow to divert rejected chips to a scrap collector.

The major equipment items required for this station are:

- 80-ton truck scale with a digital readout printer.
- Prefab metal building for chip control office.
- Outdoor floodlights in the chip yard area.
- Two Caterpillar D4 bulldozers (one used as equipment for backup).
- Blacktopped chip pile area.
- Hydraulic truck dumper.
- Railcar pit unloading system.
- Screening and rechipping area.
- Chip pile recovery pit.
- Chip washer system.
- Conveyors and blowing equipment.

TMP Refining

From the chip washer, washed chips flow daily via the screw feeder into a vertical impregnator-preheater. In the Prex impregnator section, the chips expand, absorbing the liquid bleaching chemicals like sponges. This ensures that there is no gradient of chemical treatment from the outer surface to the center of the chip.

The following is a list of recommended chemicals to be added in the impregnator. The amounts are typical application levels; exact amounts depend on the exact condition of the chips used in the process and the characteristics of the finished pulp.

Newsprint-grade pulp	12 lb/ton aluminium sulfate for pitch control 9 lb/ton bisulfite for mild bleaching 6 lb/ton sodium hexametaphosphate for resin control
Sanitary-tissue and magazine-grade pulp	In addition to the above three chemicals, add the following: 11 lb/ton sodium hydroxide for pH balance 13 lb/ton sodium hydrosulfite for full bleaching

The chemically impregnated chips are lifted from the impregnator section and dropped into the preheater section, where steam is applied at 45 psi, 200 pounds per ton, 130 to 140°C, $2\frac{1}{2}$ to 3 minutes.

The steamed chips are transported via a twin-screw conveyor to two pressurized single-disc American Defibrator RLP-54S refiners. Refining occurs at 25 to 30%, 110 to 120°C, so that the lignin-rich middle lamella section of the chip fiber is completely separated.

From the pressurized refiners, the pulp is discharged through a blow valve system to the cyclone. In the 80-inch-diameter blow cyclone separators, steam is separated from the pulp and vented off.

The pulp is then carried via cross-screw transfer conveyors, at 22 to 24% consistency, to two single-disc American Defibrator RL-54S atmospheric refiners. One refiner receives 90% of the pulp flow, while the other receives 10% plus the reprocessable pulp rejected by the screens and cleaners. Both refiners are sized to handle equal flow capacities for maintenance switchover periods. This refining stage further develops the pulp into the particular characteristics the final product is to achieve.

The pulp is quenched at the refiner outlet with white water to achieve 3% consistency and gravity-dropped into an agitated stock chest. The pulp remains in the stock chest from 30 to 60 minutes for latency removal.

The major equipment items for this section are:

- Vertical impregnator-preheater.
- Two RLP-54S, 9000-hp pressurized refiners.
- Two blow-valve systems.
- Two cyclone systems.
- Two RL-54S, 9000-hp atmospheric refiners.
- 75-hp agitated stock chest.

Pulp Screening and Cleaning

The pulp from TMP refining is normally sufficiently shive-free, so that no screening is normally required. However, most pulp plant operators prefer a single-stage screening system to ensure optimal pulp quality during system irregularities.

From the stock chest, the pulp is pumped to a Model 400 Bird Centrisorter pressure screen and then to a three-stage Bauer modular Centricleaner system. The acceptable pulp flows to a Beloit Jones Polydisk decker, where the consistency is changed from 0.67 to 3% for proper flow to either a third-stage flow-through refiner or to a roll press for flash-drying preparation.

The rejected pulp (averaging 42 tons per day from screening and 31 tons per day from cleaning) enters an IMPCO Sudor press, where it is dewatered to 23% consistency. The pulp is then pumped to the second-stage refiner for reprocessing.

Major equipment items for this section are:

- Bird Model 400 Centrisorter pressure screen.
- Bauer three-stage modular Centricleaner system.
- Two Beloit Jones Polydisk deckers.
- IMPCO Model 50-A Sudor press.
- IMPCO Series 600 Cloverotor thick stock pumps.

Pulp Drying

Optimum flash-drying requires a constant rate of pulp at low but constant moisture content. The IMPCO Vari-nip roll press allows automatic changes in pressability characteristics. The consistency-controlled and metered pulp enters the roll press at 3% consistency and is discharged from the shredder-conveyor section at 48% consistency.

From the dewatering press, a mat of pulp with 48% dryness is conveyed to the fluffer, where it is disintegrated into small pieces which are ideal for feeding into the dryer. The fluffing stage is of vital importance for the heat economy of the plant as well as for the quality of the product, because a greater pulp surface area contact with hot air in the flash-dryer means a faster drying cycle.

The feed to the flash-dryer takes place by means of a pneumatic transport system which utilizes air from the pulp dryer conditioning stage.

The flash-drying facility is arranged as a two-stage countercurrent system, thus utilizing the air from the second drying stage by returning it to the first stage in order partially to dry the wet pulp.

In the first drying stage, the pulp is introduced into the hot air stream coming from the second drying stage. At the point of introduction, the air temperature is 287°F. After the pulp has been partially dried in the first drying stage, the air temperature drops to about 187°F, with the dryness of the pulp at approximately 55%.

At the inlet to the second stage, the pulp is dispersed in the hot air stream from the direct gas-fired air heater. At this point the temperature of the air is 500°F. On completion of the drying process, the dryness of the pulp is 90% bone dry.

The major equipment items for this section are:

- IMPCO Vari-nip roll press.
- Niro fluffer and flash-dryer.

Pulp Baling

Flash-dried pump flows from the dry conveying stage directly into a Sunds PF-400 slab press, where it is compressed and enters the baling line.

The major equipment components are:

- Sunds pulp bale presses.
- Lambs-Gray-Harbor bale finishing line.
- Ovalstrap wire-tying equipment.

Electrical Distribution System

The electrical load for a TMP plant varies from 29,410 to 33,200 kilowatts, depending on the pulp grade. For example, the anticipated connected electrical load for a newspaper-grade TMP plant is 32,000 kilowatts with an 80% demand factor. This results in a plant electrical demand of approximately 1675 amperes at 13.8 kilovolts.

Power is purchased from a public utility company. The utility company provides an on-site electrical substation to transform the incoming line voltage from 115,000 to 13,800 volts. A reactor has been installed to reduce transmission line load fluctuations.

Via a radial distribution network, power is conveyed to the various areas of the plant through an interlocked armour aerial cable (four-wire with neutral grounded). The distribution loads for various electricity requirements are given in Table 6.22.

Refiner voltage is transformed from 13.8 to 4.16 kilovolts. Motor load areas over 350 maximum horsepower (miscellaneous refining and pulp drying areas) have the voltage transformed to 2300 volts, while load areas of small horsepower motors have the voltage reduced to 480 volts.

Most of the electrical wiring and cable within the buildings is installed in conduits, except the lighting system wiring, which is installed in mineral-insulated cables. Exposed conduit in buildings is galvanized electrical metallic tubing with compression fittings. Conduit buried in the ground or embedded in concrete floors is galvanized, rigid, heavy-wall steel conduit with threaded fittings.

Table 6.22   Power Requirements in Different Components of a TMP Mill

Item	Maximum Motor hp	Recommended Voltage	Total kW Load		
			Tissue	Newsprint	Magazine
Chip preparation	150	480	445	445	445
Refining					
TMP	9,000	4,160	24,125	26,860	28,060
Miscellaneous	400	2,300	540	540	540
Pulp screening and					
cleaning	150	480	525	525	525
Pulp drying	450	2,300	1,170	1,170	1,170
Baling	300	480	485	485	480
Boiler	250	480	485	485	480
Water	75	480	290	290	290
Waste	75	480	500	350	350
Miscellaneous					
equipment and					
lights	50	480	850	850	850
Total			29,410	32,000	33,200

The plant ground system consists of bare copper grid buried under the building floor and connected to the plant installation at several points. Building steel is grounded by connecting every other column to the plant ground system. Motors of 10 horsepower and larger are grounded by a copper conductor. Smaller motors are adequately grounded through a continuous metallic conduit system.

The lighting illumination levels conform to the recommendations of the Illumination Engineers Society as applied to the various areas of the facility.

All electrical equipment and its installation comply with applicable standards of the National Electrical Manufacturers Association, and to the latest requirements of state and local electrical codes.

Water Supply System

Only drinking and sanitary water is obtained from the city water system (35 gpd per employee); all other water utilized comes from an on-site water supply. Two wells (average depth of 600 feet) provide ample water for plant operation, and each well is capable of supplying 1,000,000 gpd.

Two 600-gpm pumps carry the well water to a 4-acre ground-level reservoir. One 500-gpm diesel motor-powered pump draws off 300,000 gallons of well water to maintain fire protection water storage in an elevated storage tank.

Depending on the quality of the well water (especially the amount of iron and pH level), pretreatment of the water prior to reservoir storage may be required. To attain a pH level of 8.0+, either sodium hydroxide or hydrochloric acid must be added. To remove iron particles from the water (iron discolors the pulp), chlorine treatment followed by pressure sand filtration is recommended.

It should be noted that along a 75-mile-wide belt of land along the Georgia-Florida border, the well water is excellent "as is." The water has a high pH, is low in iron, and contains hydrogen sulfide (nature's bleaching agent).

Three 700-gpm pumps distribute the water at 75 psi to the various plant areas as follows:

TMP plant use	675,000 gpd
Boiler water	29,000 gpd
Fire system	296,000 gpd minimum

Only 29,000 gpd (boiler water) must be treated before use ($30 per day treatment cost). No additional workers are required for the water system. The effluent control chemist maintains quality checks on the water, and a regular roving maintenance man performs preventive maintenance on the pumps and other equipment.

Effluent Control System

Any new pulp mill is required to make either a "negative declaration" or an "environmental impact statement" to the Georgia Environmental Protection Division (EPD). A negative declaration applies to a mill that generates a negligible amount of polluting materials and causes no harm to existing surroundings. An environmental impact statement applies to a mill that generates excessive polluting materials but has taken steps to reduce them to a level conforming with effluent limitation standards established by the U.S. Environmental Protection Agency (EPA). The proposed TMP mill would have to make an environmental impact statement. Effluent limitations on BOD5, TSS, pH, and zinc for a new TMP mill were promulgated in December 1975. These limitations are presented in Table 6.23.

In designing an effluent control system for the proposed TMP mill, the EPA effluent limitations set for 1983 should be adopted. The wastewater treatment system for the TMP process residues described below is based on the following criteria, which are better than the minimum federal EPA standards set for 1983 for discharge into rivers:

Total wastewater per day	1,000,000 gpd (3800 m³/day)
Total BOD per day	10,000 lb (4.5 metric tons) (1200 mg/1)
Allowable daily BOD discharge	0.7 tons (185 mg/1), 86% reduction
Typical plant daily BOD discharge	0.2 tons (52 mg/1), 95% reduction
TSS per day	30,000 lb (13.5 metric tons) (3600 mg/1)
Allowable daily TSS discharge	0.6 tons (150 mg/1), 96% reduction
Typical plant daily TSS discharge	0.1 tons (26 mg/1), 99% reduction

Eight-inch sewer lines carry the waste discharge from the chip washer, boiler-house and TMP plant areas to the effluent control treatment facility. An automatic front-raked, front-return bar screen removes bark, knots, and wood trash from the waste prior to gravity discharge into the clarifier (the terrain is graded so as to avoid need for a lift station). A 50-foot-diameter clarifier (2-hour detention) removed 70 to 80% of the remaining solids from the wastewater. Solid particles settle to the bottom of the collection tank, where they are removed via a collector mechanism.

Table 6.23   Effluent Limitations for a New TMP Mill (pounds per ton of product output)

	By 1977		By 1983	
Item	Maximum for Any One Day	Daily Average for 30 Days	Maximum for Any One Day	Daily Average for 30 Days
BOD5	10.7	5.2	5.0	2.8
TSS	8.8	4.0	9.2	3.3
Zinc	0.26	0.19	0.26	0.19
pH	Shall not exceed 6.0 to 9.0			

Source. Environmental Protection Agency, *Development Document for Advanced Notice of Proposed or Promulgated Rule Making for Effluent Limitations Guidelines and New Source Performance Standards*, Group I, Phase II, August 1975.

The wastewater then flows to an aeration lagoon for 10 to 13 days' retention to reduce the BOD to an acceptable discharge level. This lagoon is 8 feet deep by 4 acres surface area (2.4 meters by 1.7 hectares). Four 50-horsepower floating aerators are positioned in the lagoon to allow sufficient BOD reduction. Nitrogen or ammonia may be insufficient to produce an optimum quantity of suspended solids in the aeration lagoon for high-quality discharge. Hence it may be necessary to add up to 500 kilogram of ammonia and 50 kilogram of phosphate per day for the required BOD discharge level.

The wastewater flows to a second 50-foot-diameter settling tank for a 2-hour stay following the aeration lagoon to allow further separation of the suspended solids. The majority of the solids removed (sludge) is returned to the aeration lagoon, while a portion is conveyed with the other collected sludge to the boiler house.

All extracted sludge is conveyed to the boiler-house area, where it is dewatered and burned in the bark boiler. Only the boiler ash is deposited in a landfill.

Polyelectrolyte coagulation may be required by the Georgia EPD for a high-quality discharge. This would require a third settling tank, with a mixing chamber and floculator.

Because of the high purity (5% BOD and 3% TSS) of the treated 1,000,000 gpd effluent, it is possible to recirculate for fire and plant use up to 90% of the treated water. This reduces the amount of well water necessary, possibly enabling the plant to operate on one standby fire protection well and to utilize city water as the main supply.

Furthermore, with only 10% (100,000 gpd) of discharge wastewater, it is possible to locate the plant either near a small stream or in a city capable of accepting this quantity of pretreated wastewater into its sewerage system.

The EPA/EPD requires the plant to provide proof of compliance with discharge guidelines. Instrumentation is required for proper control of the aeration tank's pH and dissolved oxygen levels. A chemist should operate the facility and test the discharge effluent for BOD, TSS, and pH.

Steam Generation

Rejected chips from the unloading screen, pressed pollution sludge, and 68 to 85 tons per day of bark are conveyed to a boiler feed bin, through a fuel shredder, and into an outdoor storage shed. Reclaim conveyors transport the wood–waste fuel mixture into a bark boiler to generate process steam. A steam reduction system splits the generated steam for distribution throughout the plant. The steam distribution is given below:

First-stage refining	5,000 lb/hr
Flash-dryer preheat	12,500 lb/hr
Miscellaneous pulp heating	3,750 lb/hr
Total	21,250 lb/hr

The bark boiler is designed to use wood waste as primary fuel but has the capability to use bunker oil as auxiliary fuel. The boiler is designed for 50,000 pounds of steam per hour at 200 psig. This overcapacity allows for inconsistent fuel mixtures and for future expansion to TMP production of 450 tons per day.

Mechanical ash collectors and wet stack scrubbers provide the required air pollution control of the boiler smoke emission. Major equipment items for this system are:

- Montgomery Industries bark shredder.
- McBurney Stokers Company fuel handling system, storage shed, bark boiler, boiler water treatment, air pollution controls, and control instrumentation.

Optional Full (Second-Stage) Bleaching

A second-state bleaching is required if pulp brightness of 70 general electric (ge) or more is desired. The levels of bleaching chemicals that must be added to obtain various degrees of ge brightness are given below:

Level of Bleaching Chemicals Added	Pulp Brightness (ge)
No chemicals added	55–59
First stage or semibleaching, add 1%	61–64
First stage or semibleaching, add 2%	64–66
First stage or semibleaching, add 3%	66–69
Second stage, add 4%	69–72
Second stage, add 5%	72–75

Second-stage bleaching would require an IMPCO press different from the one previously specified. The new press would change the finished pulp consistency from 2 to 18%. The bleaching agent is added at the inlet of the steam shredder-mixer. After increasing the pulp temperature from 45 to 50 to 60 to 70°C, the pulp is pumped by a high-density pump to a retention tower for 35-minute retention. An IMPCO drum filter washes out the residue bleaching agent, and the bleached pulp proceeds to the drying process.

It is recommended that Ventron Corporation's Borol process be used to manufacture the bleaching agent at the plant site.

Infrastructure

Infrastructure of the mill includes plant site preparation, roads, rail connections, sewers, and fire protection. These facilities are discussed below.

1. *Plant site characteristics and preparation.* Buildings and installations are located to best suit the operating convenience of the plant and to make efficient use of the plant site.

   The plant site was chosen for its proximity to adequate water, power, and transportation routes. Comprising a minimum of 40 acres, the site is near adequate wood raw material supply. The land is relatively flat and composed mostly of alluvial clay overlaying sand and gravel.

   All TMP plant departments, with the exception of the chip station area, are aligned along a north–south centerline to provide access throughout the plant and permit easy expansion to 450 ADT/D. A central corridor carries all process piping and power distribution cables.

   A substantial buffer zone of grassland has been established between the plant areas and the adjacent property.

   Mill roads, most of which are hard-surfaced up to the main loading doors of all buildings, form a loop system around the main plant, with a turn-around at the chip dumper. Primary roads within the mill are arranged so the main flow of traffic, including chip trucks, does not cross railroad tracks. Rail tracks are located to facilitate delivery of chemicals and wood and shipment of finished products from the warehouse.

   To permit unrestricted movement of construction vehicles during rainy weather, much of the site has been stripped to a depth of 1 foot and back-filled with compacted gravel to an elevation above the adjacent ground.

   Heavily loaded structures (TMP plant) are supported on piles, while lightly loaded structures are on spread footings. Ground-floor slabs are on compacted granular fill, except in some localized areas that are heavily loaded, where pile-supported slab and beam systems are used.

2. *Paved roads and areas.* All roads and paved areas accessible to truck traffic have a base course consisting of 6 inches of stabilized aggregate placed on compacted subgrade. Surfacing consists of $1\frac{1}{2}$ inches of plant-mixed surfacing material.

3. *Railroads.* A spur line serves the plant. All track construction was done in accordance with American Railroad Engineers Association (AREA) standards, with 20% maximum curves. All cross-ties were treated in accordance with AREA standards. The rails are good, used 90-pound track rails.

4. *Sewers.* A septic tank has been constructed sized for a daily plant population of 100 persons. It has an automatic dosing siphon to provide for the most efficient utilization of the leaching field.

   All sanitary sewers projecting from within buildings to 5 feet out are cast-iron soil pipe. All road crossings and sewer catch basins also are cast-iron pipe. All other sewer pipe is of concrete or vitrified clay pipe, per American Society for Testing and Materials (ASTM) standards.

5. *Fire protection.* In addition to the yard fire system, carbon dioxide (CO_2)

fire extinguishers are provided in all buildings, plus sprinkler systems in the warehouse, plant, and office buildings. All materials, systems, and procedures are in accordance with National Board of Fire Underwriters or Factory Mutual recommendations.

ECONOMIC ANALYSIS AND FINANCIAL PROJECTIONS

Capital Costs

All capital requirements for a new TMP mill with a capacity of 300 ADT/D are presented in this section. In the feasibility study, financial data were compiled for three different types of pulp—sanitary tissue grade, newsprint grade, and magazine grade. For the sake of simplicity, however, profit and loss, cash flow, and balance sheet projections are shown only for the sanitary tissue–grade mill. The bulk of these capital costs is for fixed capital outlay, and a small portion is for working capital. Most of these data on capital and production costs were obtained during a 5-month period between June and October 1975, and thus are subject to change because of subsequent inflation and the fluctuation of foreign exchange rates. Prices quoted by the various companies generally include provisions for an escalation clause. Commodity and price indexes published by government sources are a good guide to expected future price increases.

Fixed Capital Requirements. Fixed investment requirements include land, site preparation, roads, buildings, chip station, refining, screening and cleaning, pulp drying, baling and finishing, chemical additive system, water supply system, effluent control, steam generation, electrical distribution system, sanitary sewer, laboratory equipment, fire protection, maintenance equipment and parts, materials handling, installation and erection, engineering, contingency, and interest cost during construction period. These fixed investment costs are given in Table 6.24 for sanitary tissue grade.

Total fixed capital outlays for a 300 ADT/D TMP mill were estimated at $26,740,140. A detailed breakdown of the costs for each item and descriptions of them are presented below.

1. *Land.* An estimated 40 acres are needed for buildings, chip yard, water reservoir, effluent control, and buffer area. Land cost was estimated roughly at $1000 per acre in the Dublin, Georgia, area.

   40 acres × 1000 = $40,000

Table 6.24   Fixed Investment Requirements for Sanitary Tissue–Grade TMP Mill (based on 300 SDT/D capacity)

Item	$
Land, 40 acres	40,000
Ground and site preparation	1,087,440
Road and rail connections	113,350
Buildings	543,000
Chip station and storage	900,450
TMP refining system	3,860,400
Pulp screening and cleaning	1,217,000
Pulp drying, baling, and finishing	4,600,000
Chemical additive system	137,500
Water supply system	1,285,000
Effluent control and waste disposal	2,600,000
Steam generation	919,000
Electrical distribution system	810,000
Sanitary sewer	118,000
Laboratory equipment	55,000
Fire protection	92,000
Maintenance equipment and parts	523,000
Materials handling	75,000
Installation and erection	2,393,000
Engineering	1,819,000
Contingency	2,137,000
Interest cost during construction period	1,415,000
Total	$26,740,140

2. *Ground and site preparation.* A total of 47,280 square feet of building area must be graded, of which 29,280 square feet is for buildings and 18,000 square feet for miscellaneous areas. Grading and preparation costs were estimated at $23 per square foot.

$$47,280 \text{ ft}^2 \times 23 = \$1,087,440$$

3. *Road and rail connections.*

- Road. Blacktop-paved access road to main highway, 25×600 ft
  Blacktop-paved employee parking lot, 80×100 ft
  Spread gravel truck access road to chip yard, 25 to 500 ft

$2.40/ft^2 blacktop =	
$(600)(2.40)(25) + (80)(2.40)(100) =$	$55,200
$1.10/ft^2 spread gravel = $(500)(1.10)(25) =$	13,750
Total	$68,950

- Rail. 256-ft chip-car storage track
  256-ft chemical tank-car siding
  256-ft warehouse railcar siding
  550-ft siding track to main lines
  $33.70/ft = (256)(3)(33.70) + (550)(33.70) = $ 44,400

  Total cost = 68,950 + 44,400 = $113,350

4. *Buildings.*

- Chip-yard control building.
  180-ft^2, 12 × 15 ft, one-story, prefab metal building
  Concrete pad, window air conditioning, lights
  180 ft^2 × $7.80 = $1,404
- Maintenance building.
  1000-ft^2, 25 × 40 ft, one-story, prefab metal building
  Concrete pad, lights, roof exhaust fans, heavy electrical
    load wiring
  1000 ft^2 × $9.36 = $9,360
- Chemical solution building.
  800-ft^2, 20 × 40 ft, one-story, prefab metal building
  Concrete pad, lights, roof exhaust system
  800-ft^2 × $9.36 = $7,488
- Warehouse/finishing line.
  Plant warehouse holds 12 days' production = (300)(12)(4
    bales/ton) = 14,000 bales
  Each bale 3 × 3 ft or 9 ft^2 floor space = (14,400)(9) =
    129,600 ft^2 floor space
  Store bales 10 high = (10) (2 ft high bales) + 2 ft clearance =
  22-ft high building
  Need 130 × 100 ft warehouse space
  13,000-ft^2, 100 = 130 ft, one-story, prefab metal building
  Roof exhaust blowers, lights, concrete pad, 22 ft height
  13,000 ft^2 × $9.36 = $121,680
- TMP plant.
  10,500-ft^2, 140 × 75 ft, 2$\frac{1}{2}$-story, prefab, concrete walls
  Roof blowers, heavy concrete reinforced flooring
  10,500 ft^2 × $27 = $283,500
- Office building.
  3200-ft^2, two-story, prefab metal building with false stone
    facing, central air conditioning, fully lighted
  First floor 3200 ft^2 × $20 = $64,000
  Second floor 3200 ft^2 × $20 × 0.7 = $44,800

- Personnel/guard house.
  600-ft², 20 × 30 ft, one-story prefab metal building with false stone facing, located adjacent to office building, fully lighted, central air conditioning
  600 ft² × \$18 =   \$10,800
  _____
  Total building costs   \$543,032
5. Chip station and storage.
  Total machinery*   \$501,810
  Mechanical installation   150,543
  Electrical controls   60,217
  Electrical installation   100,362
  Used 920 loader—Yancey Bros.   30,533
  D4 bulldozer—Yancey Bros.   38,485
  50-ton truck scale—Wiggins Scales   18,500
  _____
  Total   \$900,450
6. *TMP refining system.*
  Chip bin—American Defibrator   \$ 106,540
  Chip washing—American Defibrator   94,500
  TMP pulping and refining—Defibrator   1,446,200
      RLP54S pressurized refiners (two)
      RS54S atmospheric refiners (two)
  Transport system—American Defibrator   250,200
  Relay panels—American Defibrator   27,000
  Start motors—Defibrator   96,160
  Main motors—Defibrator   814,000
  Secondary equipment and shipment   1,000,800
  Start-up service   25,000
  _____
  Total   \$3,860,400
7. *Pulp screening and cleaning.*
  Agitated latency chest   \$370,000
  Model 400 Centrisorter screen system   38,000
  Three-stage Centricleaner system   101,500
  Deckers, Sudor reject press and two pulp pumps—IMPCO   392,000
  Secondary equipment and shipment   315,500
  _____
  Total for tissue and newsprint grades   \$1,217,000
  Third-stage pump-through refiner and miscellaneous—American Defibrator   259,200
  _____
  Total for magazine grade   \$1,476,200

* Included are hydraulic truck dumper, railcar pit unloading system, screening and rechipping equipment, chip pile recovery pit, chip washer system, conveyors and blowing equipment.

8. *Pulp drying, baling, and finishing.*

Fluffer and flash dryer system—Niro	$2,800,000
Bale press, baling and unit-tie system—Sunds	1,200,000
Shipment	600,000
Total	$4,600,000

9. *Chemical additive system.* A chemical additive system will be housed in a prefab metal building, 20 × 40 ft, located adjacent to the chemical unloading facility. Provisions will be made for unloading the raw chemicals from truck or railcar. The system will handle the receiving, storing, mixing, and pumping of the chemicals to the impregnator.

Tissue grade, five chemicals, five-tank system =	
(5)(27,500) =	$137,500

10. *Water supply system.*

Fire system tank	$150,000
Reservoir	370,000
Two wells	140,000
Pumps	20,500
Controls	186,000
Piping	155,000
Miscellaneous and installation	263,500
Total	$1,285,000

11. *Effluent control system and waste disposal.*

Sewers, piping, bar screen, clarifiers, aerated lagoon, discharge station—Peabody Welles, Inc.	$1,900,000
Effluent control monitoring equipment—Parker Engineering Chemicals	150,000
Secondary equipment and shipment	410,000
Optional coagulation tank	140,000
Total	$2,600,000

12. *Steam generation (boiler house).*

Bark shredder	$ 20,500
Boiler system	622,500
Feed conveyors	11,000
Secondary equipment and shipment	265,000
Total	$919,000

13. *Electrical distribution system.*

Main facilities.	$600,000

      Indoor metal-clad switchgear line-up

      Transformers for refiner motors

      Low-voltage load center unit substation

Medium voltage starter substation
Grounding resistor for 2400-V. substation
Secondary equipment and shipment.   210,000

| Total | $810,000 |

14. *Sanitary sewer.*

| Septic tank system and piping | $ 87,000 |
| Miscellaneous and installation | 31,000 |

| Total | $118,000 |

15. *Laboratory equipment.* Two kinds of equipment are needed for testing wood chips and pulp. These materials will be tested for the following:

Wood chips: moisture content, density, size classification, age.
Wood pulp: drainage, freeness, brightness, PFI, shive content, tensile strength, tear factor, burst factor, water- or moisture-absorbing capacity.

Basic equipment such as a Sommerville flat screen, Bauer McNett fiber classifier, finish wet web tester, and so on, are needed. Budgeted equipment costs are $55,000.

16. *Fire protection equipment.* Main fire facilities are CO_2 fire extinguishers and a sprinkler system. Fire extinguishers should be installed one every 1000 square feet, and sprinkler heads should be placed one every 20 square feet in some buildings. The facilities needed, their locations, and their costs are as follows:

Pump and alarm system	$28,500
Yard fire piping	17,350
Chip yard area—1 CO_2 extinguisher	9
Maintenance—1 CO_2 extinguisher	9
Chemical solution area—1 CO_2 extinguisher plus foam fire hoses	609
Warehouse/baling line—13 CO_2 extinguishers, 650 sprinkler heads	13,117
TMP plant—22 CO_2 extinguishers, 300 sprinkler heads	6,198
Office building—6 CO_2 extinguishers, 70 sprinkler heads	1,454
Personnel guard house—1 CO_2 extinguisher, 40 sprinkler heads	809
Miscellaneous and installation	23,945

| Total | $92,000 |

17. *Maintenance equipment and parts.*

| Spare parts, TMP plant (1.5% total TMP cost) | $ 95,340 |
| Spare parts, chip yard (1.5% total chip yard cost) | 15,145 |

Spare parts, dryer-baler (1.5% total equipment cost)	70,055
Cleaning supplies and equipment	3,500
Ground maintenance equipment and supplies	8,750
Machine shop equipment	85,000
Electrical shop equipment	34,750
Welding and sheet metal shop equipment	26,000
Hoists, lifts, and so on	74,000
Two-way radios for communication	550
Pickup trucks (two)	9,000
Miscellaneous racks, tools and supplies ($+$ 10%)	42,210
Spare parts, electrical system	15,000
Spare parts, water system	3,500
Spare parts, boiler system	12,000
Spare parts, waste treatment system	28,200
Total	$523,000

18. *Materials handling.* Bales will be unitized at the plant into increments of 2 (2, 4, 6, 8) per customer. Baled pulp will be loaded onto railcars (120 per car) and containerized trucks (150 per container).

Forklifts to handle bales (two at $12,000 each)	$24,000
Ovalmatic unitizer	50,000
Pallets	1,000
Total	$75,000

19. *Installation and erection.* A large sum will be needed for labor, materials, related service, and overhead costs in installing all equipment and machinery. The amount estimated is about $2.4 million or 8 to 9% of the total fixed-capital outlay.

20. *Engineering expenses.* The engineering function includes the preparation of all flow diagrams and layouts, and the drawing up of equipment and construction specifications with accompanying detailed blueprints. The engineering function also includes the issuing of tenders for equipment, evaluation of bids entered by contractors, and the negotiation and finalizing of contracts with contractors. Once contracts for equipment have been granted, it will be necessary to maintain an inspection and expediting service to ensure that the equipment is in fact being manufactured in accordance with specifications and that the schedule of delivery dates is maintained.

The cost of an engineering study was estimated at $1.8 million or about 7% of all fixed-capital outlays.

21. *Contingency.* Provisions have been made for unexpected delays, poor work scheduling, or late deliveries. A little over $2 million has been earmarked for these purposes.

22. *Interest during construction period.* It was estimated that 24 months will be required to construct a TMP mill with all equipment and facilities installed. Progress payments on contracts and equipment orders will have to be met by equity funds, short-term borrowing, or long-term borrowing. A significant portion of the capital outlay during the construction period will have to come from short-term borrowing. Long before the enterprise is in operation, substantial interest costs will have accrued. These costs are usually capitalized to reflect the true costs of putting the facilities into operation. Of the total fixed-capital outlay of $26,740,140 plus $1,000,000 for preoperational expenses, $15,700,000 was estimated to come from short-term borrowing for various lengths of time at an annual interest rate of 10%. Interest costs were estimated at $1,415,000.

23. *Working capital.* Estimated working capital for the TMP mill is given in Table 6.25. Working capital was estimated on the basis of wood chip supplies for $1\frac{1}{2}$ months, finished pulp for 1 month, accounts receivable for 1 month, chemicals and other mill supplies for 1 month, and a cash reserve of $1 million. Total working capital was estimated at a little over $5 million.

Table 6.25   Estimated Working
Capital Requirements (based on
a 300 ADT/D capacity TMP mill)

Item	$
Wood chips	485,000
Finished pulp	1,773,000
Receivables	1,773,000
Chemicals and supplies	127,000
Cash reserve	1,000,000
Total	$5,158,000

24. *Preoperational and start-up expenses.* Prior to the actual mill start-up, money should be provided for various activities to put the mill in operation. These expenses are salaries for management and supervisory personnel, the hiring and training of mill staff, preparation of mill operating manuals and instructions, establishment of operational and control systems, and miscellaneous office expenses. Finally, start-up expenses should be provided for specialists, raw materials, and labor. These preoperational expenses were estimated at $1 million; they will be amortized in a 5-year period after the mill becomes operational.

25. *Total capital requirements.* Total capital requirements for the entire project include all fixed capital investment, working capital, and

preoperational and start-up expenses. These requirements were estimated at $32 million. (See Table 6.26.)

Table 6.26 Estimated Total Capital Requirements (based on a 300 ADT/D capacity TMP mill)

Item	$
Fixed capital investment	26,740,140
Working capital	5,158,000
Preoperational and start-up expenses	1,000,000
Total	$32,898,140

26. *Construction schedule and expenses.* Mill construction and machinery delivery schedules were projected according to established trade practices. These projections are essential in making financial plans and cash flow forecasts. Contracts for major machinery generally require 30% cash down payment on order, 60 to 65% payment on shipment, and 5 to 10% on start-up. Delivery time varies from 3 to 18 months, depending on the item. Projected mill construction, machinery order, delivery, erection and installation time, and start-up period, together with cash outlays involved in each item, are presented in Table 6.27.

The first cash outlay for an individual fixed investment shown in the table means that an order has been placed. A second payment indicates delivery if the item is machinery. Dashed lines following payments on an item signify either erection and installation of machinery or continued construction on buildings and roads. Engineering expenses are paid in installments at the beginning of the project, while erection and installation costs are spread out over the second year of the construction period. Contingency funds will be used whenever there is an unexpected cash outlay. These cost outlays are consistent with the given fixed-capital requirements plus the $1 million projected for preoperational and start-up expenses. All these cost outlays are summed up on a monthly basis.

Production Costs

Manufacturing costs consist of basically two major classifications—variable costs and fixed costs. Variable costs can be defined as those that vary in accordance with the level of production. This classification usually consists of the materials directly consumed in the production of mill products, such as wood chips, chemicals, power, gas, and miscellaneous operating materials (such

Table 6.27 Construction Schedule and Expenses: Tissue-Grade TMP Mill

Year 1976	July	August	September	October	November	December
Fixed investments						
Land						
Road and rail connections						
Buildings						
Chip station and storage						
TMP refining system						
Pulp screening and cleaning						
Pulp drying, baling, and finishing						
Chemical additive system						
Water supply system						
Effluent control and waste disposal						
Steam generation						
Electrical distribution						
Sanitary sewer						
Laboratory equipment						
Fire protection						
Maintenance equipment and parts						
Materials handling						
Installation and erection						
Engineering	$300,000			$300,000		
Contingency						
Interest cost during construction period						
Preoperational expenses						
Salaries	6,000	$6,000	$6,000	6,000	$6,000	$6,000
Hiring and training						
Establishing control system						
Miscellaneous expenses	2,000	2,000	2,000	2,000	2,000	2,000
Start-up costs						
Specialists						
Materials						
Miscellaneous						
Total	$308,000	$8,000	$8,000	$308,000	$8,000	$8,000

Table 6.27 (Continued)

Year 1977	January $	February $	March $	April $	May $	June $	July $	August $	September $	October $	November $	December $
Fixed investments												
Land	40,000											
Ground and site preparation	300,000											
Road and rail connections	45,000		68,350			187,440						
Buildings				600,000			200,000		200,000			143,000
Chip station and storage							135,000					
TMP refining system	1,158,000											
Pulp screening and cleaning				365,000								
Pulp drying, baling, and finishing	1,380,000											
Chemical additive system					385,000							
Water supply system												
Effluent control and waste disposal						780,000						
Steam generation							300,000					
Electrical distribution							110,000					
Sanitary sewer									35,000			83,000
Laboratory equipment												
Fire protection												
Maintenance equipment and parts												
Materials handling												
Installation and erection												
Engineering	300,000			300,000			300,000			319,000		
Contingency	100,000	50,000	50,000	50,000	50,000	50,000	100,000	50,000	50,000	50,000	50,000	50,000
Interest cost during construction period												
Preoperational expenses												
Salaries	9,000	9,000	9,000	9,000	9,000	9,000	9,000	9,000	9,000	9,000	9,000	9,000
Hiring and training												
Establishing control system												
Miscellaneous expenses												
Start-up costs												
Specialists	3,000	3,000	3,000	3,000	3,000	3,000	3,000	3,000	3,000	3,000	3,000	3,000
Materials												
Miscellaneous												
Total	3,335,000	62,000	130,350	1,327,000	447,000	1,029,440	1,157,000	62,000	297,000	381,000	62,000	288,000

Table 6.27 (Continued)

Year 1978	January	February	March	April	May	June	July	August	September	October	November	December
	$	$	$	$	$	$	$	$	$	$	$	$
Fixed investments												
Land												
Ground and site preparation												
Road and rail connections												
Buildings												
Chip station and storage			500,000				265,450					
TMP refining system			2,316,000	730,000				122,000	386,400			
Pulp screening and cleaning												
Pulp drying, baling, and finishing			2,760,000							460,000		
Chemical additive system	40,000					90,000			7,500			
Water supply system	770,000							130,000				
Effluent control and waste disposal		600,000				700,000				520,000		
Steam generation					550,000				69,000			
Electrical distribution	300,000		200,000			200,000						
Sanitary sewer												
Laboratory equipment												
Fire protection	30,000					62,000			55,000			
Maintenance equipment and parts	75,000	75,000										
Materials handling								200,000		125,000	123,000	
Installation and erection	50,000	100,000	300,000	300,000	300,000	300,000	300,000	300,000	200,000	100,000	100,000	43,000
Engineering	100,000	100,000	100,000	100,000	100,000	100,000	100,000	100,000	100,000	100,000	100,000	337,000
Contingency												
Interest cost during construction period												1,415,000
Preoperational expenses												
Salaries	16,000	16,000	16,000	16,000	16,000	16,000	21,000	21,000	21,000	21,000	21,000	21,000
Hiring and training										40,000	60,000	100,000
Establishing control system										10,000	10,000	10,000
Miscellaneous expenses	4,000	4,000	4,000	4,000	4,000	4,000	4,000	4,000	4,000	4,000	4,000	4,000
Start-up costs												
Specialists											50,000	50,000
Materials											53,000	100,000
Miscellaneous											20,000	35,000
Total	1,385,000	895,000	6,196,000	1,150,000	970,000	1,472,000	690,450	877,000	842,900	1,380,000	541,000	2,115,000

as wire, metal straps, cover paper). Fixed costs can be defined as those that remain constant and are not influenced by the level of production under normal operating conditions. This classification includes labor, administrative salaries, mill maintenance, insurance, ad valorem taxes, and miscellaneous expenses such as telephone and telegraph, office supplies, and so on. Two major fixed costs—(1) interest and debt retirement and (2) depreciation—must be added in order to complete a list of total production costs.

The terms used in connection with production costs in this study are defined as follows.

- *Variable costs.* Wood chips, power, natural gas, chemicals and miscellaneous.
- *Fixed costs.* Labor, administrative salaries, maintenance and supplies, boiler fuel, insurance, ad valorem taxes, and miscellaneous.
- *Manufacturing costs.* Variable costs plus fixed costs.
- *Out-of-pocket costs.* Manufacturing costs plus interest and debt retirement.
- *Total production costs.* Out-of-pocket costs plus depreciation.

Table 6.28 Estimated per-Ton Production Costs of TMP (based on 300 ADT/D capacity)

Variable costs	$
Wood chips	35.93
Power	35.84
Gas	3.15
Chemicals	8.33
Miscellaneous supplies	2.13
Subtotal	85.38
Fixed costs	
Labor	13.25
Salaries	3,49
Maintenance	9.18
Boiler fuel	1.20
Insurance	2.41
Ad valorem taxes	2.82
Miscellaneous supplies	2.45
Subtotal	34.80
Manufacturing costs	120.19
Interest and debt service	23.89
Out-of-pocket costs	144.07
Depreciation	12.90
Total production costs	156.97

The proposed TMP mill would operate 24 hours per day and 345 working days a year. Based on a 300 ADT/D capacity, a summary of production costs for the TMP mill is given in Table 6.28. These costs are quoted per ton of thermomechanical pulp produced. Variable costs constitute nearly one-half of the total production costs. Wood chips and power costs are the dominant variable costs. Fixed costs, excluding interest and depreciation, constitute about 22% of the total production costs. Manufacturing costs were estimated at $156.97 per ton. Costs for interest and debt service were estimated at about $23 or about 14% of the total costs. Depreciation, a noncash cost, was estimated at about $13 or about 8% of the total costs. Total production costs were estimated at $156.97 per ton.

Detailed calculations for each cost element are presented separately for both variable costs and fixed costs.

1. *Variable costs.*
   - *Wood chips.* The cost of wood chips would be $18 per green ton (about 50% moisture), $16 for the wood chips themselves and $2 for delivery. One ton of wood chips weighs 2000 lb, which yields about 963 to 1002 lb of pulp in air-dry condition (10% moisture), depending on what grade of pulp is to be produced. Details of processing losses, yields, and unit costs are:

Item	Unit	Tissue
Green wood chips input	lb	2000
Screening and handling losses at 3%	lb	60
Wood chips in washer	lb	1940
Moisture content at 50%	lb	970
Fiber content at 50%	lb	970
Washing loss at 3%	lb	29
In refiners	lb	941
Refiner losses (3%, 3.5%, or 5%)	lb	27
In screening and cleaning equipment	lb	914
Screening and cleaning losses (1.3%, 1.5%, or 3%)	lb	12
Fiber yields	lb	902
Fiber yields	%	93
Moisture content in pulp	lb	100
Pulp yield (air-dry weight)	lb	1002
Pulp yield per ton of green wood chips	%	50.1
Green wood chips per ADT pulp	tons	1.996
Greenwood chip cost per ADT pulp	$	35.93

- *Power.* Power would be purchased from the Georgia Power Company, which would provide a substation at Dublin, Georgia. Power requirements were estimated at 31,500 kW with 80% diversity.

31,500 kW $\times$ 1.34 = 42,000 hp $\div$ 300 tons = 140.7 hp/ton per day
31,500 kW $\times$ 730 hr/month $\times$ 0.80 = 18,396,000 kW-hr/month

Power rate was quoted at 18.3 mills/kW-hr by the Georgia Power Company.

The power requirements for the proposed TMP mill are given below in kilowatts:

Item	Tissue-Grade	
	Peak	Normal
Chip preparation	445	445
Refining	24,665	19,730
Pulp preparation	525	525
Pulp drying	1,170	1,170
Baling	485	485
Steam generating (boiler)	485	485
Water supply	290	290
Effluent and waste control	500	500
Miscellaneous equipment and lights	850	850
Total	29,415	24,480

Power costs are based on normal requirements.
Tissue-grade pulp:

24,480 kW $\times$ 24 hr = 587,520 kW-hr/day
587,520 kW-hr $\times$ 0.0183/kW-hr = \$10,752/day
\$10,752 $\div$ 300 tons = \$35.84 per ton of pulp produced

- *Natural gas.* Gas is required for flash-drying of pulp. Dublin, Georgia, has 6-inch gas mains and an adequate supply of gas. Gas cost was estimated at 9 cents/therm (100,000 Btu). Consumption estimates:

1583 Btu/lb of pulp for flash dryer
3,166,000 Btu/ton of pulp or about 32 therms
Miscellaneous usages require 3 therms/ton
Total gas requirements are 35 therms/ton of pulp
35 $\times$ 9c = \$3.15/ton

- *Chemicals.* Chemicals required for bleaching and for boiler water treatment are:

Item	Pounds/Ton of Pulp	Tons/ Day	Cost/Ton of Chemical	Cost/ Day	Cost/Ton of Pulp
Alum	12	1.8	$ 62	$ 112	$0.37
Sodium bisulfite	9	1.35	232	313	1.04
Sodium hexameta- phosphate	6	0.9	445	400	1.34
Sodium hydroxide	11	1.65	145	239	0.80
Sodium hydro- sulfite	13	1.95	720	1404	4.68
Chemicals for boiler water				30	0.10
Total				$2498	$8.33

Additional chemicals are necessary for treating wastewater. The types and amounts needed would vary according to local streamflow conditions and water characteristics.

- *Miscellaneous supplies.* Wire, steel strapping, wrapping paper, labels, pallets, water and effluent treatment chemicals, lubricants, and so on, were estimated at $2.13 per ton of pulp produced.

2. *Fixed costs.*

- *Labor.* About 76 workers are required to operate a TMP mill for three shifts per day plus one extra shift per week to allow five working days per worker per week. Wage rates were based on current rates prevailing in the industry plus 15% fringe benefits. The number of workers required for major operations, base rates, and base cost per day are as follows:

Operation	Crew Size	Shifts/ Day	Total Persons	Total Hours	Base Rate	Base Cost/Day
Chip yard	2	3	6	48	$ 5	$ 240
TMP control	1	3	3	24	10	240
TMP roving tester	1	3	3	24	10	240
Drying and baling	1	3	3	24	9	216
Warehouse and forklift	2	3	6	48	5	240
Maintenance	6	3	18	144	9	1296
Utility	2	3	6	48	5	240
Boiler and water	3	3	9	72	9	648
Clean-up	1	3	3	24	4	96
Total	19		57*	456		$3456

* Add one extra shift of 19 persons per week to permit a five-working-day schedule per shift in a week.

$3456 plus fringe benefits of 15% or $518 = $3974/day
$3974 × 345 days a year = $1,371,030/year
$1,371,030 ÷ 103,500 tons = $13.25/ton of pulp produced

- *Administrative salaries.* About 72 persons are included as the administrative personnel needed for the proposed TMP mill. Their titles, salaries, fringe benefits, and annual expenses are given as follows:

Title	No.	Annual Salary	Fringe Benefits		Total
President	1	$30,000	25%	$7,500	$37,500
Vice president, sales	1	24,000	20%	4,800	28,800
Plant manager	1	21,000	20%	4,200	25,200
Assistant plant manager	1	16,000	20%	3,200	19,200
Accountant	1	13,200	20%	2,640	15,840
Purchasing manager	1	13,200	20%	2,640	15,840
Personnel manager	1	13,200	20%	2,640	15,840
Chemist	1	13,200	20%	2,640	15,840
TMP foreman	4	13,200	15%	1,980	60,720
Lab technician	2	10,000	15%	1,500	23,000
Medical	1	10,000	15%	1,500	11,500
Clerk-typist	4	8,000	15%	1,200	36,800
Payroll clerk	1	8,000	15%	1,200	9,200
Guard	4	8,000	15%	1,200	36,800
Janitor	1	8,000	15%	1,200	9,200
Total	25				$361,280

$361,280 ÷ 103,500 tons = $3.49 per ton

- *Maintenance and supplies.* Provisions must be made to supply necessary replacements on parts, repair and adjustment supplies, and other maintenance materials. Estimated annual cost and per-unit cost are given below.

Parts and replacements	$550,000
Other maintenance requirements	400,000
Total	$950,000
Per ton	$9.18

- *Boiler fuel.* Bark, sawdust, and other kinds of wood residues from sawmills would be used as boiler fuel. The boiler should be in operation 24 hours a day throughout the year except when shut down for cleaning or repair.

  Tissue-grade mill: fuel for boiler requires 68 tons of wood waste per day at $5 per ton delivered.

68 tons $\times$ \$5 = \$340 per day $\times$ 365 days = \$124,100 per year

\$124,100 $\div$ 103,500 tons = \$1.20 per ton of TMP produced

- *Insurance.* Insurance rates on an industrial plant depend on water availability at the plant, fire prevention equipment installed, building materials, and products and raw materials stored at plant. Annual rates vary from \$0.75 to \$1.00 per \$100. A rate of \$0.90 per \$100 is adopted to cover all damage liabilities.

Inventories, 2 weeks

Wood chips	\$ 151,000
Pulp	827,400
Miscellaneous	50,000
Total inventories	\$1,028,400
Fixed investments less land	26,700,140
Total insured amount	\$27,728,540
Insurance @ \$0.90/\$100	249,557
Cost per ton	\$2.41

- *Ad valorem taxes.* Using ad valorem taxes at Dublin (Laurens County, Georgia) as the basis for calculation, the rate is \$26.30 per \$1000 at 40% of actual value.

Fixed investments	\$26,740,140
Two weeks' inventories	1,028,400
Total	\$27,768,540
At 40% valuation	11,107,416
At \$26.30/\$1000 tax rate	292,125
Cost per ton	\$2.82

- *Miscellaneous.* Miscellaneous annual expenses are given below:

Office supplies	\$ 60,000
Laboratory supplies	40,000
Telephone and telegraph	20,000
Dues and subscriptions	100,000
Lights	32,220
Water and sewage	1,400
Total	\$253,620
Cost per ton	\$2.45

- *Interest and debt retirement.* The capital required will be supplied from two sources—equity capital and long-term borrowing. It is assumed that one-third of the expenditures will be financed by equity capital and two-thirds will come from borrowing. It is further assumed that the entrepreneurs will put up about \$3 million in cash to meet immediate needs, while about $7 million will be raised through common stock sales. (See cash flow projections in a later section.) With one-third of the capital required funded by equity capital, the remainder can be financed through issuance of bonds. Interest and debt retirement have been worked out on a 20-year basis at 9% per annum on borrowed capital. The calculations are as follows:

Total capital required	$32,898,140
Equity capital	10,000,000
Long-term borrowed capital	22,898,140
20-year debt retirement plan at	
9% per annum	2,472,999
Cost per ton	$23.89

- *Depreciation.* Depreciation is a noncash cost. It is important for entrepreneurs to set aside a sufficient fund for the cost of depreciation. However, no one can predict accurately the useful life of a piece of machinery. The rate of depreciation depends largely on subjective judgment on specific working conditions and the intensity of uses. There are several methods in setting depreciation costs. Some are for bookkeeping purposes, and some are for tax-reporting purposes. For this study, a 20-year straight-line depreciation method is adopted. The calculations are given below:

Fixed investment less land	$26,700,140
Annual 20-year straight-line	
depreciation	1,335,007
Cost per ton	$12.90

Financial Projections

The financial projections for this study include five basic statements which constitute the basis of financial analysis for the proposed TMP mill:

1. The profit and loss statement, which indicates whether the operations of the enterprise will generate a reward for its owners during a 10-year period.
2. The cash flow statement, which indicates the amount of money to be received from mill operations, loans, equity contributions, or common stocks, and the amount that must be paid for capital expenditures, debt retirement, labor, materials, overhead, and so on, during a period of $12\frac{1}{2}$ years.
3. The projected balance sheet, which indicates the nature of the assets and liabilities of the proposed mills and the equity of the owners during a 10-year period.
4. The profitability analysis, which provides measures of returns in relation to investments at different given times within a projected period.
5. The sensitivity analysis, which indicates the risks involved concerning

changes in sales price, sales volume, manufacturing costs, and fixed capital requirements.

It should be noted that all projections were made on the basis of 1975 constant dollars, and no attempt has been made to estimate the future changes in sales prices and costs related to capital outlays, labor, materials, overhead, sales revenue, and so on. Projections involving other economic factors, such as tax rates, sale commissions, and export expenses, also are based on 1975 standards. The five statements mentioned above are presented separately.

Pro Forma Profit and Loss Statement.   A 10-year projection, 1979 to 1988, is provided for a TMP mill producing tissue-grade pulp. (See Table 6.29.) The volume of pulp production increases from 76,800 tons in the first year of operation to 114,000 tons (maximum output) in the fifth year of operation. Tonnage given is based on 2000 pounds per ton in air-dry condition or 10% moisture content. Gross sales are based on f.o.b. mill prices per ton of pulp, as follows:

	Tissue Grade	Newsprint Grade	Magazine Grade
First year	$187	$185	$190
Following year	$197	$195	$200

These prices are competitive with mechanical pulps offered by Scandinavian producers in the EEC countries. (See Table 6.18.) Unit prices are constant over the projected period.

Brokerage and sales expenses account for 5% of gross sales. Brokerage commissions actually were calculated on 3% of gross sales and various sales expenses at 2%. Gross sales minus brokerage and sales expenses are equal to net sales.

Manufacturing costs comprise both variable and fixed costs, which were presented in detail in the previous section. Operating profits are the result of net sales minus manufacturing costs. Preoperational and start-up expenses are amortized in the first 5-year operating period. After the deduction of interest on debt and depreciation, net loss or profit before taxes is derived. Taxes were calculated on the basis of 48% on the profit for federal taxes and 6% for state taxes. Net profit is the remainder after taxes have been deducted.

The first year's operation ends in a loss. However, net profit after taxes may exceed $1 million to $2 million a year, depending on the specific year. (See details in Table 6.29.)

Table 6.29 Projected Profit and Loss Statement: Tissue-Grade TMP Mill (based on 300 ADT/D, start-up January 1, 1979, at nominal capacity of 103,500 tons per year)

	1979	1980	1981	1982	1983	1984	1985	1986	1987	1988
	$	$	$	$	$	$	$	$	$	$
Production in tons[a]	76,800	102,000	106,000	110,000	114,000	114,000	114,000	114,000	114,000	114,000
Gross sales[b]	14,361,600	20,094,000	20,882,000	21,670,000	22,458,000	22,458,000	22,458,000	22,458,000	22,458,000	22,458,000
Brokerage and sales expenses, 5%	718,080	1,004,700	1,044,100	1,083,500	1,122,900	1,122,900	1,122,900	1,122,900	1,122,900	1,122,900
Net sales	13,643,520	19,089,300	19,837,900	20,586,500	21,335,100	21,335,100	21,335,100	21,335,100	21,335,100	21,335,100
Manufacturing costs										
Variable costs at $85.38/ton	6,557,184	8,708,760	9,050,280	9,391,800	9,733,320	9,733,320	9,733,320	9,733,320	9,733,320	9,733,320
Fixed costs	3,601,712	3,601,712	3,601,712	3,601,712	3,601,712	3,601,712	3,601,712	3,601,712	3,601,712	3,601,712
Operating profits	3,484,624	6,778,828	7,185,908	7,592,988	8,000,068	8,000,068	8,000,068	8,000,068	8,000,068	8,000,068
Less:										
Preoperational and start-up expenses[c]	200,000	200,000	200,000	200,000	200,000	0	0	0	0	0
Interest	2,043,398	2,015,036	1,946,342	1,923,444	1,854,749	1,808,953	1,740,259	1,671,564	1,579,972	1,511,277
Depreciation	1,335,007	1,335,007	1,335,007	1,335,007	1,335,007	1,335,007	1,335,007	1,335,007	1,335,007	1,335,007
Net profit before taxes	(93,781)[d]	3,135,004[d]	3,704,599	4,134,537	4,610,312	4,856,108	4,924,802	4,993,497	5,085,089	5,153,784
Income taxes, 54%	0	1,692,902	2,000,462	2,232,650	2,489,568	2,622,298	2,659,393	2,696,488	2,745,948	2,783,043
Net profit after taxes	0	1,442,102	1,704,097	1,901,887	2,120,744	2,233,810	2,265,409	2,297,009	2,339,141	2,370,740

[a] Annual mill production increases until the fifth year of its operation, when it levels off at the estimated maximum production. The first year is a shakedown period.
[b] Sales during the first year are priced below market prices in order to gain entry. The first-year price is $187/ADT, f.o.b. Prices in succeeding years are $197/ADT, f.o.b.
[c] Preoperational and start-up expenses, $1,000,000, are amortized over a 5-year period.
[d] Deducted 1979 loss.

Projected Cash Flow Statement.   Cash flow is the most important financial tool used for analyzing capital expenditures. Cash flow is not equivalent to income, profits, or earnings. In most cases, operating cash flow is the sum of after-tax profits plus annual depreciation charges. In these projections, after-tax profit is allowed to accumulate in the cash account and no provisions are made for reinvestments and for cash dividends on common stocks.

The projections are made for two periods: (1) planning and construction, July 1976 to December 1978, a $2\frac{1}{2}$-year period; and (2) mill operation, 1979 to 1988, a 10-year period. Monthly projections are made for the planning and construction period and for the first year of the operating period, while annual projections are made from 1979 to 1988.

During the planning and construction period, about one-third of the cash receipts would come from equity capital, which consists of founders' stock and net from sales of common stock. Two-thirds would come from short-term borrowing. Long-term borrowing would occur during the last month of the construction period in order to pay off short-term loans and interest accrued. Cash disbursements during this period reflect largely capital outlays for fixed investments presented in Table 6.27.

Cash-flow projections for the operating period differ markedly from those for the planning and construction period. Cash receipts during this period would come largely from collection of receivables or, more precisely, the sales of pulp produced. Cash disbursements during this period reflect all manufacturing costs plus interest payments, long-term debt retirement, corporate income taxes, and local property tax assessments.

Cash is allowed to accumulate during the projected period. At the end of the period, the cash balance would be close to $28 million for a tissue-grade pulp mill. Details of these cash-flow projections are presented in Table 6.30.

Balance Sheet Statement.   The balance sheet represents the financial position of the proposed TMP mill at a given date. The statement was projected for a 10-year period, 1979–1988. Detailed projections are given in Table 6.31.

Two major components of the balance sheet are (1) assets and (2) liabilities and owners' equity. Under current assets are cash, accounts receivable, miscellaneous prepayments, and inventories. Cash reflects the cash flow given in Table 6.30. Accounts receivable reflect 2 months of gross sales as shown in Table 6.29. Miscellaneous prepayments indicate a whole year's ad valorem taxes. Inventories include 2 weeks' finished goods, 1 day of work in process, 2 weeks' raw materials, and 2 weeks' expendable supplies. Plant assets consist of land value and depreciated values on buildings and equipment. Total assets, which represent the sum of current assets and plant assets, are projected to increase gradually from slightly over $32 million in 1979 to $47 million and $48 million in 1988. They reflect general cash-account increases during this period.

Liabilities include current and long-term liabilities. Current liabilities consist of (1) accounts payable, which mean 2 weeks' raw material supplies; (2) accrued wages and other expenses, which include 2 weeks' wages, 1 month's salaries, and three months' insurance expenses; (3) estimated income taxes payable for a 3-month period; and (4) other current liabilities, which consist of 1 month's expenses for power, gas, and other utilities. Long-term liabilities reflect the standing long-term debt on that date.

Total assets minus total liabilities are equal to total equity. Total equity minus capital stock is equal to retained earnings. The TMP mill would show negative retained earnings figures in the first year's operation. Retained earnings would increase to $20 million at the end of the projected period, while total equity would increase to $30 million.

Profitability Analysis. Under this analysis, five methods are employed to measure the returns on the proposed investments. They are (1) net return on equity investment, (2) ratio of operating profit to total assets, (3) net return on sales, (4) debt service ratio, and (5) payback time. These profitability measures are discussed below.

1. *Net return on equity investment.* This is probably the most important measure of investment. It is a ratio of net earnings (profits) to equity investment and is expressed in percentage. Two measures can be employed: (1) net profit to capital stock and (2) net profit to tangible net worth. Capital stock is the money entrepreneurs and common stock holders put up for the investment, while tangible net worth is the sum of capital stock and retained earnings. Capital stock remains constant, while retained earnings increase over the years.

   Three years (1980, 1984, and 1988) were chosen for comparison purposes. Ratios for the TMP mill model are presented in Table 6.32 for the 3 years. In the case of tissue-grade TMP, net profit to capital stock will increase from 14.4% in 1980 to 23.7% in 1988, while net profit to tangible net worth will decrease from 12.4% to 7.7% in the same period. The rise in the former reflects the excellent profitability of the proposed project, while the decline in the latter indicates that the retained earnings can be better employed elsewhere. As mentioned previously, the retained earnings from accrued after-tax profits can be used for new ventures, for expansion of the existing mill, or for cash dividends to stockholders.

Table 6.30 Cash Flow Projections: Tissue-Grade TMP Mill

Year 1976	July	August	September	October	November	December
Opening Balance	$ 0	$192,000	$184,000	$176,000	$168,000	$160,000
Cash Receipts						
Collection of Receivables						
Net from Sales of Common Stock						
Investments (Founders' Stock)	500,000					
Short-Term Borrowing during Construction						
Long-Term Borrowing				300,000		
Total	$500,000	$192,000	$184,000	$476,000	$168,000	$160,000
Cash Disbursements						
Preoperational and Start-up Expenses	$ 8,000	$ 8,000	$ 8,000	$ 8,000	$ 8,000	$ 8,000
Payment for Raw Materials						
Payment for Labor						
Manufacturing Overhead						
Selling Expenses						
General and Administrative Expenses						
Payment for Fixed Assets	300,000			300,000		
Interest Payments						
Loan Repayments						
Payment on Income Taxes						
Other Taxes and Assessments						
Total	$308,000	$ 8,000	$ 8,000	$308,000	$ 8,000	$ 8,000
End Balance	$192,000	$184,000	$176,000	$168,000	$160,000	$152,000

(Continued)

Table 6.30 (Continued)

Year 1977	January	February	March	April	May
Opening Balance	$ 152,000	$817,000	$755,000	$ 624,650	$ 97,650
Cash Receipts					
Collection of Receivables					
Net from Sales of Common Stock	4,000,000				
Investments (Founders' Stock)				800,000	400,000
Short-Term Borrowing during Construction Period					
Long-Term Borrowing					
Total	$4,152,000	$817,000	$755,000	$1,424,650	$497,650
Cash Disbursements					
Preoperational and Start-up Expenses	$ 12,000	$ 12,000	$ 12,000	$ 12,000	$ 12,000
Payment for Raw Materials					
Payment for Labor					
Manufacturing Overhead					
Selling Expenses					
General and Administrative Expenses	3,323,000	50,000	118,350	1,315,000	435,000
Payment for Fixed Assets					
Interest Payments					
Loan Repayments					
Payment on Income Taxes					
Other Taxes and Assessments					
Total	$3,335,000	$ 62,000	$130,350	$1,327,000	$447,000
End Balance	$ 817,000	$755,000	$624,650	$ 97,650	$ 50,650

260

June	July	August	September	October	November	December
$ 50,650	$ 21,210	$1,864,210	$1,802,210	$1,505,210	$1,124,210	$1,062,210
1,000,000	3,000,000					
$1,050,650	$3,021,210	$1,864,210	$1,802,210	$1,505,210	$1,124,210	$1,062,210
$ 12,000	$ 12,000	$ 12,000	$ 12,000	$ 12,000	$ 12,000	$ 12,000
1,017,440	1,145,000	50,000	285,000	369,000	50,000	276,000
$1,029,440	$1,157,000	$ 62,000	$ 297,000	$ 381,000	$ 62,000	$ 288,000
$ 21,210	$1,864,210	$1,802,210	$1,505,210	$1,124,210	$1,062,210	$ 774,210

(Continued)

Table 6.30 (Continued)

Year 1978	January	February	March	April
Opening Balance	$ 774,210	$ 70,210	$ 175,210	$ 179,210
Cash Receipts				
Collection of Receivables				
Net from Sales of Common Stock				
Investments (Founders' Stock)				
Short-Term Borrowing during Construction Period	700,000	1,000,000	6,200,000	1,000,000
Long-Term Borrowing				
Total	$1,474,210	$1,070,210	$6,375,210	$1,179,210
Cash Disbursements				
Preoperational and Start-up Expenses	$ 20,000	20,000	20,000	20,000
Payment for Raw Materials				
Payment for Labor				
Manufacturing Overhead				
Selling Expenses				
General and Administrative Expenses				
Payments for Fixed Assets	1,365,000	875,000	6,176,000	1,130,000
Interest Payments				
Loan Repayments				
Payment on Income Taxes				
Other Taxes and Assessments	19,000			
Total	$1,404,000	$ 895,000	$6,196,000	$1,150,000
End Balance	$ 70,210	$ 175,210	$ 179,210	$ 29,210

May	June	July	August	September	October	November	December
$ 29,210	$ 59,210	$ 87,210	$ 96,760	$ 19,760	$ 26,860	$ 46,860	$ 55,860
1,000,000	1,500,000	700,000	800,000	850,000	1,400,000	550,000	22,898,140
$1,029,210	$1,559,210	$787,210	$896,760	$869,760	$1,426,860	$596,860	$22,954,000
20,000	20,000	25,000	25,000	25,000	75,000	218,000	320,000
950,000	1,452,000	665,450	852,000	817,900	1,305,000	323,000	380,000
							1,415,000
							15,700,000
$ 970,000	$1,472,000	$690,450	$877,000	$842,900	$1,380,000	$541,000	$17,815,000
$ 59,210	$ 87,210	$ 96,760	$ 19,760	$ 26,860	$ 46,860	$ 55,860	$ 5,139,000

(Continued)

263

Table 6.30 (Continued)

Year 1979	January	February	March	April	May
Opening Balance	$5,139,000	$3,862,933	$2,860,045	$2,829,311	$2,817,031
Cash Receipts					
Collection of Receivables			991,100	1,028,500	1,065,900
Net from Sales of Common Stock					
Investments (Founders' Stock)					
Short-Term Borrowing					
Long-Term Borrowing					
Total	$5,139,000	$3,862,933	$3,851,145	$3,857,811	$3,882,931
Cash Disbursements					
Payment for Raw Materials	$ 452,514	$ 469,590	$ 486,666	$ 503,742	$ 520,818
Payment for Labor	114,252	114,252	114,252	114,252	114,252
Manufacturing Overhead	89,500	89,500	89,500	89,500	89,500
Selling Expenses	49,555	51,425	53,295	55,165	57,035
General and Administrative Expenses	72,038	72,038	72,038	72,038	72,038
Interest Payments	171,736	171,478	171,219	170,957	170,694
Loan Repayments	34,347	34,605	34,864	35,126	35,389
Payment on Income Taxes					
Other Taxes and Assessments	292,125				
Total	$1,276,067	$1,002,888	$1,021,834	$1,040,780	$1,059,726
End Balance	$3,862,933	$2,860,045	$2,829,311	$2,817,031	$2,823,205
Monthly Production in Tons	5,300	5,500	5,700	5,900	6,100

June	July	August	September	October	November	December
$2,823,205	$2,847,832	$2,890,914	$2,952,449	$3,032,439	$3,130,883	$3,247,781
1,103,300	1,140,700	1,178,100	1,215,500	1,252,900	1,290,300	1,327,700
$3,926,505	$3,988,532	$4,069,014	$4,167,949	$4,285,339	$4,421,183	$4,575,481
$ 537,894	$ 554,970	$ 572,046	$ 589,122	$ 606,198	$ 623,274	$ 640,350
114,252	114,252	114,252	114,252	114,252	114,252	114,258
89,500	89,500	89,500	89,500	89,500	89,500	89,600
58,905	60,775	62,645	64,515	66,385	68,255	70,125
72,038	72,038	72,038	72,038	72,038	72,038	72,039
170,429	170,161	169,892	169,620	169,347	169,071	168,794
35,655	35,922	36,192	36,463	36,736	37,012	37,290
						0
$1,078,673	$1,097,618	$1,116,565	$1,135,510	$1,154,456	$1,173,402	$1,192,456
$2,847,832	$2,890,914	$2,952,449	$3,032,439	$3,130,883	$3,247,781	$3,383,025
6,300	6,500	6,700	6,900	7,100	7,300	7,500

(Continued)

Table 6.30 (Continued)

Operating Year	1979	1980	1981	1982
Opening Balance	$ 5,139,000	$ 3,383,025	$ 5,562,552	$ 8,143,799
Cash Receipts				
Collection of Receivables	11,594,000	19,660,600	20,750,800	21,505,700
Net from Sales of Common Stock				
Investments (Founders' Stock)				
Short-Term Borrowing				
Long-Term Borrowing				
Total	$16,733,000	$23,043,625	$26,313,352	$29,649,499
Cash Disbursements				
Payment for Raw Materials	$ 6,557,184	$ 8,708,760	$ 9,050,280	$ 9,391,800
Payment for Labor	1,371,030	1,371,030	1,371,030	1,371,030
Manufacturing Overhead	1,074,100	1,074,100	1,074,100	1,074,100
Selling Expenses	718,080	1,004,700	1,044,100	1,083,500
General and Administrative				
Expenses	864,457	864,457	864,457	864,457
Interest Payments	2,043,398	2,015,036	1,946,342	1,923,444
Loan Repayments	429,601	457,963	526,657	549,555
Payment on Income Taxes	0	1,692,902	2,000,462	2,232,650
Other Taxes and Assessments	292,125	292,125	292,125	292,125
Total	$13,349,975	$17,481,073	$18,169,553	$18,782,661
End Balance	$ 3,383,025	$ 5,562,552	$ 8,143,799	$10,866,838

266

1983	1984	1985	1986	1987	1988
$10,866,838	$13,805,839	$16,710,610	$19,578,287	$22,408,868	$25,189,989
22,359,500	22,458,000	22,458,000	22,458,000	22,458,000	22,458,000
$33,226,338	$36,263,839	$39,168,610	$42,036,287	$44,866,868	$47,647,989
$ 9,733,320	$ 9,733,320	$ 9,733,320	$ 9,733,320	$ 9,733,320	$ 9,733,320
1,371,030	1,371,030	1,371,030	1,371,030	1,371,030	1,371,030
1,074,100	1,074,100	1,074,100	1,074,100	1,074,100	1,074,100
1,122,900	1,122,900	1,122,900	1,122,900	1,122,900	1,122,900
864,457	864,457	864,457	864,457	864,457	864,457
1,854,749	1,808,953	1,740,258	1,671,564	1,579,972	1,511,277
618,250	664,046	732,740	801,435	893,027	961,722
2,489,568	2,622,298	2,659,393	2,696,488	2,745,948	2,783,043
292,125	292,125	292,125	292,125	292,125	292,125
$19,420,499	$19,553,229	$19,590,323	$19,627,419	$19,676,879	$19,713,974
$13,805,839	$16,710,610	$19,578,287	$22,408,868	$25,189,989	$27,934,015

Table 6.31 Balance Sheet: Tissue-Grade TMP Mill

Operating Year As of	1979 Jan. 1	1979 Dec. 31	1980 Dec. 31	1981 Dec. 31
ASSETS				
Current Assets				
Cash	$ 5,139,000	$ 3,383,025	$ 5,562,552	$ 8,143,799
Accounts Receivable		2,767,600	3,110,000	3,458,000
Miscellaneous Prepayments	292,000			
Inventories				
Finished Goods		691,900	777,500	864,500
Work in Process		13,200	17,500	18,200
Raw Materials	75,000	106,000	141,000	146,500
Expendable Supplies	52,000	68,800	91,400	95,000
Total Current Assets	$ 5,558,000	$ 7,030,525	$ 9,699,952	$12,725,999
Plant Assets				
Land	40,000	40,000	40,000	40,000
Buildings	1,743,000	1,655,850	1,568,700	1,481,550
Equipment	24,957,140	23,709,283	22,523,819	21,397,628
Total Assets	$32,298,140	$32,435,658	$33,832,471	$35,645,177
LIABILITIES AND OWNERS' EQUITY				
Current Liabilities				
Accounts Payable	$ 127,000	$ 234,640	$ 316,125	$ 328,508
Accrued Wages and Other Expenses		145,200	145,200	145,200
Estimated Income Taxes Payable		0	423,226	500,116
Other Current Liabilities		293,100	332,180	351,566
Total Current Liabilities	$ 127,000	$ 672,940	$ 1,216,731	$ 1,325,390
Long-Term Liabilities				
Mortgage Loan	22,898,140	22,463,075	22,005,112	21,478,455
Total Liabilities	$23,025,140	$23,136,015	$23,221,843	$22,803,845
Owners' Equity				
Capital Stock	$10,000,000	$10,000,000	$10,000,000	$10,000,000
Retained Earnings	(727,000)	(700,357)	610,628	2,841,332
Total Equity	$ 9,273,000	$ 9,299,643	$10,610,628	$12,841,332
Total Liabilities and Owners' Equity	$32,298,140	$32,435,658	$33,832,471	$35,645,177

1982 Dec. 31	1983 Dec. 31	1984 Dec. 31	1985 Dec. 31	1986 Dec. 31	1987 Dec. 31	1988 Dec. 31
$10,866,838	$13,805,839	$16,710,610	$19,578,287	$22,408,868	$25,189,989	$27,943,015
3,584,000	3,727,000	3,743,000	3,743,000	3,743,000	3,743,000	3,743,000
896,000	931,750	935,750	935,750	935,750	935,750	935,750
18,800	19,500	19,500	19,500	19,500	19,500	19,500
152,000	157,500	157,500	157,500	157,500	157,500	157,500
98,500	102,000	102,000	102,000	102,000	102,000	102,000
$15,616,138	$18,743,589	$21,668,360	$24,536,037	$27,366,618	$30,147,739	$32,900,765
40,000	40,000	40,000	40,000	40,000	40,000	40,000
1,394,400	1,307,250	1,220,100	1,132,950	1,045,800	958,650	871,500
20,327,747	19,311,359	18,345,791	17,428,502	16,557,077	15,729,223	14,942,762
$37,378,285	$39,402,198	$41,274,251	$43,137,489	$45,009,495	$46,875,612	$48,755,027
$ 340,792	$ 353,075	$ 353,075	$ 353,075	$ 353,075	$ 353,075	$ 353,075
145,200	145,200	145,200	145,200	145,200	145,200	145,200
558,163	622,392	655,575	664,848	674,122	686,487	695,761
364,833	371,260	371,260	371,260	371,260	371,260	371,260
$ 1,408,988	$ 1,491,927	$ 1,525,110	$ 1,534,383	$ 1,543,657	$ 1,556,022	$ 1,565,296
20,928,900	20,310,650	19,646,604	18,913,863	18,112,429	17,219,401	16,257,679
$22,337,888	$21,802,577	$21,171,714	$20,448,246	$19,656,086	$18,775,423	$17,822,975
$10,000,000	$10,000,000	$10,000,000	$10,000,000	$10,000,000	$10,000,000	$10,000,000
5,040,397	7,599,621	10,102,537	12,689,243	15,353,409	18,100,189	20,932,052
$15,040,397	$17,599,621	$20,102,537	$22,689,243	$25,353,409	$28,100,189	$30,932,052
$37,378,285	$39,402,198	$41,274,251	$43,137,489	$45,009,495	$46,875,612	$48,755,027

2. *Operating profit to total assets.* This ratio measures the earnings of the business from all its assets before taxes and compensation to the contributors of these assets. The operating profits are derived from the profit and loss statements given in the previous section, and the total assets come from the balance sheets. For the tissue pulp mills, the ratio will be about 20% in 1980 and will decline gradually to about 16.5% in 1988. The details are given in Table 6.32.

Table 6.32 Profitability Ratios for TMP Mill, 1980, 1984, and 1988 (based on 300 ADT/D capacity and 345 operating days a year)

Equation and Ratio	1980	1984	1988
Net profit	$1,442,102	$2,233,810	$2,370,000
Capital stock	$10,000,000	$10,000,000	$10,000,000
Ratio	14.4%	22.3%	23.7%
Net profit	$1,442,102	$2,233,810	$2,370,000
Tangible net worth	$11,610,628	$20,102,537	$30,932,052
Ratio	12.4%	11.1%	7.7%
Operating profit	$6,778,828	$8,000,068	$8,000,068
Total assets	$34,832,471	$41,274,251	$48,755,027
Ratio	19.5%	19.4%	16.4%
Net profit	$1,442,102	$2,233,810	$2,370,740
Net sales	$19,089,300	$21,335,100	$21,335,100
Ratio	7.6%	10.5%	11.1%
Initial capital investment		$32,898,140	
Annual cash flow		$2,233,810 + $1,335,007	
Payback time		9.2 years	

3. *Net return on sales.* This measure indicates the relationship between the net profit earned and the net selling value of the pulp produced. The ratio can vary substantially, purely on the basis of the financing structure of the company. Projections made for this study indicate a ratio of 7.6 to 11.1% for the tissue-grade mill. See details in Table 6.32.
4. *Debt service ratio.* This is calculated by dividing the estimated gross profit or operating profit of the enterprise for any year by the payments of both interest and debt retirement which are due under an agreement. In general trade practices, a ratio below 200% is regarded as poor, while a ratio above 200% is regarded as good. The ratio for the tissue-grade pulp mill is between 274 and 323%. Obviously, the returns are good enough to meet the loan

criteria of any lending institutions which might be approached to lend the capital required for such a venture. Details are given in Table 6.32.

5. *Payback time.* The payback or payout time is designed to estimate the number of years required to recover the capital invested in the proposed TMP mill. It is calculated by dividing initial capital investment by annual cash flow. Annual cash flow is the sum of after-tax profit and depreciation. The year 1984 was chosen as the estimating index point because it is the time in the projected period when the operational peak will be reached. Payout time is about 9 years for the tissue-grade TMP mill. The detailed calculations are given in Table 6.32.

Sensitivity Analysis. This is essentially a technique designed to measure the consequences of changing market conditions. There are certain unknown elements in any feasibility study. Changing demands, changing techniques in production, and changing price levels of end products, as well as raw material supplies, may give an entirely different outlook to a proposed project. Two methods of measuring these risk elements were used in this study: break-even analysis and sensitivity analysis of changes in price, sales volume, manufacturing cost, and fixed investment.

1. *Break-even analysis.* This method of evaluating risk determines the level of capacity at which a mill can work without incurring losses or making a profit. In most pulp mills the output of the mill exceeds the designed capacity. Under this study, the maximum output (114,000 ADT per year) exceeds the designed nominal capacity of 300 ADT/D by 10%. The break-even point is the level of production at which the total production costs are exactly covered by the sales revenues generated from the tonnage produced and sold. Two other break-even points are also calculated to cover manufacturing costs and to cover out-of-pocket costs. (See definitions of manufacturing costs, out-of-pocket costs, and total production costs on page 248.)

Detailed calculations and break-even points for the proposed TMP mill are given in Table 6.33. To break even with the total production costs, tissue-grade mills would have to produce and sell 72,808 tons annually; to cover out-of-pocket costs, tissue-grade mills would have to sell 59,691 tons annually; and to cover manufacturing costs, tissue-grade mills would have to sell 35,391 tons.

These break-even points are presented in graphic form for visual evaluation in Figure 6.5. The break-even point amounts to less than 70% of the full operational level of 114,000 tons a year. If sales go beyond the break-even point for total production costs, profit will occur. However, if sales lag behind the break-even point for total production costs, losses will take place.

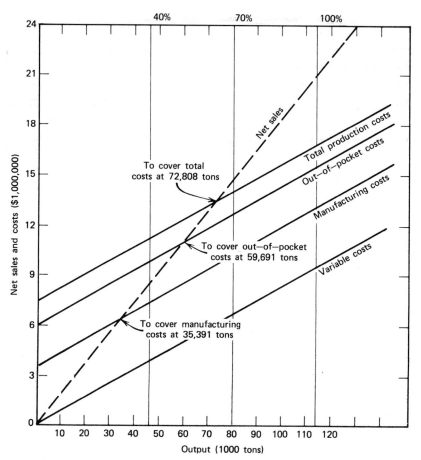

Figure 6.5 Break-even chart for a TMP mill, based on annual production of 114,000 tons of tissue-grade pulp.

2. *Sensitivity analysis.* This technique indicates how variations from the estimates of price, volume, manufacturing costs, and capital requirements made for this study would affect the enterprise. Alternative possibilities on sales price, sales volume, manufacturing cost, and fixed investments are given for the TMP mill in Table 6.34. If the sales prices are cut by 10%, the return on investment will decrease by 7%. If the sales volumes drop by 10%, the return on investment will drop by 5%. If the manufacturing costs rise by 10%, the return on investment will fall by 5%. If the fixed investments increase by 10%, the returns will decrease by about 3%. Finally, if the fixed investments are 10% less than the basic study amount, the returns will increase by 2%. It is obvious that the sales price of the end product has a

greater impact on the returns than any other factor. The impacts of manufacturing costs and sales volume on the returns are significant, but less than that of sales price. The fixed-investment changes have the least influence on the returns.

Table 6.33 Break-Even Points for TMP Mill (based on 114,000 ADT/year output)

Basic Calculation and Break-Even Points	Unit	
F.o.b. sales per ton	$	197.00
Sales expenses, 5%	$	9.85
Net sales per ton	$	187.15
Variable costs per ton	$	85.35
Profit before fixed costs, A	$	101.77
Annual fixed costs, B	$	3,601,712
Interest and debt service, C	$	2,472,999
Depreciation, D	$	1,335,007
Break-even for Manufacturing costs: B/A	Tons	35,391
Break-even for out-of-pocket costs: $(B + C)/A$	Tons	59,691
Break-Even for Total Production costs: $(B + C + D)/A$	Tons	72,808

CONCLUSION

The thermomechanical pulp mill proposed for construction in the Coastal Plains region of the United States is feasible from both the technical and social standpoints.

On the technical side, major concerns are raw material supplies, technologies, locational factors, market potentials for end products and investment requirements and projected returns. Raw material supplies have proved to be more than sufficient to build one TMP mill of 300 ADT/D capacity at Dublin and Montezuma in Georgia, Camden in South Carolina, and Selma in North Carolina. The supplies would come from sawmills willing to commit their wood chips and residues within a 100- to 150-mile radius of each chosen location.

TMP is regarded as the major breakthrough in pulping technology since the development of the kraft process four decades ago. The merits of TMP are high yields, improved quality of mechanical pulp, minimal pollution, and small operating units with small investment requirements relative to chemical pulp mills. Although TMP requires a larger power input per ton of pulp produced than other processes, the total power requirements of a TMP mill are not too

Table 6.34

| Item | Basic Study | Alternative Possibilities* (thousand $) | | | Fixed Investments | |
		Sales Price Cut by 10%	Sales Volume Cut by 10%	Manufacturing Cost Increased by 10%	Increased by 10%	Decreased by 10%
Net sales	21,335	19,201	19,201	21,335	21,335	21,335
Total manufacturing costs	13,335	13,335	12,500[b]	14,668	13,335	13,335
Operating profit	8,000	5,866	6,710	6,667	8,000	8,000
Fixed investment	26,740	26,740	26,740	26,740	29,414	24,066
Working capital	5,158	4,900[a]	4,900[a]	5,674	5,158	5,158
Total investment	31,898	31,640	31,640	32,414	34,572	29,224
Operating profit as percent of total investment	25.7%	18.5%	21.2%	20.6%	23.1%	27.4%
Difference between each alternative and basic study	0%	−7.2%	−4.5%	−5.1%	−2.6%	1.7%

[a] The working capital requirements vary with the volume of sales income and the level of manufacturing costs.

[b] A cut of 10% in sales volume with an accompanying cut in the volume of production does not result in a 10% savings in manufacturing cost. The fixed-cost items remain.

274

large and are within the supply capacities of power companies in Georgia, South Carolina, and North Carolina.

All four chosen locations have adequate supplies of wood raw materials, power, water, and labor. Each location is near a river which can be used as an outlet for waste-processing water after treatment. Adequate transportation networks exist for both incoming raw materials and outgoing products. Good industrial sites are available at each location.

Based on a worldwide market survey conducted under this study, it is obvious that the market pulp potentials for TMP lie in sanitary-tissue grades. Major markets would be ih the EEC countries, and domestic markets would be second in importance. In quantitative terms, the market is large enough to support a market sanitary-tissue TMP mill with a 300 ADT/D capacity. However, numerous private contacts with individual companies during the term of this study indicate that opportunities also exist for contract sales of TMP in board grade, newsprint grade, and magazine grade. Several major pulp and paper companies are interested in participating in financing the proposed TMP mills.

Fixed-capital investments for a TMP mill with a 300 ADT/D capacity would be about $26.7 million plus about $5.1 million working capital. Total production costs per ton of TMP would be about $157 for sanitary-tissue grade. This production cost compares favorably with f.o.b. net sales of $197 per ton for sanitary-tissue grade. The payout period for total capital invested would be 9 years.

From the social point of view, TMP mills in the region would provide an outlet for surplus wood chips and wood residues generated by participating sawmills. Income from the sale of wood chips and residues is essential to many sawmills. In addition, TMP produced in the region would alleviate the shortage of wood fiber supplies in the EEC countries. It also is possible that the produced TMP could reach Japan, which is one of the major pulp-importing nations. Establishment of TMP mills in the region would also mean jobs and incomes for many rural communities far beyond the wages and salaries projected in this study.

Chapter Seven

SOCIAL PROFITABILITY ANALYSIS

This chapter is aimed primarily at government loan officers, especially those in developing countries, who are concerned with how valuable a project will be to the economy, that is, its social profitability. If the analyst is interested only in the commercial profitability of a project, this chapter can be eliminated.

The rationale behind the appraisal criterion may be to select those projects for which the country's resources are most appropriate and to avoid the others. The appraisal criterion, then, is based on national objectives such as minimum use of foreign exchange, minimum fuel consumption per worker, maximum use of labor, minimum use of capital, or other factors. The project must be evaluated to estimate its contributions to the achievement of these objectives, and the appraisal criteria used are based on some form of investment guidelines.

In place of investment guidelines, the appraisal can involve a cost-benefit analysis to ascertain the social benefits and costs of the project so that social profitability can be estimated. Rather than focusing on a few important factors, cost-benefit analysis attempts to include all factors attributable to the project, both measurable and nonmeasurable.

The following discussion is not intended to be extensive but to provide a basic understanding of social profitability analysis and its relationship to the analysis of commercial profitability, which results from the economic feasibility study discussed in the preceding chapters.

Also, it should be remembered that both investment guidelines and cost-benefit analysis depend on government policy decisions. Social profitability cannot be determined using investment guidelines unless the government has provided them; likewise, social profitability cannot be determined using cost-benefit analysis unless government policy has provided guidelines on such factors as the discount rate to use and, if needed, shadow prices.

THE NEED FOR SOCIAL PROFITABILITY ANALYSIS

While the private sector is able to apply a yardstick of commercial profitability to make a choice among alternative projects, such a criterion is inadequate for the government analyst for several reasons.

Market imperfections, externalities, and income distribution are some of the factors that distort commercial profitability as a measure of the value of a project to the economy. For example, because of market imperfections, the current prices of the goods and resources involved in a project may not always reflect their real value to the economy as a whole. Therefore the use of commercial profits to determine the value of a project to the economy is not an accurate guide.

The role of the government, especially in developing countries, indicates a need for social profitability analysis. The government is faced with a continuous appraisal of projects, both those conducted by the private sector but financed with government funds and those in the private sector but subject to government permits. The government also must appraise private projects that require some form of government assistance such as tax relief, tariff protection, tax exemptions on imports of machinery or raw materials, or foreign exchange allocation. In actuality, then, particularly in developing countries, a great number of projects are within the range of government influence.

INVESTMENT GUIDELINES

For projects undertaken by the government, investment guidelines take the form of a set of administrative procedures, while for the private sector investment guidelines are often enacted into investment laws or investment priorities plans. Investment guidelines, whatever their form, are supposed to reflect national development objectives and provide a means of assigning priorities to projects. If self-sufficiency in food production is considered a national objective, agricultural projects may be assigned the highest priority. In different

circumstances, industrial projects may be favored if the growth of manufacturing is considered essential to overall economic development. Frequently, an
impediment to the growth of the economy, and therefore a consideration in
project selection, may be the scarcity of foreign exchange required for the im-
portation of fertilizers, capital equipment, or other items.

Investment guidelines are usually translated into more specific appraisal
criteria to assist in the selection of projects. For example, in countries with
foreign exchange difficulties, the usual procedure is to select projects solely on
the basis that they will be net savers or earners of foreign exchange, that is, a
"net foreign exchange savings" criterion.

In reality, this appraisal criterion, calling for the selection of projects whose
outputs can be exported or substituted for imports, eliminates very few projects. If it is considered that the prices of imported finished products comprise
payments for labor, capital services, and other inputs, the price when importing
raw materials or semifinished products will of course cover fewer of these costs.
Therefore, for a project that produces an imported product, it can be seen that
by importing its component parts rather than the product itself a saving of
foreign exchange takes place.

The net foreign exchange savings measure does not consider the basic
question of whether the proposed project can earn or save foreign exchange
better than alternative investments. The analyst must choose from efficient
and inefficient foreign exchange saving projects, that is, he must consider the
domestic resources required to save or earn a unit of foreign exchange. Even
with a more sophisticated net foreign exchange savings criterion, there are
other factors, such as employment generation, which need to be considered.

Investment guidelines also take the form of investment priorities plans. An
example of an investment priorities plan is the Eighth Investment Priorities
Plan[1] for the Philippines. This plan contains a list of priority projects which
have been identified by the Board of Investments as socially desirable and
therefore eligible to receive government assistance. The primary considerations
in the selection of priority projects are the general policy objectives:

- Promotion of labor-intensive projects.
- Regional dispersal of industries.
- Development of small- and medium-scale industries.
- Promotion of more manufactured exports.

The Eighth Investment Priorities Plan includes a list of projects as well as

[1] Board of Investments, "Eighth Investment Priorities Plan and First Public Utilities Priorities
Plan 1975" (Manila, Philippines, May 1975).

essential information related to scale, location, market orientation (export or domestic), and other factors.

The economic feasibility study should be conducted prior to the cost-benefit analysis because it provides these basic figures, as well as because the commercial profitability of the project is important to the government analyst. For instance, under certain conditions, the project may show a positive social profitability but a negative private profitability, or the opposite may be true. In order to induce investment by the private sector in a project with a high social profitability, government action in the form of subsidies or tax relief may be justified. In the opposite case, where private profitability is high but social profitability is negative, government action such as credit constraints to conserve scarce resources is necessary.

The manner in which cost-benefit analysis and social profitability differ from the commercial profitability resulting from an economic feasibility study becomes apparent in the following discussion. There are several texts which extensively cover the problems involved in conducting a cost-benefit analysis. Therefore the following discussion presents only the major considerations entailed in such a study.

COST-BENEFIT ANALYSIS

Cost-benefit analysis represents another approach to quantifying the social profitability of a project. There is no single prescribed procedure for conducting a cost-benefit analysis, but during the examination of a wide variety of projects a range of evaluation procedures has evolved.

Procedures for conducting a cost-benefit analysis have developed along two lines. In the more advanced countries, the majority of cost-benefit studies have been executed for projects whose outputs generate no revenue, such as education or recreation.

In the developing countries, however, cost-benefit analysis has been used primarily for projects that produce an output. Hence market prices exist, but market prices do not always reflect the social valuation of the goods produced or resources utilized. Since this text is concerned with the latter type of project, the following discussion concentrates on cost-benefit analysis as applied to revenue-generating projects.

The economic feasibility study provides the basic figures, that is, quantities of raw materials used, from which the commercial profitability can be measured. By means of cost-benefit techniques, these figures can be used in calculating the social profitability of a project. Although the economic feasibility study provides the raw data with which the analyst can begin, these data can be collected without undertaking such a study.

National Objectives

The relationship between cost-benefit analysis for project appraisal and national objectives is that the criteria to be employed in a cost-benefit analysis must be derived from, or consonant with, national objectives and reflect this relationship. For example, benefits are quantifications of the extent to which advantageous effects take place. In order to be aware of what is preferable, one must be familiar with national objectives. In cost-benefit analysis, then, one has to consider as a benefit any contribution to the accomplishment of a national objective, and as a cost any employment of resources that might have been otherwise used.

In the more advanced countries cost-benefit analysis has concentrated almost exclusively on the objective of achieving an efficient economy, that is, one in which output, utility, and therefore welfare are maximized. The welfare of the nation is presumed to be a function of the national income; consequently, the national income is often suggested as a measure.

Problems are encountered when the national income is used as a measure of welfare. For instance, the national income includes certain factors such as pecuniary spillovers which should not be included when efficiency is the objective, but does not consider factors such as leisure which increase welfare. However, although real national income is not an adequate measure of welfare, changes in the national income do provide, under most circumstances, an indication of changes in welfare. Hence the measure of the change in welfare for the efficiency objective, then, is the value of the incremental output minus its cost.

There are several objectives, such as the equitable distribution of income either by region or by class, which are sometimes argued to be as important as maximizing economic welfare. Multiple objectives present problems, because it is difficult to incorporate them into a measure by which to ascertain the net benefits of a project. Suggested approaches have been to maximize a weighted sum of net benefits by assigning, in some manner, weights to each objective, which can then be applied to the project's benefits satisfying each objective. Another way to treat multiple objectives is to structure them as constraints. In this instance the approach may be to maximize efficiency benefits subject to constraints on regional income benefits and the quality of the environment.[2]

---

[2] For further discussion, see Leonard Merewitz and Stephen H. Susnick, *The Budget's New Clothes* (Chicago: Markham Publishing Co., 1971), Chaps. 8 and 9, and Hartmut Schneider, *National Objectives and Project Appraisal in Developing Countries* (Paris: OECD, 1975).

An approach to the incorporation of multiple objectives, which has been developed and used in developing countries, is to reflect such objectives in shadow prices. For example, if employment is an objective, the government may assign a shadow price of zero for unskilled labor and use it in the cost-benefit analysis rather than using the market price, or more likely the social value, for labor. Such treatment of labor reflects the government objective of measuring employment by assigning no social cost for the utilization of unskilled labor.[3]

Another treatment of multiple objectives in a cost-benefit analysis is to maximize national welfare but to provide exhibits which indicate regional income benefits, foreign exchange benefits, class income redistribution benefits, and others. With the present state of the art in cost-benefit analysis, this approach has certain appeal. Since in most countries weights have not been explicitly assigned to objectives by a government planning organization, this procedure allows the decision maker to use his judgment in attaching weights to the efficiency objective, income redistribution objective, and others. A disadvantage of such an approach is that there is not a single measure that can be used to rank projects.

Project Definition

The starting point for a cost-benefit analysis is a definition of the proposed project, which includes a technical description of the project, alternatives which should be considered, and any pertinent constraints.

The technical description of the project should include an assessment of the quantities and types of resource inputs, as well as the time frame in which they are utilized. Similar information is required concerning the final goods of the project, along with the nature and physical dimensions of known "externalities." If an economic feasibility analysis has been completed prior to the cost-benefit analysis, the majority of the required technical information can be obtained from it.

The study approach can consider only cost-benefits that arise from either implementation or nonimplementation of the project, or it can be more comprehensive and consider other alternatives. For instance, if the objective is to manufacture a specific output, other, perhaps more realistic, alternatives to consider may involve alternative technologies which embody different

[3] See United Nations Industrial Development Organization, *Guidelines for Project Evaluation* (New York: United Nations, 1972), and I. M. D. Little and J. A. Mirrlees, *Project Appraisal and Planning for Developing Countries* (New York: Basic Books, 1974).

combinations of labor and capital as well as alternative economies of scale. In the construction of a new plant, another alternative may be to expand an existing plant. Each alternative should be compared with the "status quo" scenario, which is defined as society without the alternative. The net benefits or the difference each alternative makes as compared with the status quo can then be compared with each other.

Considering appropriate alternatives is most important in cost-benefit analysis. Suppose, for example, that the construction of a new plant shows positive net benefits for the society. This project, nevertheless, would still be the wrong choice if even higher net benefits could result by expanding the existing plant.

The consideration of alternatives involves more work for the analyst, yet it is not so much as it may seem at first. Any cost or benefit not affected by the alternatives under consideration can be disregarded. For instance, in the case of a cost-benefit analysis of manufacturing the proposed project output by using alternative technologies, the administrative, distribution, and selling expenses need not be considered because it is unlikely that they will differ.

Recognition of relevant constraints also should be included in the project definition, because this quickly eliminates any alternatives that do not qualify and also provides guidelines for the analyst as he selects the alternatives to consider. Prest and Turvey provide a discussion and classification of constraints: physical, legal, administrative, budgeting, and distribution.[4]

The previous discussion on national objectives and their relationship to the project indicates that the cost-benefit analysis cannot always be made solely on the grounds of *efficiency* but may have to take into account other considerations such as income distribution.

The project definition also should include a definition of society. Some of the benefits, as well as costs, of a project affect the vicinity where the project is located, some are statewide, and still others may be spread throughout the nation. Therefore the boundaries of society must be defined in order to determine the costs and benefits to be counted.

Enumeration of Costs and Benefits

The project feasibility analysis conducted from the private viewpoint is concerned with the receipts and expenditures generated and the resultant commercial profitability. The inputs and outputs of the project attached to these

[4] A. R. Prest and R. Turvey, "Cost-Benefit Analysis: A Survey," in *Surveys of Economic Theory*, Vol. III (New York: St. Martin's Press, 1967), pp. 172–174.

receipts and expenditures provide the basis for identifying the internal social costs and benefits of the project. The technical description taken from the project definition will yield the necessary data if an economic feasibility analysis has not been completed.

In addition to the internal costs and benefits that occur, there is also a class of costs and benefits which are imposed on others during the construction and operation of the project and for which nothing is received or paid. These effects are external costs and benefits or, collectively, externalities or spillovers of the project. Pecuniary and technological externalities are the two types that have been identified.

Technological Externalities. A technological externality of a project involves physical effects on others and should be included in the cost-benefit analysis. Technological externalities can result from uncompensated effects of the project which affect the physical outputs possibility, either in quantity or quality, that other producers can achieve from their physical inputs. Similarly, technological externalities can involve uncompensated effects on the satisfaction consumers receive from their inputs, such as the quality of the goods they consume or its effect on the environment. Technological externalities, then, can be distinguished by the fact that they affect the amount of output that other producers or consumers receive from a fixed amount of input. Such externalities occur with the uncompensated use of a resource that is shared with others. For instance, if a project pollutes the atmosphere, the result is a genuine cost to the neighborhood, which is difficult to measure. Another cost is that incurred by the local manufacturer who can no longer utilize the outdoors to dry his product because of the pollution and therefore must find an alternative means.

Pecuniary Externalities. Pecuniary externalities are composed of the financial effects of the project upon others. A cost-benefit analysis conducted with the objective of economic efficiency and including pecuniary externalities is double counting. However, if the objective of the cost-benefit analysis includes income redistribution, for example, the pecuniary externalities are relevant because they represent the income transfer or distributional effects of the project.

McKean classifies pecuniary externalities into four types; considering whether the project increases factor rates of hire, cuts down prices of substitute products, raises prices of complementary products, or lowers the price of the output.[5]

[5] For detailed discussion, see Roland N. McKean, *Efficiency in Government through Systems Analysis* (New York: Wiley, 1958), pp. 136–141.

For example, where a project results in the expansion of an industry and the increased output lowers the price of the project's output, it is incorrect to include the reduced price as a benefit to consumers. Nor can the damages resulting from the lower price be included as a cost by the original producers, since such items represent transfers.

Secondary Benefits.   Secondary benefits can be regarded as a form of pecuniary externalities, although they do not fit exactly into any of the categories mentioned. Except for special circumstances where persistent unemployment exists, capital is underutilized, or increasing returns to scale exist, they should not be included in a cost-benefit analysis where the main concern is an efficient economy.[6] If, however, the objective is regional redistribution of income, the above conditions do not have to apply and secondary benefits should be included.

Secondary benefits are composed of incomes *stemming from* or *induced by* the project. Stemming benefits are the increase in profits that can be attributed to the increased activity of processors, truckers, railroads, merchants, and others using or handling the project's output before it reaches the consumer. Induced benefits are the increase in profits from activities which supply inputs to the project.

Intangibles.   Intangibles are costs and benefits that cannot be readily translated into the common denominator being used, which in most studies is dollars.[7] Some effects of the project, such as the destruction of a scenic historic site or the loss of prestige, cannot be quantified at all. Others, such as air pollution, although they cannot be measured with market prices, can be quantified by using some other unit of measure.

Intangibles should not be eliminated from the cost-benefit analysis merely because they do not lend themselves to quantification in terms of dollars. The treatment of intangibles should be to provide a concise description and, if possible, present some quantitative indicators.

The various categories of project effects such as internal costs and benefits, technological and pecuniary externalities, secondary benefits, and intangibles are useful in the identification of the costs and benefits of a project. It is possible, however, that a benefit or cost fits into more than one category, and the analyst must be careful to avoid double counting.

[6] *Ibid.*, pp. 154–163, and Otto Eckstein, *Water Resource Development* (Cambridge, Mass.: Harvard University Press, 1958), pp. 211–212.
[7] McKean, p. 58.

Since, in the majority of cases, economic efficiency is one of the project's objectives, only increases in income from the project that result in an increase in national income are of primary interest, and not the income transfers, although exhibits showing income distribution can be prepared. The following questions are helpful in this regard.

- Is there any real output or production that is destroyed or not undertaken because of the project?
- Are any resources or productive inputs destroyed or caused to lie idle because of the project?
- Is there any loss of consumption or investment because of the project?[8]

Measurement of Costs and Benefits

After the analyst has identified the costs and benefits emanating from the project, he must then measure them. The process of measurement requires the quantification of the costs and benefits and their valuation. The valuation of costs and benefits can be accomplished using market prices and shadow prices.

For some benefits and costs no meaningful monetary valuation may be possible. Such would be the case if the project were sited so that the destruction of a beautiful landscape or historic site resulted. Although no valuation is possible, these intangible benefits and costs should not be dropped from the analysis, but presented, if only in a descriptive form, along with the other results.

Market Prices.   For those items in the cost-benefit analysis for which market prices exist, the initial inclination is to use them to evaluate costs and benefits. Cost-benefit studies in the more advanced countries have assumed that the price mechanism works and, for the most part, have used market prices where available, except for special circumstances such as in the case where the project's output is large relative to the total market. Also, in the more advanced countries, cost-benefit analysis has concentrated on the valuation of costs and benefits for which no market prices exist but appropriate social values can be approximated in money terms. However, the important question, especially for developing countries, is whether the market prices reflect the real costs and the real benefits to the society.

Shadow Prices.   To better reflect the real costs of inputs to society and the

---

[8] Harley H. Hinrichs and Graeme M. Taylor, *Systematic Analysis* (Pacific Palisades, Calif.: Goodyear Publishing Co., Inc., 1972), pp. 19–20.

real benefits of the outputs attributable to the project, shadow prices are used in place of market prices. Shadow prices are used in cost-benefit analysis when no market prices exist, when market imperfections are present, or when political and social objectives are incorporated into the valuation process.

For costs and benefits where no market prices exist, shadow prices can be constructed if social values can be approximated in money terms by inferring the price that consumers would be willing to pay if the product were available.

In developing countries market imperfections are the primary reason why adjustments to market prices are necessary. The shadow prices of labor, for example, in the case where unemployment exists, can be valued as zero even though market wages are paid. This is because, in terms of other goods or services foregone, it costs society nothing to have the unemployed labor used. Some examples of other market imperfections are listed below:

- Price controls are used for selected items, and this disturbs the relationship between relative prices.
- Import controls often cause a distortion between the market price of goods and the real cost of producing them.
- The price of foreign exchange is set by the government, and this results in the country's currency being either undervalued or overvalued, hence a distortion in domestic prices relative to world prices.
- Interest rates have an enormous range, as a result of factors such as government intervention and monopoly elements in the supply of capital.[9]

Shadow prices also can be used to incorporate political and social judgments into the valuation process. If society considers unemployment undesirable, the shadow price of labor can be set by an act of policy and assigned a negative value. This treatment of labor means that the employment of labor should be considered a benefit and not a cost.

The need for shadow prices, especially in developing countries, has resulted in several publications on the correct manner to calculate such values. One approach to determining the shadow prices for a project's inputs and outputs is to use world prices.[10] The cost to the economy, that is, the shadow prices, of the project's inputs and outputs, which are traded or substituted for traded goods, are either c.i.f. import prices or the f.o.b. prices. Techniques have been developed to derive shadow prices for nontraded goods and services, as well as

[9] Adapted from Little and Mirrlees, pp. 29–36.
[10] *Ibid*, and Lyn Squire and Herman G. van der Tak, *Economic Analysis of Projects* (Baltimore: Johns Hopkins University Press, 1975). Also, for a critique, see the *Bulletin of the Oxford* University Institute of Economics and Statistics, **34** (Feb. 1972).

shadow wage rates. Although the concept of shadow prices is intuitively appealing, the practical aspects of cost-benefit analysis suggest that, unless a complete set of shadow prices is provided by the government, the calculation of such values is beyond the means of the analyst.

Final Considerations

At this point in the cost-benefit analysis the analyst has collected the majority of the data needed for analysis. To complete it he must determine the rate to discount the costs and benefits of the project, the life of the project, what adjustments to make for uncertainty, and the decision criteria to use. And finally, he must explore the sensitivity of the analysis to the variation of critical parameters such as the discount rate.

Choice of Interest Rate. Unfortunately, there is no universal agreement, in principle, concerning the rate to choose for discounting the costs and benefits of a project. The debate is concerned with whether to use the social time preference rate or the social opportunity cost rate of interest and how to determine the values of each.[11] In practice, however, these theoretical discussions need not concern the analyst, because the discount rate is usually a policy variable, that is, it is set by the government. For presentation in the cost-benefit analysis, it is useful to compute the critical discount rate, defined as the rate of interest that will move the project from the acceptance to the rejection category.

Life of the Project. The analyst must decide how far into the future to forecast the costs and benefits arising from the project, and therefore the extent to which they are counted into the net present value of the project. Values far into the future, depending on the discount rate, usually have small present value. The higher the discount rate, the smaller the present value for a given time horizon. For instance, $1.00 received 40 years from now has a present value of $0.14 when the discount rate is 5% per year, and a present value of $0.02 when the discount rate is 10% per year. The estimate of the project life can be based on the physical or economic life of the primary capital inputs coupled with a subjective evaluation of the possibility of technological

[11] For concise discussion, see H. G. Walsh and Alan Williams, *Current Issues in Cost-Benefit Analysis*, C A S Occasional Paper No. 11 (London: Her Majesty's Stationery Office, 1969), pp. 11–14.

obsolescence and changes in future demand and competition, or the life of the project can be a policy decision by the government.

Decision Criteria. The computational procedures for the different criteria— net present value, internal rate of return, benefit/cost ratio, and others—that can be used to rank and evaluate alternative projects are discussed in the Appendix. The net present value criterion is, in general, the preferable for most cost-benefit analyses.

Sensitivity Analysis. Sensitivity analysis or parameterization can be used to examine how the project's net benefits (e.g., net present value) vary with changes in the parameters of the study, especially those where uncertainty in their values exist. For instance, the decision maker may want to know the effects of changes in the discount rate on the net present value. The analyst can calculate net present value for the project at a low, medium, and high discount rate, or he can use a graphical presentation as in Figure 5.3. The sensitivity techniques used in the financial analysis also are applicable to cost-benefit analysis.

Adjustments for Risk. Many risks are intrinsic to a project. Construction or start-up operations may take longer than projected; the prices of raw materials, labor, or other inputs, as well as finished products, may differ from expectations; a new technology may render the project obsolete; or the finished products may not meet the operational or quality expectations.

The techniques for treating risk in a project, which were discussed in the financial analysis, are equally applicable in cost-benefit analysis. See Pouliquen for examples of the use of risk analysis in a cost-benefit study.[12]

Presentation of Results. The presentation of the cost-benefit analysis should include all the following elements: the project definition; a display of the costs and benefits to society where society is defined as a nation, a region, or a specific group; the net present value for the alternative or alternatives; the sensitivity analysis for critical uncertain parameters; and appropriate supplementary exhibits on uncertainty, intangibles, and distributional effects associated with the project.

[12] Louis Y. Pouliquen, *Risk Analysis in Project Appraisal*, World Bank Staff Occasional Papers No. 11 (Baltimore: Johns Hopkins Press, 1972).

BIBLIOGRAPHY

Bryce, Murray D. *Industrial Development.* New York: McGraw-Hill, 1961.

Dasgupta, Ajit K., and D. W. Pearce. *Cost-Benefit Analysis.* New York: Harper & Row, 1972.

Dasgupta, Partha. "An Analysis of Two Approaches to Project Evaluation in Developing Countries," in *Industrialization and Productivity,* Bulletin 15. New York: United Nations, 1970.

Ekstein, Otto. *Water Resources Development.* Cambridge, Mass.: Harvard University Press, 1958.

Hinrichs, Harley H., and Taylor M. Graeme. *Systematic Analysis.* Pacific Palisades, Calif. Goodyear Publishing Co., 1972.

Howe, Charles W. *Benefit-Cost Analysis for Water System Planning.* Water Resources Monograph 2. Baltimore: Publication Press, 1972.

Lesourne, Jacques. *Cost-Benefit Analysis and Economic Theory.* New York: American Elsevier Publishing Co., 1975.

Little, I. M. D., and J. A. Mirrlees. *Project Appraisal and Planning for Developing Countries.* New York: Basic Books, 1974.

McKean, Roland N. *Efficiency in Government through Systems Analysis.* New York: Wiley, 1958.

Mears, Leon A. *Economic Project Evaluation.* Manila: University of the Philippines Press, 1969.

Merewitz, Leonard, and Stephen H. Sosnick. *The Budget's New Clothes.* Chicago: Markham. 1971.

Mishan, E. J. *Economics for Social Decisions.* New York: Praeger, 1973.

Noriega, Bienvenido M., Jr. "An Analysis of the Investment Priorities Plans and the Export Priorities Plans of the Board of Investments," *NEDA Journal of Development,* 1, No. 1 (1974).

Pearce, D. W. *Cost-Benefit Analysis.* London: Macmillan, 1971.

Pouliquen, Louis Y. *Risk Analysis in Project Appraisal.* World Bank Staff Occasional Papers No. 11. Baltimore: Johns Hopkins Press, 1972.

Prest, A. R., and R. Turvey. "Cost-Benefit Analysis: A Survey," in *Surveys of Economic Theory,* Vol. II. New York: St. Martin's Press, 1967.

Reutlinger, Shlomo. *Techniques for Project Appraisal under Uncertainty.* World Bank Staff Occasional Papers No. 10. Baltimore: Johns Hopkins Press, 1972.

Sassone, Peter G., and William A. Schaffer. *Cost-Benefit Analysis: A Handbook.* New York: Academic Press, in press.

Schneider, Hartmut. *National Objectives and Project Appraisal in Developing Countries.* Paris: Organization for Economic Cooperation and Development, 1975.

Scitovsky, Tibor. "Two Concepts of External Economics," *Journal of Political Economy,* **62.** (April 1954).

Scitovsky, Lyn, and Herman G. Von der Tak. *Economic Analysis of Projects.* Published for the World Bank. Baltimore: John Hopkins Press, 1975.

UNIDO, *Guidelines for Project Evaluation,* P. S. Dasgupta, S. A. Marglin, and A. K. Sen. New York: United Nations, 1972.

Walsh, H. G., and Alan Williams. *Current Issues in Cost-Benefit Analysis.* CAS Occasional Papers No. 11. London: Her Majesty's Stationery Office, 1971.

Chapter Eight

FINANCING
THE PROJECT

As one experienced entrepreneur stated, "The best way for an entrepreneur or businessman to raise money is to know people who have money and who are willing to lend it to him." Since almost everyone knows people who have money and yet the difficulties in venture funding are widely acknowledged, the crucial part of the statement must be "willing to lend it." Generally speaking, most people are unwilling to part with their money unless they have great assurance that it will be returned with an adequate gain to compensate them for its use and also for the risk involved. The higher the risk, the higher the required gain. If the maximum anticipated gain is insufficient to offset the risk, an investor would be foolish to back a project. In order to obtain money, the businessman or entrepreneur must indeed know people who have money and are willing to lend it. The point is that he must *make them willing to lend it*. This means that he must convince them that the anticipated returns are more than adequate for the risk involved. To do this he must present a credible picture of both the anticipated returns and the risk.

Previous chapters have provided step-by-step procedures for a feasibility analysis, the primary purpose of which is to convince the entrepreneur that his project idea is or is not financially attractive. This chapter is concerned with convincing potential investors that they should back the project. While they are certainly interested in the sales plan, manufacturing plan, and financial analysis developed in the feasibility study, they are not likely to be concerned about the details, nor do they want to wade through the entire feasibility analysis to obtain crucial information. In fact, the investment proposal will quite likely compete with dozens of others for the attention of a busy investor. If it cannot convince him of the merits of the project in about 5 minutes, it will be passed over. In that short time he wants to know more than the results of the feasibility analysis. Who is the entrepreneur? Does he have the capability to manage the business? What is his track record? Who else is involved? What is his management plan? How much money does he have? How much more does he want? What is he going to do with it? These questions and more must be answered.

The objective of this chapter is to demonstrate how to prepare an investment proposal which will be effective in selling the project to potential investors. In order to do this, we first discuss briefly some considerations in venture financing decisions, legal structures and their effects on financing, sources of funds (i.e., where to look for money), and what potential investors will want to know about the entrepreneur, his current business (if he has one), and his proposed venture.

FINANCING CONSIDERATIONS

If it is at all possible, the entrepreneur should furnish his own initial funding even if he is forced to mortgage his home, borrow on the cash value of his life insurance, and sacrifice his standard of living. In many cases, however, no amount of sacrifice can produce the required money, and he must seek help from outsiders. His all-important question is, "Where can I get the money?" The answer to this question depends on the answers to several questions which must precede it:

- Should "outside" money be equity or debt financing?
- What legal structure should I choose and how will it affect financing?
- How much equity do I need?
- How much money must I raise and when will it be needed?

Equity versus Debt

Depending on the legal structure chosen for the company, the entrepreneur may have a choice between debt, equity funding, and/or some combination of these. Kelley et al. explain that the financial needs of a company are met by renting, leasing, or buying funds. A loan or short-term debt is *rented* by paying interest. Money is *leased* through debentures or bonds with a relatively long fixed payback period. Money is *bought* by selling shares in the business.[1]

Rented and leased funds are classed as debt. The principal advantage of debt financing is that the founding entrepreneur does not have to give up any of the ownership. Moreover, interest paid on the debt is treated as an expense of business operation and deducted from gross profits before taxes. On the negative side, the debt must be repaid in amounts and at times specified by the terms of the loan. Since the profits of the new firm are not guaranteed as to either timing or amount, there is always the possibility that it will find itself unable to service a large debt obligation. It is little wonder, then, that debt money is difficult to obtain for the new venture. Even if borrowed money can be obtained, an excessive amount may jeopardize the company's flexibility in obtaining future short-term credit to meet unexpected needs.

The financial foundation for the new firm must be equity capital, that is, money that is bought. Equity money represents ownership in the business. It has the advantage that no interest is paid, and it does not have to be paid back. Further, its use to purchase unencumbered assets provides the collateral necessary to obtain loans when debt money is needed.

In order to obtain equity capital from outsiders, the entrepreneur must give up part of his company. Thus he will have to share not only the future profits of the enterprise, but also its control. Since the new venture has no earnings record and no tangible assets, it is difficult to set a price on its common stock. A reasonable estimate can be obtained by applying the average price/earnings ratio of similar companies already in operation to the pro forma earnings projections. Needless to say, potential investors are likely to view an estimate obtained in this manner with skepticism. The actual price will be established by what the market will pay.

Legal Structure

The legal form of organization chosen for the new business may not be critical to its success, but it does have considerable influence on business financing, taxes, and other matters. Patrick Liles in his book, *New Business Ventures and the Entrepreneur*, discusses seven considerations which should affect the choice of business structure.

[1] Albert J. Kelley, Frank B. Campanella, John McKiernan, *Venture Capital—A Guidebook for New Enterprises* (Boston: The Management Institute, School of Management, Boston College, 1971), p. 4.

1. Organization requirements and their cost.
2. Liability of owners.
3. Continuity of the concern.
4. Transferability of interest.
5. Management and control.
6. Attractiveness for raising capital.
7. Tax treatment.[2]

The relative importance of these considerations is a matter for legal advice, and the decision should not be made without consulting a lawyer. In fact, if the new business is started, it is certain that a lawyer will be needed and the legal structure decision provides a good occasion to establish a relationship with a lawyer. Liles offers four rules regarding legal advice that the entrepreneur should keep in mind:

1. Find a lawyer.
2. Find the best lawyer available.
3. Base the choice on the lawyer's reputation, particularly in the area of new ventures. Avoid choosing a lawyer merely because he is a friend or (worse) a relative.
4. Attempt to understand as many of the legal issues as possible.[3]

The most common legal structures for businesses in the United States are the *sole proprietorship*, *general partnership*, *limited partnership*, and *corporation*. The discussions that follow attempt only to present an overview of important differences in these forms of organization, with particular attention to how each affects the financing of the business.

The Sole Proprietorship. The sole proprietorship is complete ownership by one individual. It is the most simple form of business organization and the most frequently used. If he operates in his own name, anyone can start a business. No legal procedure is necessary to set up a business as a sole proprietor and there are no organization costs.[4] Moreover, the type of business and its location can be changed without legal action. The proprietor has complete freedom in

---

[2] Patrick R. Liles, *New Business Ventures and the Entrepreneur* (Homewood, Ill.: Richard D. Irwin, 1974), p. 79.

[3] *Ibid.*, p. 75.

[4] A license for certain types of businesses may be required. A check of such requirements should be made in the locality where the business will be located. Also, if the business is operated under a tradename, a filing fee may be required.

all management and policy decisions, subject of course to the plethora of red tape and regulations imposed by federal regulatory agencies, which are a cross all businesspeople must bear. He may sell the business or end it at any time he chooses. However, since the proprietor *is* the business, it has no more permanence than he does. When the proprietor dies, so does the business.

For tax purposes, profits of the business are treated as ordinary income of the proprietor, and losses from the business can be used to offset against other income. Since the business itself pays no taxes on its profits, there is no double taxation as in the case of corporate profits distributed to the owners.

The sole proprietorship, however, is not without disadvantages. The entire assets—business and nonbusiness—of the sole proprietor are at risk and will be seized to satisfy creditors if the business fails. (It should be noted that this probably is true for other forms of business organization. Lenders generally insist that business principals pledge their personal assets along with business assets as collateral for loans.) Moreover, legal judgments against the company will be satisfied by the proprietor's personal assets. This is perhaps the strongest disadvantage of the sole proprietorship.

The sole proprietor has some disadvantages in raising capital. He must furnish every penny of equity capital. If others invest in the business, they will do so on the basis of loans. Since they cannot share in the potential growth, there is little incentive for an investor to risk his money. The result is that the funds the proprietor can borrow are severely restricted.

The General Partnership. A general partnership is formed when two or more persons co-own the business. Partnerships are often formed to pool the resources or talent of the individual partners. Management responsibilities customarily are divided among the partners. Persons with diverse backgrounds and business experience therefore can constitute an effective management team.

A written agreement of the partnership arrangement is not required, but it is highly recommended. Without it, the partnership arrangement is likely to be a source of unending disagreements which jeopardize the success of the company. Murphy suggests that the partnership agreement include:

1. The name of the company and a description of the business to be conducted.
2. The capital contribution of each partner.
3. The amount and nature of the services to be contributed by each partner.
4. Salaries and withdrawals to be made by each partner.
5. An explanation of how profits (or losses) will be divided among the partners.

6. Restrictions, if any, on the authority of each partner.
7. The method to be used when admitting new partners.
8. The procedure to be followed in the event of voluntary dissolution of the partnership.
9. The procedure to be followed in the event of the death or disability of a partner. This commonly includes some provision for life insurance and a method for computing the value of the partnership interest.[5]

Needless to say, this document should be written by a competent lawyer. With the exception of the desirability of written articles of agreement, the partnership is no more difficult to form than the sole proprietorship and enjoys the same freedoms. However, the freedom of any individual partner cannot approach that of the sole proprietor, since each must share management prerogatives with the other partners. Moreover, actions of any partner on behalf of the company are binding on all partners whether or not they agreed to the act.

Partners are individually and collectively responsible for the liabilities of the company. As with the proprietorship, the general partners have unlimited liability, and legal judgments against the company can be satisfied by the personal assets of the partners. The general partnership has other disadvantages unless they are specifically provided for in the articles of agreement.

1. *The partnership is dissolved on the withdrawal or death of one of the partners.* The articles of agreement may stipulate how each of these events is to be handled in order to ensure continuity of the company. For example, the agreement may provide a method for computing the value of a partnership interest and provide for an option for purchase by the other partners of any partner's interest on his withdrawal or death.
2. *A partner may not sell his interest without the consent of all other partners.* The partnership agreement may, for example, provide for transferability of any partner's interest after first offering that interest to the remaining partners at a specified price.

The ability to raise capital is strengthened by the partnership. It pools the resources of two or more people along with their credit. If the partnership agreement is well written, this form of business organization offers more stability and permanence than the proprietorship and is therefore more attractive to a lender.

[5] Thomas P. Murphy, *A Business of Your Own* (New York: McGraw-Hill, 1956), pp. 205–206.

The Limited Partnership. The limited partnership is always a contractual agreement between one or more general partners and one or more limited partners. The general partners may invest cash, tangible property, or services and are responsible for the operation of the business. They share unlimited personal liability for all obligations of the business. The investment of the limited partners may be in the form of cash or tangible property, but not services. However, the liability of limited partners cannot exceed their invested capital. These individuals may not participate in any way in the management of the business or otherwise exercise control over the business, or they will lose their special status as limited partners.

The limited partnership form of organization is created by statute, and most states require the filing of a written document with a specified statutory authority. This document must designate general partners and limited partners and the amount of contribution of each. Some states also require the filing of the written articles of agreement, and it may be necessary to give public notice in a newspaper that the limited partnership has been formed and to list the limited partners. The liability limitation is binding only in states where statutory requirements are met. If the firm does business in other states, it must meet their requirements or be regarded as a general partnership with unlimited liability for all partners.

Unless the partnership agreement provides otherwise, the limited partnership is automatically terminated by death or withdrawal of any of the general partners. Also, unless the agreement provides otherwise, a general partner cannot sell his share of the business without the consent of all the other general partners. Limited partners, since they have no active role in the business, are permitted to transfer their interests at will. From a tax standpoint, the limited partnership operates like the general partnership. Each partner's pro rata share of the business profits is taxed as ordinary income, whether or not the profits are actually distributed.

The limited partnership structure offers some advantage over the general partnership in raising capital. This structure provides an opportunity for an investor to own part of the business and to share in its financial success without assuming unlimited personal liability for business obligations. Like the corporate investor, he may be an "absentee" owner and may transfer his interest to another. Thus the arrangement has some of the features of the corporation while retaining much of the freedom of the general partnership.

The Corporation. A corporation is a legal "person" created by statute. The laws regarding formation and registration of corporations vary from state to state. However, most statutes provide broad powers for the corporation with regard to acquiring and transfering property (including other corporations), making contracts, appointing or hiring officers, employees, and other agents, and so forth. In fact, corporations are permitted "to have and exercise all powers necessary or convenient to effect any or all of the purposes for which the corporation is organized."[6] Usually it is required that the articles of incorporation set forth the following.

1. The name of the corporation.
2. The purpose or purposes for which the corporation is being organized.
3. Information concerning the share of stock in the corporation.
4. Information concerning the initial board of directors.
5. The name and address of each incorporator.

The corporate structure is certainly the most complex form of business organization. However, it possesses several advantages. Since the corporation is a legal entity, it is liable for its own debts. Creditors' claims are limited to the corporation's assets. Investors can lose no more than the funds they have invested. Ownership is in the form of shares of stock, which may be held by anyone. As a legal entity the corporation has perpetual life unless a limited period of duration is stated in its articles of incorporation. Thus insolvency, withdrawal, or death of any of the owners does not affect the existence of the organization. Moreover, the ownership may be divided into as many shares as desirable to attract investors, and classes of ownership with different voting privileges and dividend rights may be created. The shareholders usually elect a board of directors (which may include incorporators) and vote on certain policy matters at the required annual meetings, but otherwise do not participate in the management of the corporation. The board of directors then appoints or elects the executive staff to operate the corporation.

All profits of the corporation are subject to state and federal corporate taxes prior to payment of dividends. In most states the corporation must also pay personal property taxes and an annual business or occupation tax. It should be pointed out that dividends are actually taxed twice—first as corporation profits and then as personal income when received by individual shareholders. This double taxation can be avoided of course by retaining the profits in the business for the purpose of expansion. If the result of such retention is to increase the value of the stock, the shareholder may enjoy a tax advantage since the increase in stock value will usually be taxed as a capital gain when the stock is sold.

[6] Georgia Code, Section 22–202.

Depending on the tax bracket in which the corporate stockholder finds himself, this tax rate may be significantly lower than that on ordinary income.

Double taxation can also be avoided by small corporations which qualify under Subchapter S of the Internal Revenue Code by meeting the following requirements:

1. The corporation must be a domestic corporation.
2. There must be only one class of stock.
3. There can be a maximum of 10 shareholders who must be either individuals or estates.
4. A maximum of 20% of the corporate income may be derived from other than operating sources (e.g., rents, interest, dividends, royalties and gains on the sale of securities).

If the corporation qualifies, it enjoys the same tax advantages as a partnership.

While the corporate organization has many advantages, it also has a potential disadvantage for the founding entrepreneur. The free transferability of shares may be a threat to the original stockholders in that they ordinarily have no control over who the new shareholders will be. This may be particularly important in a small, closely held corporation in which the founder has sold a substantial, if not controlling, interest in order to obtain starting capital. The approach most frequently used to alleviate this problem is to place restrictions in the articles of incorporation which give the corporation or other shareholders an option or right of first refusal to purchase the shares any stockholder desires to sell. Similar provisions may give shareholders first rights to purchase on a pro rata basis any additional stock the corporation may issue.

The corporation is superior to other forms of business organization when it comes to raising capital. The shares in the corporation offer a convenient means for the sale of equity, and the flexibility in creating special classes of stock may be used to retain control and/or make certain classes of stock attractive to investors. The equity capital raised from the sale of stock may be used to purchase fixed assets of the corporation, and these may be used as collateral for loans. For the new venture, however, these advantages may be somewhat illusory. The entrepreneur may find that the price he is able to obtain for stock is so low that he must virtually give away a large portion of his company in order to get started and that the new owners then will be breathing down his neck at every move. Nonetheless, the corporate structure is the most attractive form of organization for raising capital.

How Much Money Must Be Raised?

The amount of money that must be raised is the difference between total funding needs and the portion of these needs that the entrepreneur himself can furnish. Total investment needs were obtained in the financial analysis. However, the entrepreneur may wish to reexamine expenditures to determine if any can be reduced or at least delayed so as to reduce the initial financing. The following are possibilities.

1. *Major suppliers may accept delayed payment for raw materials and components.* Suppliers of raw materials and purchased components are of course interested in the success of the new business. They hope to gain new sales and may agree to extended terms on purchases during start-up in return for assurance of preferential consideration for future purchases. If they are optimistic concerning the success and future growth of the new venture, it may be rather easy to obtain this concession.
2. *Officers may be willing to defer salary payments or accept a reduced salary for a limited time.* It is not unusual for the founders of a new venture to draw substantially reduced salaries during the period in which they are attempting to establish a business. If this is done, however, it should be clear that the reduction will be short-lived. Financial projections should indicate when deferred compensation will be made up and full salaries paid. A business plan that indicates a long period of reduced or deferred salaries for management is not likely to impress a potential investor. He knows that managers and their families must have reasonable living standards and wants assurance that the fledgling company will receive the complete, dedicated attention of its management. If they have personal financial problems, this is not likely to be the case.
3. *Equipment manufacturers may be willing to finance production equipment on terms favorable to the new company.* It is likely that production equipment will be available from several manufacturers who are anxious to sell to the new company. They may be willing to accept an amortized note secured by the equipment or a lease-purchase arrangement.
4. *Customers may be willing to make C.O.D. or advance payment.* Although customary trade terms may be net 30 or net 60, it is possible that customers of the new firm may want to encourage development of an alternative supply source and will agree to pay on delivery or even in advance. This is most likely in the case of local customers who are paying high shipping costs on goods purchased from distant vendors.

In effect, each of these potential alternatives involves the granting of credit by friends of the new venture. None of them reduce the total funds needed, but they do change the timing of the needs and perhaps make it possible to meet needs from earnings rather than outside funds.

After reducing initial funding needs as much as possible, the entrepreneur's next question is, "How much money must I put into the business?" In most cases, the answer is simply stated, "All that you have!" The attitude of most investors is that of the Small Business Investment Company executive who stated, "Before we make an investment in a new venture we want the founder to have every penny he has in it. We can then be certain that he will give it his utmost effort and if it does fail, his money will go first." Investors are cold-hearted people.

How Much Equity?

How much equity is needed in starting a business? Certainly the entrepreneur does not want to sell any more of his company than he has to. If the company is successful, it will be worth far more in a few years than can be obtained from the initial sale. Robert S. Morrison suggests that for a company set up to produce a proven but not yet marketed proprietary product, an estimate of equity money is the total of the following.

1. Thirty-four percent of the cost of buildings and land.
2. Forty percent of the installed cost of standard, general-purpose equipment.
3. Sixty percent of the cost of specialized equipment.
4. One hundred percent of the cost of tooling.
5. Two hundred percent of estimated start-up costs.
6. One hundred percent of monthly sales volume expected in 12 months.[7]

A strong equity base has the advantage of providing a margin of security for the new venture and is of course looked on favorably by creditors. It eases the problem of obtaining credit from suppliers, banks, and other lenders and may permit the company to weather unexpected problems in reaching the planned level of production and profit.

SOURCES OF FINANCING

In addition to the legal structure decision and the choice of debt or equity financing, the list of potential sources of funds is affected by the stage of de-

---

[7] Robert S. Morrison, *Handbook for Manufacturing Entrepreneurs* (Cleveland: Western Reserve Press, 1974), p. 66.

velopment of the company. Stages of venture development have been described in various ways. The following seem to describe the early stages of a new venture very well.[8]

- *Stage 0.* This is the conceptual or fetal stage. All that exists is a product concept and possibly a proposed entrepreneurial group. Technical aspects of product and process development are yet to be considered. This stage is characterized by the engineer who says, "I have designed a revolutionary process to convert coal to a fluid powder which can be burned with great efficiency."
- *Stage I.* A prototype has been developed and tested; a feasibility study has been conducted, which indicates potential commercial feasibility; and a management team has been selected. The investment proposal has been prepared but the business does not yet exist.
- *Stage II.* The company is in existence. It has produced and sold products and has a short operating history which permits financial analysis. It is in the process of planning long-term growth.

The successful company will continue, of course, through further stages of growth and development. We are concerned here, however, only with putting the new venture into existence.

Money for stage 0 is most likely to come from the entrepreneur, his family, and close friends. This represents the highest risk situation, and conventional financing sources are generally uninterested. Any outside funds usually come from wealthy individuals in the community. The reason for this lies in the federal income tax on capital gains versus ordinary income. If the project fails, the federal government will share a major part of their loss via the tax deduction route and, if the project succeeds, they will be able to retain a major part of the gain via the capital gains route.

In most instances, stage I is the earliest point at which the entrepreneur should approach investors. For convenience of discussion, financial sources for stages I and II are divided into two groups—sources of debt financing and venture capital sources.

Sources of Debt Financing

Debt financing, as defined earlier in this chapter, is money lent to the company. The lender may make an *unsecured* loan solely on the basis of the borrower's good character and credit rating. More commonly, however, the loan is secured

---

[8] See J. Kelley et al., p. 30.

by the assets of the entrepreneur and/or his company. Most lending agencies prefer to make short-term loans (1 year or less) which are to be repaid by the sale of goods and collections of receivables in the normal course of business. Intermediate-term loans (up to 5 years) are made for the purchase of income-producing assets which may also serve as collateral to secure the loan. The lender expects that the loan will be self-liquidating from income produced by the asset. Long-term loans (more than 5 years) frequently are made for the purchase of real estate and are secured by a security deed to the property. If not secured by real property, long-term loans may be in return for debentures or bonds. Bonds may be secured by chattels of buildings and equipment. A debenture, by definition, is an unsecured bond.

For the proprietorship and general partnership, debt financing is the only alternative available. It is an important and often desirable form of financing for any business, since it preserves ownership and provides leverage.

Commercial Banks.   Commercial banks are the department stores for loans and other financial services. Most can provide short-term, intermediate-term, and long-term loans. They are also very conservative in making such loans. A rather common claim is that a bank will lend money "only if you can prove that you don't need it." In truth, the bank, like any other lender, wants assurance that the borrower will be able to pay interest and repay the loan when it is due. It is up to the applicant to furnish this assurance.

A commercial bank is the first place to which the entrepreneur should turn for debt financing. Interest rates are likely to be lower than from most other sources and a good banking relationship is invaluable to the new business. Robert S. Morrison makes these points concerning banking relationships:

1. Banking should involve a personal rapport between the bank and its customers with someone in the bank carrying a torch for each borrower.
2. A smaller bank is likely to be more attentive to the needs of small and medium-sized borrowers than a large bank.
3. Large banks show favoritism toward large borrowers when money is tight. The small and medium-sized borrowers may have the rug pulled out from under them.
4. It may take years to build up both confidence and a top credit standing with a bank.
5. A good banking connection is a very valuable asset to a business; treat it with care, like your best customer.[9]

[9] Morrison, pp. 75–76.

Insurance Companies. Some insurance companies are now making loans to businesses. Life insurance companies are governed by state laws which affect loan policies. Such regulations may specify that (a) the borrower must be a corporate entity; (b) the borrower must have been in business for a specified period of time; and (c) historical and current earnings of the borrower must meet specified requirements. In states that have such requirements, new-venture loans are ruled out. However, in other states life insurance companies do make loans to new businesses. Moreover, property and casualty insurance companies are subject to less stringent state regulations and are much more active in financing new ventures.

Insurance company loans may carry higher interest charges than bank loans, but they have the advantage that they are usually for a longer period of time and do not usually interfere with short-term bank loans.

Consumer Finance Companies. Consumer finance companies specialize in small loans to individuals whose credit ratings may not permit them to obtain a bank loan. The interest rate is on the order of $1\frac{1}{2}$ times the prevailing bank interest rate for the same size loan. This is an expensive source of funds and should be a last resort for any business.

U.S. Small Business Administration.[10] When financing is not otherwise available on reasonable terms, the Small Business Administration (SBA) may guarantee up to 90%, or $350,000, whichever is less, of a bank loan to a small firm.

If the entire loan is not obtainable from a private lender and if an SBA guaranteed loan is not available, SBA will consider advancing funds on an immediate participation basis with a bank. SBA considers making a direct loan only when other forms of financing are not obtainable and funds are available for direct lending.

The agency's share of an immediate participation loan may not, at the present time, exceed $150,000. Direct loans may not exceed $100,000 and at times may not be available as a result of federal fiscal restraints. SBA business loans may be for as long as 10 years, except portions of loans for new-construction purposes, which may have a maturity of 15 years. Working capital loans are usually limited to 6 years.

SBA loan restrictions require, among other things, that the applicant have

[10] From *SBA Business Loans*, (Washington, D.C.: U.S. Small Business Administration, April 1976).

enough capital in an existing firm so that, with the new loan, he can operate on a sound financial basis. At least three out of four SBA loans—probably more —are made to established businesses.

Other Loan Sources in the Federal Government. Generally speaking, to be eligible for a government loan, certain requirements must be met. They are:

- Financing from private, commercial sources must not be available on reasonable terms.
- There must be reasonable assurance of repayment.
- The loan must be in the public interest.

Under these conditions, loans for various specialized purposes are available from the following agencies:

- Farmers Home Administration.
- Veterans Administration.
- Overseas Private Investment Corporation (OPIC).

Detailed information concerning these loan sources can be obtained by writing to the appropriate federal agencies.

Private Pension Funds. Private pension funds may supply long-term financing for fixed assets. The arrangement may be sale-leaseback in which the pension fund purchases the property and leases it back to the borrower with options for renewal or purchase after a specified time.

Small Business Investment Companies. Small Business Investment Companies (SBICs) were created by the Small Business Investment Act of 1958 as a vehicle for providing equity capital and long-term loan funds for small businesses. In practice, most SBICs provide loan funds only if "sweetened" by stock warrants or convertible debentures. The companies expect to share in the capital gains of the business. Since equity financing is involved in most of their investments, SBICs are discussed in the following section.

Venture Capital Sources

There appears to be no firmly established definition of venture capital. However, it is characterized as being high risk with the principal objective of capital gains. Additionally, and probably more importantly, venture capital is characterized by a continuing active relationship between the small business and the venture capitalist.

According to Dominguez,

> Venture capital financing is generally the first capital to be invested by sources outside the firm, and the last to exit. In the parlance of the market, it is the "front money" or funds that are normally subordinated to all other financial commitments of the enterprise. Aside from common stock financing, the most common forms of alternative equity instruments issued in venture capital investments are convertible debentures, warrants, and letter stock options.[11]

Thus the distinguishing characteristic of venture capital sources is an investment policy aimed at achieving most of the profit through capital gains. This is not to say, however, that venture capital firms never use debt. They often combine notes and stock in a financing package.

The amount of ownership the entrepreneur must surrender in the venture capital deal is of course a matter of negotiation. Considering the risks involved, the venture capitalist is likely to feel that his dollars are more important to the new firm than the contributions of the entrepreneur. Depending on the stage of development of the company, he is quite likely to seek a controlling interest.[12]

From the venture capitalist's viewpoint, a fairly large rate of gain will be needed on investments that turn out to be successful, to make up for many that fail and result in losses. Also, he must make his profit through the sale of his equity in the new business—back to the entrepreneur, to the public, or to another company—and it takes time to develop an equity investment to the point where it can be sold at a gain. Rotch shows that in order for a hypothetical venture capital firm to make 10% on total assets, it must, over a 5-year period, make gains averaging 150% on investments that produce some capital gain.[13] Also, the venture capital firm is not likely to be interested in small deals, because selling the investment in a small company will be more difficult than selling the investment in a large company—particularly if a public issue is involved. Most venture capitalists prefer investments of at least $100,000 to $500,000.

---

[11] John R. Dominguez, Venture Capital (Lexington, Mass.: Lexington Books, 1974), p. 1.

[12] For a more detailed discussion of venture capital raising, see Liles, pp. 461–495.

[13] William Rotch, "The Pattern of Success in Venture Capital Financing," *Financial Analysts Journal*, **24** (Sept.–Oct. 1968), pp. 141–147.

There are several publications that offer detailed lists of venture capital companies, their investment preferences, investment limits, and other information. Some of them are listed in the bibliography at the end of this chapter. However, such lists invariably become outdated quickly. Furthermore, the entrepreneur who seeks venture capital is likely to turn first to local sources of funds, which may or may not be listed in these references. As a matter of practicality, the nearest office of the SBA is likely to be a fruitful starting place for the entrepreneur who wants to learn where venture capital may be found locally.

The following sections list only the major classes of venture capital sources and discuss some of their characteristics.

Small Business Investment Companies.[14]   An SBIC is a privately owned and privately operated small business investment company licensed by the SBA to provide equity capital and long-term loans to small firms. Often, an SBIC also provides management assistance to the companies it finances. Many SBICs are owned by relatively small groups of local investors. However, the stock of over 40 SBICs is publicly traded, and more than 80 SBICs are partially or wholly owned by commercial banks.

A major incentive for SBICs to risk their capital in small businesses is the chance to share in the profits if the businesses grow and prosper. Three types of investments are commonly used by SBICs to give them an opportunity to participate in this growth:

- Loans with warrants.
- Convertible debentures.
- Common stock.

While most SBICs want an opportunity to share in the growth and potential profits of the small companies they finance, some make loans that involve no equity features. The small business that obtains a straight loan is usually required to provide security, but this may take the form of a second mortgage, a personal guarantee, or some other type of collateral.

In order for a firm to qualify for financing from an SBIC, it must meet SBA requirements as a "small" business. The SBA generally considers a business small if (*a*) its assets do not exceed $5 million, (*b*) its net worth does not exceed $2.5 million, and (*c*) its average net income after taxes for each of the preceding

---

[14] From *SBIC Financing for Small Business* (Washington, D.C.: Small Business Administration, 1968).

2 years was not more than $250,000. In determining the size of a business, the SBA also considers the size of any affiliates, including a parent company which can control the firm, and any other companies controlled by the same parent company.

Since an SBICs ultimate success is linked to the growth and profitability of its so-called portfolio companies—that is, those it has financed—many SBICs offer management services as a supplement to financing. These services sometimes are as valuable as the financing itself, although few small businesspeople are aware of this when they first approach an SBIC.

A recent extension of SBICs are Minority Enterprise Small Business Investment Companies (MESBICs) which have been formed for the purpose of providing venture capital and equity financing to small businesses owned by persons who are socially or economically disadvantaged. Usually included in this clientele group are blacks, Puerto Ricans, Mexican-Americans, Indians, and Eskimos. MESBICs have a structure similar to SBICs, except that the nature of SBA leverage is different and certain rules and regulations of the SBA have been liberalized to enable MESBICs to overcome certain financing problems unique to businesses owned by members of minority groups.

Privately Owned Venture Capital Companies. The attractiveness of investing in relatively new businesses with potential for rapid growth has resulted in the formation of a number of venture capital companies organized as partnerships or corporations. In some cases these investment companies view their role as more than mere suppliers of venture capital and retain a management and technical staff for the purpose of assisting companies in which they hold an interest. They view themselves as "business developers" as opposed to the more passive venture capitalists.

Private Investors. For most new businesses that seek outside funds, the most likely sources are individuals of wealth in the local community. These people usually have incomes from their own business or profession that put them in a high tax bracket, and they may be very interested in participating in a venture that elects Subchapter S status or which qualifies under Section 1244 of the Internal Revenue Code.

Subchapter S, as stated previously, permits certain corporations to elect to be taxed as a partnership—thereby avoiding the corporate tax and passing gains and losses to the shareholders as ordinary gains and losses. Section 1244 permits an individual to treat a loss from investment in the common stock of a qualifying small business as an *ordinary* loss rather than a capital loss. Thus losses can be deducted from income (taxed at a high rate), while gains are taxed at a maximum rate of 25%. The restrictions pertaining to both Subchapter S and Section 1244 are available from the Internal Revenue Service.

Another potential financing source is made up of successful entrepreneurs who themselves have gone through the "birthing" of a new venture and are sympathetic to similar efforts. Such persons may be willing to contribute their own entrepreneurial expertise in addition to money. Individuals who may be interested in participating in a new venture may be located through bankers, stockbrokers, insurance agents, or professional investment advisory services.

Fiduciary Funds. For the most part, funds held in trust for others (e.g., pension funds, insurance) are closely regulated by state laws and are not used to make equity investments in new ventures. However, the potential for substantial capital gains and the success history of traditional venture capital firms have attracted some fiduciary institutions into the venture capital business.

Their policies are not usually a matter of public knowledge, and it is quite difficult for the entrepreneur to establish contact. At the present time, they cannot be regarded as significant sources of funds for small businesses. Nonetheless, they are a potential source for venture capital.

Closed-End Investment Funds. The first publicly held venture capital firm was the American Research and Development Corporation (ARD), established in 1946. ARD has since made over 100 investments and is the largest closed-end investment company in the venture capital field. There are about 13 others, all of which operate nationally.[15]

Closed-end investment companies are organized to own and trade in the securities of other firms. While there are many success stories concerning their investments in young companies, they seldom invest in a new venture without at least some history of operations.

Industrial Corporations. Several large corporations have created investment divisions or venture capital subsidiaries to invest in new businesses. Their objectives are likely to be distinctly different from those of conventional venture capital sources. Primarily they are interested in new ventures which, in some

---

[15] Information on these companies and many other sources of venture capital is given in A. J. Kelley, F. B. Campanella, J. McKierman, *Venture Capital—A Guidebook for New Enterprises* (NTIS Document No. COM–71–01099), available from the National Technical Information Service, U.S. Department of Commerce, Springfield, Va. 22151.

fashion, relate to their basic business. Possibilities are companion products to their own, products that utilize their own products and sources of supply, and products that involve technology useful in their own operations.

To a new business, a large industrial corporation as a source of venture capital offers advantages in the form of management and technical assistance, markets, and perhaps distribution channels. There are, however, disadvantages which should cause the entrepreneur to be wary. Baty lists several, among them:

- Industrial corporations are usually not anxious to see the new venture go public. They are more disposed toward the acquisition of new divisions and/or subsidiaries.
- The entrepreneur may find a buy-out formula (based on performance) or a right of first refusal to buy any founder's stock as a condition of the venture capital deal.
- The corporation may insist that the new business not sell its product to competitors of the corporation.
- The corporation may require policies, accounting conventions, and banking relationships, and make other demands which reduce the autonomy of the new business.[16]

Choosing a Venture Capital Partner. It is worthwhile to emphasize again that venture capital is primarily equity capital and should not be sought as seed money. Two things are likely to occur if venture capital is sought early in the development of a new company: (1) The request will probably be refused, and (2) if not, it will be very costly. The earlier venture capital is obtained, the more it costs in terms of equity.

When the time does come, where should the entrepreneur look and how should he choose a venture capital partner? The first place to look is in the local community. Several months before the money is actually needed, the entrepreneur will likely find a visit to the nearest SBA regional office helpful. There he can obtain a list of SBICs and advice concerning other sources of financing. He should then talk with bankers, investment bankers, attorneys, and investment advisors who may know of venture capital sources. Next, he should learn as much as possible about the sources of venture capital that might meet his needs. What types of investments do they make? How much do they have available for investment? Will they be able to assist in obtaining additional financing later? Do they have contacts which would be helpful in a future

---

[16] Gordon B. Baty, *Entrepreneurship—Playing to Win* (Reston, Va.: Reston Publishing Co., 1974), p. 101.

public offering? Do they offer management services? The ultimate choice will have a far-reaching effect on the future of the firm and must be made carefully.

Going Public

All the preceding sources of equity capital involve the *private* sale of shares or other rights in the business. The entrepreneur, however, may seek to raise equity capital by selling shares in his company to the public. In doing this, he may turn to an *underwriter* (an individual who agrees to market all or a part of an issue of stock to the public as a service to the seller), or he may attempt a public offering himself.

The public offering of securities is a complex, strictly regulated business which requires legal assistance and supervision. The entrepreneur who wishes to follow this path should consult with the staff of the Securities and Exchange Commission (SEC) and retain the best corporation lawyer he can find.

WHAT THE INVESTOR LOOKS FOR IN THE INVESTMENT PROPOSAL

Preceding sections have dealt with financing considerations and sources for loans and venture capital. They have attempted to answer the question, "Where can I get the money?" What remains is to convince someone actually to part with the money. As stated earlier, this requires a credible presentation of the anticipated returns and risks involved in the venture. Such a presentation is called an *investment proposal* or, quite frequently, a *business plan*. It seems appropriate to distinguish between the two. The business plan is primarily an internal document to guide day-to-day business decisions and measure progress. It is a blueprint for future operations and, through periodic review and updating, provides a mechanism for management planning and control. The SBA describes the business plan as "an exciting new tool which the owner-manager of a small business can use to plot a 'course' for his company."[17]

A potential investor is obviously interested in much of the information in the business plan—market, technical, and financial. He prefers a condensed version, however, and he must have some additional information concerning the management group—personal and financial histories, capabilities, and accomplishments. Hence the investment proposal is a special-purpose document based on the business plan and specifically created for fund raising. Its purpose

---

[17] Small Business Administration, *Business Plan for Small Manufacturers*, Management Aid for Small Manufacturers No. 218 (Washington, D.C.: Small Business Administration, 1973).

is *to attract the potential investor's interest.* As a matter of fact, if the investment proposal enables the proposed project to survive the initial screening, it will have been successful.

The contents and emphasis of the investment proposal differ according to the financing being sought and the investor(s) to whom it will be submitted. Baty offers the following good advice:

> Remember your audience. Where possible, tailor the material to the knowledge, interests, and needs of the person whose OK is necessary for your deal to move ahead. Is he an engineer? Then summarize the market data and financial plans in graphs, and beef up technical areas. Is your target reader an SBIC officer? Then show how your cash flow allows for servicing of convertible debt and, possibly, for some management consulting a CPA or, better, a security analyst check your pro formas for out-of-whack ratios, etc.[18]

Bear in mind that, regardless of the audience, the investment proposal must contain certain information necessary to appraise the project. While there may be a difference in emphasis, any potential investor looks for answers to the following questions.

1. What is the proposition?
2. What are the characteristics of the product, the company, and the industry?
3. What are the qualifications of the people involved?
4. Is there a market and can the venture successfully serve it?
5. What is the growth potential?
6. Can the proposed enterprise produce the product competitively?
7. What is the projected profitability?
8. What are the risks?

In the discussions that follow, it is presumed that the business is at least at stage I, more likely stage II, of development and that the potential investor is either a venture capitalist or lender.

1. *What is the proposition?* Specific information the potential investor needs is:
   - Total project cost and proposed capitalization.
   - If equity financing is sought, the structure (common stock, convertible debt, etc.) and pricing.

[18] Baty, p. 120.

- Timing of the financing.
- Is subsequent financing will be needed, the timing and how it is to be obtained.
- Use of the requested funds.
- In a nutshell, the projected returns from the project.

2. *What are the characteristics of the product, the company, and the industry?*

- Product description and purpose.
- History of product development.
- Proprietary features.
- Competitive products.
- What makes the product different.
- Background of the company.
- History and growth of the industry and its markets.

3. *What are the qualifications of the people involved?* Each year Dun and Bradstreet publishes data on business failures. According to these statistics, the average life span of all companies in the United States is about 7 years—16 out of 17 companies fail. These data include businesses of all types, including "shoestring" operations which never had a chance and should never have been started. However, it is true that many new businesses fail and that the undisputed leader among causes of failure is lack of managerial ability.

Most investors state emphatically that the people involved are more important to the success of the venture than the venture concept itself. If the idea is particularly good and there are apparent gaps in management skills, investors may identify these gaps, assist in filling them, and then support the venture. However, many venture proposals are turned down because of doubt concerning managerial abilities. Billy Robinson, commercial officer of the Trust Company Bank of Atlanta states, "The first thing you must learn when lending to small business is that small business is the small business*man*. Unless you know the businessman you can't lend to small business. You have to appreciate what his goals are . . . talk to him about his numbers. In about five minutes you know if he understands the mechanics of financing a small business. If he doesn't a loan will destroy both his dreams and him."[19]

Investors readily admit that the evaluation of people is a subjective matter and that they develop an intuitive ability based on experience in dealing with businesspeople. The characteristics they list as important—iron will, determination, enthusiasm, resourcefulness, perceptiveness, and personal committment to the business—are principally related to integrity

---

[19] Loral Dean, "Small Firms: Surviving is Fierce," *Atlanta*, 15, No. 9, pp. 66–71.

and motivation. Liles discusses the following three areas for evaluating people with the proposed venture:

- Integrity and reliability.
- Abilities and demonstrated competence.
- Attitudes and ambitions.[20]

The investor cannot and will not attempt to make these complex evaluations on the basis of the investment proposal alone. If the proposal survives initial screening, personal conferences and references will also influence his evaluation of the management group. However, the information expected in the proposal can be outlined as follows.

- The organizational structure.
- Individual resumes.
- Individual financial statements.
- Members of the board of directors (if appropriate).
- Why this is a good management *team.*

In addition, if the firm has an operating history, an analysis of its current financial statements will disclose a great deal about the management's competency. The investor looks at the latest balance sheet to make an evaluation of the following.

- Current assets/current liabilities ratio.
- Financial structure.
- Net worth.
- Quality of assets and liabilities.

4. *Is there a market and can the venture successfully serve it?* The investor examines three essential aspects of this question:

(*a*) The potential market.
  - Is there documented evidence of market growth?
  - What are the price trends?
  - If the product is new, has public acceptance been established?
  - What is the total potential market?

(*b*) The marketing strategy.
  - How will the company price its product?
  - What are the sales channels?
  - What are the sales costs?
  - What are the promotional plans and budgets?
  - What makes the product different (e.g., quality, features, service)?

[20] Liles, p. 473.

- What is the projected share of the market and estimated sales?
- Who are the key customers?

(c) The competition.
- Who are the competitors?
- What part of the market does each serve?
- Where are they located?
- What is their price structure?

5. *What is the growth potential?* The venture capitalist, as stated previously, is interested in more than just whether or not the company can make a consistent fair return on invested capital. According to Kelley et al., "The typical venture capitalist expects to increase his investment by a factor of 5 in five years."[21] Indicators of high growth potential are:

- Demonstrated customer acceptance of a new proprietary product in an area where no competitive products exist.
- Increasing market trends.
- Natural opportunities for diversification which will increase the market.
- Product involves new technology to meet a presently unserved need and therefore has the potential to open up a whole new industry.
- Innovation in product, production technology, or distribution, which provides a strong competitive advantage.

6. *Can the proposed enterprise produce the product successfully?* In order to answer this question, information from the technical analysis must be furnished.

- Process descriptions.
- Results of development work.
- Sources and costs of raw materials.
- Workpower and skills requirement.
- Quality control procedures.
- Manufacturing facilities requirements (including land, buildings, and equipment).
- Plant location and justification.
- Cost estimates (land, buildings, equipment, operating costs).
- Fixed costs and variable costs by product.
- Planned plant capacity and expansions to meet future needs.

7. *What is the projected profitability?* This question is answered by the results of the financial analysis.

- Pro forma financial statements.

[21] Kelley, et al., p. 29.

Income statement.
Balance sheet.
Cash flow projections.

- Measures of commercial profitability.

8. *What are the risks?* Of course the investor understands that risks are involved, and he is prepared to accept reasonable risk. To go into the venture without appraising the risk, however, would be foolhardy. In his attempt to assess risk he asks, "What are the factors that can adversely affect profits?" Having identified such factors, he must estimate their seriousness and their likelihood of occurrence. Since profits are a function of sales and costs, the investor may consider threats to sales and costs:

- Threats to projected sales.

    Overestimation of the potential market and its growth.
    Overestimation of the venture's market share under the proposed price structure.
    Price cuts by competitors.
    Introduction of superior competitive products.
    Product obsolescence through technology, style changes, customer whims, and so on.
    Competitive advantage lost through governmental action (e.g., additional taxes, removal of subsidies, removal of protective tariffs or import restrictions).
    Market closed by governmental action (e.g., environmental controls).
    Product quality and performance problems.
    Product service problems.
    Delivery system failure.
    Export barriers.

- Threats to costs.

    Increased prices of input materials and labor.
    Increased distribution costs.
    Increased operating costs.
    Tax increases.

Since these threats are difficult to evaluate individually, the investor is interested in a break-even analysis and in the results of risk analysis as discussed in Chapter 5.

Other risk factors that should also concern the investor are:

- Stability of the management team.
- Technical feasibility of the project.

OUTLINE FOR A VENTURE CAPITAL PROPOSAL

Many lenders and venture capitalists provide outlines or formats for investment proposals to be submitted to them. The following outline is suggested by Stephen D. Sholes.[22]

A well-prepared proposal will impress prospective venture capitalists with the planning ability and general competence of management. In addition, the process of preparing the presentation will help management understand the true extent of the opportunities and limitations of their ventures.

Above all, the venture capital proposal must be an honest presentation. All companies have weaknesses as well as strengths, and these should be discussed frankly. Because it must be readable, the main body of the proposal should be as brief as possible with adequate treatment of all relevant information. Heavy, detailed material, such as technical information, should be summarized in the main body, with complete information confined to appendices.

The following organization is effective:

1. *Basic proposition.* Begin the presentation with a page outlining the following:

   - Name and address of the company.
   - Amount of the proposed financing.
   - Desired structure (common stock, convertible debt, etc.) and pricing of the financing.
   - Timing of the need for the financing.
   - Use of the proceeds (briefly).
   - Subsequent financing needs and their timing.

2. *Summary.* In two or three pages, summarize the most important data in the proposal to facilitate the venture capitalist's review.

3. *Company.* Summarize background information on the company— date and state of incorporation, founders, business purpose, and highlights of progress to date (e.g., major developments, such as the introduction of new products, etc.). Provide a history of predecessor companies, if any. State the names of subsidiaries, if any, their date and state of incorporation, and the company's degree of ownership in each.

---

[22] From Stephen D. Sholes, "The Search for Venture Capital—Preparatory Steps," *Financial Executive,* **62**, No. 8 (1974), pp. 46, 54–58.

4. *Capitalization.* Present the company's most current balance sheet and specify the nature and terms of each type of present financing. State the names and addresses of parties that provide debt financing (trade creditors, short-term lenders, long-term lenders, and lessors) and summarize any related agreements. Provide a detailed breakdown of equity ownership. Give a chronology of the company's long-term financings.

5. *Market.* Describe the company's product or service in detail, indicating its nature, application, and patent protection, if any. Include technical material, such as engineering studies, photographs, and selling brochures. Compare the company's product to those of its competitors, explaining what sets the company's product apart. Discuss plans for new products.

6. *Market.* Define the target market for the product in terms of its nature, current size (units and total dollar volume), and growth potential. Clearly state the assumptions on which the market definition is based. To the extent possible, corroborate the market definition with studies performed by others. If the company has a track record, discuss how its product has been received in the marketplace and why.

7. *Competition.* Name and discuss all major competitors. Of relevance are the market share (by product if applicable) and relative strengths and weaknesses of each. If the company has a track record, comment on its performance in relationship to its competitors. If there are no competitors, discuss the possible development of competition and from whom it is likely to come. Discuss the possibility of technological obsolescence, if applicable, and how the company will protect itself.

8. *Marketing.* Outline the company's pricing, marketing, sales, and distribution strategies for the next 5 years and the rationale for each. Discuss the plans for implementing these strategies. Of course, if the company has a track record, comment on current pricing, marketing, sales, and distribution strategies and their future application (5 years forward). Outline pricing, by product, at each level of distribution. If the company has a track record, provide at least a partial list of customers and, if applicable, name distributors, sales agents, manufacturer's representatives, and so on.

9. *Manufacturing.* Describe how the company's product is being or will be manufactured. The following sequence is suggested:

   - Manufacturing facilities including land, building, and equipment (nature and capacity).
   - Method of manufacture.
   - Quality-control procedures.

- Raw materials or components (source, cost, and related contracts).
- Breakdown of fixed manufacturing costs.
- Breakdown of variable unit costs by product.

10. *Organization.* Show an organization chart (include names of people currently filling positions) of the present or proposed organization. Discuss the personnel needs of the company by function for the immediate future. Provide a 5-year forecast of personnel needs by function and discuss the expected evolution of the organizational structure. Comment on the labor supply and its nature (unionization, training, etc.). Fully describe the company's wage and salary structures and benefit plans (pensions, profit sharing, and stock option plans). Provide detailed biographical sketches for the key personnel and directors.

11. *Use of proceeds.* Outline specifically how the proposed financing is to be used. For example, of a $500,000 financing $200,000 may be used to purchase or build a plant, $100,000 to purchase equipment, and $200,000 to carry receivables and inventory. If all or part of the financing is to be used for a capital project, substantiate the estimated cost of the project. If the company has a track record, provide an analysis of the incremental earnings projected to result from the financing.

12. *Historical financial statements.* If the company has a track record, provide income statements, income sources, uses-of-funds statements, and balance sheets, in comparative form, for the last 5 years or from inception. Give detailed breakdowns of sales and income statement cost categories. Provide operating statistics and explain unusual fluctuations in the statistics (e.g., abrupt declines in sales or earnings, large increases in receivables or inventories unaccompanied by increases in sales, unexplained reductions in equity accounts, etc.). Explain changes in accounting methods.

13. *Forecast.* Present a 5-year forecast of the company's financial statements incorporating the proposed financing. In a blueprint or start-up situation, the forecast should be on a monthly basis for the first year, a quarterly basis for the second year, and annually thereafter. A forecast on a quarterly basis for the first year and annually thereafter suffices for a company with a track record. The following sequence is suggested:

- Income statements.
- Schedules giving detailed breakdowns of sales (units, price, and total dollar volume) and costs.

- Sources and applications of fund statements.
- Balance sheets.

Summarize and explain the numbers. Clearly state all assumptions on which the forecast is based, making sure that it is consistent with all material presented elsewhere in the proposal. Discuss the timing and purpose of future financing needs. Outline the accounting methods being used or to be used by the company and discuss present or planned financial control methods and management information systems.

BIBLIOGRAPHY

Adams, Sam. "What a Venture Capitalist Looks For," *MBA*, **7**, No. 6 (June–July 1973).

Baty, Gordon B. *Entrepreneurship: Playing to Win*. Reston, Va.: Reston Publishing Co.,1974.

Belew, Richard C. *How to Win Profits and Influence Bankers—The Art of Practical Projecting*. New York: Van Nostrand Reinhold, 1973.

Brady, Brigid. *Steps to Starting a Business*. San Francisco, Calif.: Bank of America, 1969.

Dible, Donald M. *Up Your Own Organization*. Santa Clara, Calif.: The Entrepreneur Press, 1974.

Dominquez, John R. *Venture Capital*. Lexington, Mass.: D. C. Heath, 1974.

Grass, Harry. *Financing for Small and Medium-Sized Businesses*. Englewood Cliffs, N.J.: Prentice-Hall, 1969.

Hutchinson, G. S. *Why, When, and How to Go Public*. New York: Presidents Publishing House, 1970.

Kelley, Albert J., Frank B. Campanella, John McKiernan. *Venture Capital—A Guidebook for New Enterprises*. (COM–71–01099). Boston: The Management Institute, School of Management, Boston College, 1971.

Klein, Richard H. "A Perspective on the MESBIC Program." *MSU Business Topics*, **20** (Autumn 1972), pp. 45–51.

Liles, Patrick R. *New Business Ventures and the Entrepreneur*. Homewood, Ill.: Richard D. Irwin, 1974.

Mancuso, Joseph R. "How a Business Plan is Read." *Business Horizons*. **17**, No. 4 (August 1974), pp. 33–42.

Markstein, David L. *Money Raising & Planning For the Small Business*. Chicago: H. Regnery, 1974.

Metcalf, Wendall O. *Starting and Managing a Small Business of Your Own*. Washington, D.C.: U.S. Small Business Administration, 1962.

Morrison, Robert S. *Handbook for Manufacturing Entrepreneurs* 2nd ed. Cleveland: Western Reserve Press, 1974.

Mueller, Robert Kirk. *The Innovative Ethic*. New York: American Management Association, 1971.

Mueller, Robert Kirk. "Venture Capital Movement," *Industrial Marketing Management*, **2** (1972), pp. 1–23.

Putt, William D. *How to Start Your Own Business*. Cambridge, Mass.: MIT Press, 1974.

Rotch, William. "The Pattern of Success in Venture Capital Financing," *Financial Analysts Journal*, **24** (Sept.–Oct. 1968), pp. 141–147.

Reubel, Stanley. *Guide to Venture Capital Sources*, 3rd ed. Chicago: Capital Publishing Corp.

Reubel, Stanley and E. G. Novotny, eds. *How to Raise and Invest Venture Capital*. New York: President's Publishing House, 1971.

Sholes, Stephen D. *Guidelines for Raising Venture Capital*. New York: Irving Trust Co.

Sholes, Stephen D. "The Search for Venture Capital—Preparatory Steps," *Financial Executive*, **42**, No. 8 (August 1974), p. 46.

Sinclair, Leroy, ed. *Venture Capital*. New York: Technimetrics, Inc., 1973.

Summers, George W. *Financing and Initial Operatings of New Firms*. Englewood Cliffs, N.J.: Prentice-Hall, 1962.

Zwick, Jack. *A Handbook of Small Business Finance*. Washington, D.C.: U.S. Small Business Administration, 1975.

Appendix

ECONOMIC EVALUATION OF

INVESTMENT ALTERNATIVES

The necessity for making a rational choice among investment alternatives arises frequently in project analysis and selection. Invariably there are alternative projects to be considered and, for any given project, there are alternative technologies, production equipment, buildings, and other investments. As we consider each decision we are faced with the question, "Of the various possible alternatives open to us, which is best in terms of profitability?" The criteria we choose must provide the answer to this question; they must be applicable to any type of investment and must be easily calculated. The criteria discussed are based on financial considerations only. They view the investment alternatives as sets of cash flows (costs and benefits) over the entire life of the alternative and provide a basis for comparison of dissimilar cash flows. Cash flows for four investment alternatives are shown in Table A.1.

The more common criteria for investment decisions may be identified as

Table A.1 Cash Flows for Investment Aternatives

Alternative	Net Annual Cash Flows per Year ($)					
	0	1	2	3	4	5
A	−12,000	4,278	3,200	−3,500	5,000	7,750
B	−10,000	3,200	2,700	2,200	2,000	1,800
C	−7,000	2,350	2,350	1,750	1,500	1,500
D	−10,000	2,000	2,000	2,000	2,000	7,500

nontime value approaches or *time value* approaches. Nontime value approaches attach no financial importance to the timing of cash flows. Time value approaches recognize that, if a project is expected to yield a cash flow of $1000 a year from now, the *present* value of that $1000 is worth somewhat less, depending on the interest rate it could earn. This reduction of future cash flows to reflect the time value of money is called "discounting."

The most commonly used criteria are:

1. Nontime value approaches.
   - Payback period.
2. Time value approaches.
   - Net present value.
   - Equivalent annual cost (capital recovery with a return).
   - Internal rate of return.
   - Benefit/cost ratio of discounted cash flows.

Each of these criteria has advantages and disadvantages which are discussed along with the methods for computation.

PAYBACK PERIOD

The payback period (sometimes also called the recoupment period) is the number of years required for the earnings from the investment to equal the investment with no interest. It is a measure of the speed with which invested funds are returned to the business. The earnings figure used in the calculation should be cash earnings after taxes. The payback period for alternative A is calculated as follows:

Year	Expenditures	Receipts	Cumulative Cash Flow
1	$12,000	$4,278	− $7,722
2	0	3,200	− $4,522
3	3,500	0	− $8,022
4	0	5,000	− $3,022
5	0	7,750	+ $4,728

The payback period is 4.39 year.

Advantages and Disadvantages

Because it is relatively simple to calculate and is intuitively appealing, the payback period is frequently used to evaluate investment proposals. While it is not a strong tool for measuring risk, it is nonetheless an approach to risk consideration, since it is an estimate of the length of time over which funds will be at risk. When used as the only criterion for investment decisions, the payback period is dangerous because it completely ignores all earnings beyond the payback years and may result in choosing a short-lived project rather than one that offers good returns over a long period of time.

NET PRESENT VALUE

In determining a criterion for the comparison of investment alternatives, one likely candidate is to express the total cash flows for each alternative as a single equivalent value which reflects the time value of money. Such a single value summarizes the value of all cash flows.

The present worth of discounted cash flows is an amount at present which is equivalent to a project's cash flow for a particular interest rate i. Thus, the present worth of investment proposal j at interest rate i with a life of n years can be expressed as

$$NPV_j\,(i) = \sum_{n=0}^{N} F_{jn}(1 + i)^{-n}$$

where F_{jn} is the net cash flow from project j during year n. Calculations of present worth are facilitated by tabulated values of the factor

$$(P/F, i, n) = (1 + i)^{-n}$$

for various values of i and n. (See Table A.2.)

A project's net present value is determined by subtracting the present value of the initial investment from the present value of all future cash receipts and disbursements. The interest rate chosen for discounting future cash flows is usually taken to be either the prevailing interest rate in the money market (cost of capital) or the return the company is currently earning on its own invested capital. If the net present value of the project is positive, the implication is that the investment is desirable, since the return is greater than the discount rate.

Calculations for the net present value of alternative A with interest at 8% are as follows.

$$
\begin{aligned}
NPV_A\,(i = 0.08) = {}& -\,12{,}000 + 4278(P/F, 0.08, 1) \\
& +\ 3200(P/F, 0.08, 2) - 3500(P/F, 0.08, 3) \\
& +\ 5000(P/F, 0.08, 4) + 7750(P/F, 0.08, 5) \\
= {}& -\,12{,}000 + 4278(0.926) + 3200(0.875) \\
& -\ 3500(0.794) + 5000(0.735) + 7750(0.681) \\
= {}& \quad \$935.18
\end{aligned}
$$

Table A.2 Present Value of $F = 1$ at Rate i Payable in n Years

n \ i	2 %	3 %	4 %	5 %	6 %	7 %	8 %	9 %
1	0.980	0.971	0.962	0.952	0.943	0.935	0.926	0.917
2	0.961	0.943	0.925	0.907	0.890	0.873	0.857	0.842
3	0.942	0.915	0.889	0.864	0.840	0.816	0.794	0.772
4	0.924	0.888	0.855	0.823	0.792	0.763	0.735	0.708
5	0.906	0.863	0.822	0.784	0.747	0.713	0.681	0.650
6	0.888	0.837	0.790	0.746	0.705	0.666	0.630	0.596
7	0.871	0.813	0.760	0.711	0.665	0.623	0.583	0.547
8	0.853	0.789	0.731	0.677	0.627	0.582	0.540	0.502
9	0.837	0.766	0.703	0.645	0.592	0.544	0.500	0.460
10	0.820	0.744	0.676	0.614	0.558	0.508	0.463	0.422
11	0.804	0.722	0.650	0.585	0.527	0.475	0.429	0.388
12	0.788	0.701	0.625	0.557	0.497	0.444	0.397	0.356
13	0.773	0.681	0.601	0.530	0.469	0.415	0.368	0.326
14	0.758	0.661	0.577	0.505	0.442	0.388	0.340	0.299
15	0.743	0.642	0.555	0.481	0.417	0.362	0.315	0.275
16	0.728	0.623	0.534	0.458	0.394	0.339	0.292	0.252
17	0.714	0.605	0.513	0.436	0.371	0.317	0.270	0.231
18	0.700	0.587	0.494	0.416	0.350	0.296	0.250	0.212
19	0.686	0.570	0.475	0.396	0.331	0.277	0.232	0.194
20	0.673	0.554	0.456	0.377	0.312	0.258	0.215	0.178
21	0.660	0.538	0.439	0.359	0.294	0.242	0.199	0.164
22	0.647	0.522	0.422	0.342	0.278	0.226	0.184	0.150
23	0.634	0.507	0.406	0.326	0.262	0.211	0.170	0.138
24	0.622	0.492	0.390	0.310	0.247	0.197	0.158	0.126
25	0.610	0.478	0.375	0.295	0.233	0.184	0.146	0.116
26	0.598	0.464	0.361	0.281	0.220	0.172	0.135	0.106
27	0.586	0.450	0.347	0.268	0.207	0.161	0.125	0.098
28	0.574	0.437	0.333	0.255	0.196	0.150	0.116	0.090
29	0.563	0.424	0.321	0.243	0.185	0.141	0.107	0.082
30	0.552	0.412	0.308	0.231	0.174	0.131	0.099	0.075
40	0.453	0.307	0.208	0.142	0.097	0.067	0.046	0.032
50	0.372	0.228	0.141	0.087	0.054	0.034	0.021	0.013

10 %	11 %	12 %	13 %	14 %	15 %	16 %	18 %	20 %	25 %
0.909	0.901	0.893	0.885	0.877	0.870	0.862	0.847	0.833	0.800
0.826	0.812	0.797	0.783	0.769	0.756	0.743	0.718	0.694	0.640
0.751	0.731	0.712	0.693	0.675	0.658	0.641	0.609	0.579	0.512
0.683	0.659	0.636	0.613	0.592	0.572	0.552	0.516	0.482	0.410
0.621	0.593	0.567	0.543	0.519	0.497	0.476	0.437	0.402	0.328
0.564	0.535	0.507	0.480	0.456	0.432	0.410	0.370	0.335	0.262
0.513	0.482	0.452	0.425	0.400	0.376	0.354	0.314	0.279	0.210
0.467	0.434	0.404	0.376	0.351	0.327	0.305	0.266	0.233	0.168
0.424	0.391	0.361	0.333	0.308	0.284	0.263	0.225	0.194	0.134
0.386	0.352	0.322	0.295	0.270	0.247	0.227	0.191	0.162	0.107
0.350	0.317	0.287	0.261	0.237	0.215	0.195	0.162	0.135	0.086
0.319	0.286	0.257	0.231	0.208	0.187	0.168	0.137	0.112	0.069
0.290	0.258	0.229	0.204	0.182	0.163	0.145	0.116	0.093	0.055
0.263	0.232	0.205	0.181	0.160	0.141	0.125	0.099	0.078	0.044
0.239	0.209	0.183	0.160	0.140	0.123	0.108	0.084	0.065	0.035
0.218	0.188	0.163	0.141	0.123	0.107	0.093	0.071	0.054	0.028
0.198	0.170	0.146	0.125	0.108	0.093	0.080	0.060	0.045	0.023
0.180	0.153	0.130	0.111	0.095	0.081	0.069	0.051	0.038	0.018
0.164	0.138	0.116	0.098	0.083	0.070	0.060	0.043	0.031	0.014
0.149	0.124	0.104	0.087	0.073	0.061	0.051	0.037	0.026	0.012
0.135	0.112	0.093	0.077	0.064	0.053	0.044	0.031	0.022	0.009
0.123	0.101	0.083	0.068	0.056	0.046	0.038	0.026	0.018	0.007
0.112	0.091	0.074	0.060	0.049	0.040	0.033	0.022	0.015	0.006
0.102	0.082	0.066	0.053	0.043	0.035	0.028	0.019	0.013	0.005
0.092	0.074	0.059	0.047	0.038	0.030	0.024	0.016	0.010	0.004
0.084	0.066	0.053	0.042	0.033	0.026	0.021	0.014	0.009	0.003
0.076	0.060	0.047	0.037	0.029	0.023	0.018	0.011	0.007	0.002
0.069	0.054	0.042	0.033	0.026	0.020	0.016	0.010	0.006	0.002
0.063	0.048	0.037	0.029	0.022	0.017	0.014	0.008	0.005	0.002
0.057	0.044	0.033	0.026	0.020	0.015	0.012	0.007	0.004	0.001
0.022	0.015	0.011	0.008	0.005	0.004	0.003	0.001	0.001	
0.009	0.005	0.003	0.002	0.001	0.001	0.001			

Advantages and Disadvantages

The present-worth amount has several features that make it suitable as a basis for comparison. First, it considers the time value of money according to the value of i selected for the calculation. Second, it concentrates the equivalent of any cash flow in a single index at a particular point in time ($t = 0$). In addition, the present-worth figure is an amount by which the equivalent receipts of a cash flow exceed or fail to equal the equivalent disbursements of that cash flow.

Disadvantages of this criterion are:

- It assumes inflows and outflows can be forecasted for the entire lifetime of the project and requires equal time periods for comparison of several investment alternatives.
- The choice of discount rate can affect the rankings of alternatives.

EQUIVALENT ANNUAL COST

This criterion is used to compare equipment alternatives which provide identical benefits but which have different cost streams (operating, maintenance, taxes, insurance, etc.) and different lengths of life. Suppose, for example, that the monetary transactions associated with two equipment alternatives are as follows.

	Alternative E	Alternative F
First cost	$27,000	$50,000
Annual operating costs		
1st year	3,700	5,000
2nd year	6,500	5,000
3rd year	8,000	5,000
4th year	—	5,000
5th year	—	5,000
Estimated salvage value	5,000	10,000
Estimated service life	3 years	5 years

In all other respects these alternatives are equal. They provide the same benefits—both tangible and intangible. Clearly the net present value criterion is an inappropriate basis for comparison because the alternatives have unequal lives. How should they be compared?

Under the assumption that the need for which the alternatives are being considered is at least 5 years, the equivalent annual cost method is appropriate. Let I = first cost of the asset, S = estimated salvage value, and n =

estimated service life in years. Then the equivalent annual cost of the asset itself consists of capital recovery plus a return and may be expressed as

$$CR = (I - S) \left[\frac{i(1 + i)^n}{(1 + i)^n - 1} \right] + S(i)$$

Calculations are facilitated by tabulated values of the factor

$$(A/P, i, n) = \frac{i(1 + i)^n}{(1 + i)^n - 1}$$

for various values of i and n. (See Table A.3.)

To the equivalent annual cost of the asset itself must be added the annual operating costs. These annual costs may be added directly if they are uniform. Otherwise, the net present value of the stream of unequal costs must be calculated and then converted to uniform equivalent annual disbursements (EAD). The calculations are illustrated below for an interest rate of 8%.

Alternative E

$$CR = (27,000 - 5000) (A/P, 0.08, 3) + 5000 (0.08)$$
$$= (22,000) (0.388) + 5000(0.08)$$
$$= \$8,936.00$$

Equivalent annual disbursements:
$$NPV = 3700(P/F, 0.08, 1) + 6500(P/F, 0.08, 2) + 8000(P/F, 0.08, 3)$$
$$= 3700(0.926) + 6500(0.857) + 8000(0.794)$$
$$= \$15,348.70$$
$$EAD = (15,348.70)(A/P, 0.08, 3)$$
$$= (15,348.70)(0.388)$$
$$= \$5955$$

Total equivalent annual costs $= \$8936.00 + \$5955.30 = \$14,891.30$

Alternative F

$$CR = (50,000 - 10,000) (A/P, 0.08, 5) + 10,000(0.08)$$
$$= (40,000)(0.250) + 10,000(0.08)$$
$$= \$10.800.00$$

Uniform annual disbursements $= \$5000.00$
Total equivalent annual costs $= \$10,800.00 + \$5,000.00$
$$= \$15,800.00$$

Thus it appears that alternative E has slightly lower equivalent annual costs than alternative F.

Table A.3 Annual Payment That Will Repay a Present Amount of $1 in _n_ Years with Compound Interest _i_ on the Unpaid Balance

n \ i	2 %	3 %	4 %	5 %	6 %	7 %	8 %	9 %
1	1.020	1.030	1.040	1.050	1.060	1.070	1.080	1.090
2	0.515	0.523	0.530	0.538	0.545	0.553	0.561	0.568
3	0.347	0.354	0.360	0.367	0.374	0.381	0.388	0.395
4	0.263	0.269	0.275	0.282	0.289	0.295	0.302	0.309
5	0.212	0.218	0.225	0.231	0.237	0.244	0.250	0.257
6	0.179	0.185	0.191	0.197	0.203	0.210	0.216	0.223
7	0.155	0.161	0.167	0.173	0.179	0.186	0.192	0.199
8	0.137	0.142	0.149	0.155	0.161	0.167	0.174	0.181
9	0.123	0.128	0.134	0.141	0.147	0.153	0.160	0.167
10	0.111	0.117	0.123	0.130	0.136	0.142	0.149	0.156
11	0.102	0.108	0.114	0.120	0.127	0.133	0.140	0.147
12	0.095	0.100	0.107	0.113	0.119	0.126	0.133	0.140
13	0.088	0.094	0.100	0.106	0.113	0.120	0.127	0.134
14	0.083	0.089	0.095	0.101	0.108	0.114	0.121	0.128
15	0.078	0.084	0.090	0.096	0.103	0.110	0.117	0.124
16	0.074	0.080	0.086	0.092	0.099	0.106	0.113	0.120
17	0.070	0.076	0.082	0.089	0.095	0.102	0.110	0.117
18	0.067	0.073	0.079	0.086	0.092	0.099	0.107	0.114
19	0.064	0.070	0.076	0.083	0.090	0.097	0.104	0.112
20	0.061	0.067	0.074	0.080	0.087	0.094	0.102	0.110
21	0.059	0.065	0.071	0.078	0.085	0.092	0.100	0.108
22	0.057	0.063	0.069	0.076	0.083	0.090	0.098	0.106
23	0.055	0.061	0.067	0.074	0.081	0.089	0.096	0.104
24	0.053	0.059	0.066	0.072	0.080	0.087	0.095	0.103
25	0.051	0.057	0.064	0.071	0.078	0.086	0.094	0.102
26	0.050	0.056	0.063	0.070	0.077	0.085	0.093	0.101
27	0.048	0.055	0.061	0.068	0.076	0.083	0.091	0.100
28	0.047	0.053	0.060	0.067	0.075	0.082	0.090	0.099
29	0.046	0.052	0.059	0.066	0.074	0.081	0.090	0.098
30	0.045	0.051	0.058	0.065	0.073	0.081	0.089	0.097
40	0.037	0.043	0.051	0.058	0.066	0.075	0.084	0.093
50	0.032	0.039	0.047	0.055	0.063	0.072	0.082	0.091

10 %	11%	12 %	13 %	14 %	15 %	16 %	18 %	20 %	25 %
1.100	1.110	1.120	1.130	1.140	1.150	1.160	1.180	1.200	1.250
0.576	0.584	0.592	0.599	0.607	0.615	0.623	0.639	0.655	0.694
0.402	0.409	0.416	0.424	0.431	0.438	0.445	0.460	0.475	0.512
0.315	0.322	0.329	0.336	0.343	0.350	0.357	0.372	0.386	0.423
0.264	0.271	0.277	0.284	0.291	0.298	0.305	0.320	0.334	0.372
0.230	0.236	0.243	0.250	0.257	0.264	0.271	0.286	0.301	0.339
0.205	0.212	0.219	0.226	0.233	0.240	0.248	0.262	0.277	0.316
0.187	0.194	0.201	0.208	0.216	0.223	0.230	0.245	0.261	0.300
0.174	0.181	0.188	0.195	0.202	0.210	0.217	0.232	0.248	0.289
0.163	0.170	0.177	0.184	0.192	0.199	0.207	0.223	0.239	0.280
0.154	0.161	0.168	0.176	0.183	0.191	0.199	0.215	0.231	0.273
0.147	0.154	0.161	0.169	0.177	0.184	0.192	0.209	0.225	0.268
0.141	0.148	0.156	0.163	0.171	0.179	0.187	0.204	0.221	0.265
0.136	0.143	0.151	0.159	0.167	0.175	0.183	0.200	0.217	0.262
0.131	0.139	0.147	0.155	0.163	0.171	0.179	0.196	0.214	0.259
0.128	0.136	0.143	0.151	0.160	0.168	0.176	0.194	0.211	0.257
0.125	0.132	0.140	0.149	0.157	0.165	0.174	0.191	0.209	0.256
0.122	0.130	0.138	0.146	0.155	0.163	0.172	0.190	0.208	0.255
0.120	0.128	0.136	0.144	0.153	0.161	0.170	0.188	0.206	0.254
0.117	0.126	0.134	0.142	0.151	0.160	0.169	0.187	0.205	0.253
0.116	0.124	0.132	0.141	0.150	0.158	0.167	0.186	0.204	0.252
0.114	0.122	0.131	0.139	0.148	0.157	0.166	0.185	0.204	0.252
0.113	0.121	0.130	0.138	0.147	0.156	0.165	0.184	0.203	0.251
0.111	0.120	0.128	0.137	0.146	0.155	0.165	0.183	0.203	0.251
0.110	0.119	0.128	0.136	0.145	0.155	0.164	0.183	0.202	0.251
0.109	0.118	0.127	0.136	0.145	0.154	0.163	0.182	0.202	0.251
0.108	0.117	0.126	0.135	0.144	0.154	0.163	0.182	0.201	0.251
0.107	0.116	0.125	0.134	0.144	0.153	0.163	0.182	0.201	0.250
0.107	0.116	0.125	0.134	0.143	0.153	0.162	0.181	0.201	0.250
0.106	0.115	0.124	0.133	0.143	0.152	0.162	0.181	0.201	0.250
0.102	0.112	0.121	0.131	0.141	0.151	0.160	0.180	0.200	0.250
0.101	0.111	0.120	0.130	0.140	0.150	0.160	0.180	0.200	0.250

Advantages and Disadvantages

For assets having the same service life, the equivalent annual cost criterion gives the same results as the present net value criterion. The equivalent annual cost criterion is often used to compare two assets having unequal service lives. The assumption is inherent, however, that the shorter-lived asset will be replaced with one having the same or lower equivalent annual costs. If risk is involved in this assumption, it must be considered subjectively. For example, alternative F provides a service life of 5 years at an equivalent annual cost of $15,081.40. Alternative E, however, provides service for only 3 years at an equivalent annual cost of $14,892.46. If service is needed for 5 years and alternative E is chosen, what about the remaining 2 years? There is no assurance that the replacement for alternative E will have a cost of $14,892.46 or less. If the likelihood is high that the cost will be greater, the proper choice at this time may be alternative F.

INTERNAL RATE OF RETURN

The internal rate of return is a widely accepted index of profitability. It is defined as the interest rate that reduces the present worth amount of a series of receipts and disbursements to zero. That is, the rate of return for investment proposal j is the interest rate i_j^* that satisfies the equation

$$0 = NPV_j\,(i_j^*) = \sum_{n\,=\,0}^{N} F_{jn}(1 + i_j^*)^{-n}$$

Solving for i_j^* directly is difficult and tedious unless done on a computer. The usual approach is to search for the appropriate value by trial and error. The calculations for alternative A are shown below:

$NPV_A\,(i = 0.08) = \quad 935.18$

$NPV_A\,(i = 0.10) = -\,12{,}000 + 4278(0.909) + 3200(0.826)$
$\qquad\qquad\qquad\quad -\,3500(0.751) + 5000(0.683)$
$\qquad\qquad\qquad\quad +\,7750(0.621)$
$\qquad\qquad\qquad = \quad \$131.15$

$NPV_A\,(i = 0.11) = -\,12{,}000 + 4278(0.901) + 3200(0.821)$
$\qquad\qquad\qquad\quad -\,3500(0.731) + 5000(0.659) + 7750(0.593)$
$\qquad\qquad\qquad = -\,\$214.87$

Hence i^* is approximately 10.4% by interpolation.

Advantages and Disadvantages

The internal rate of return is familiar to many businesspeople and administrators and is therefore readily accepted. It has advantages in not requiring the prior determination of a discount interest rate, and it can be directly related to profit goals. The criterion of average rate of return is enough if an alternative must be accepted or refused; if its rate of return is higher than the average rate at which capital can be obtained, the alternative may be carried out. However, it is a valid measure for comparison of alternatives only if the financial conditions under which capital can be borrowed and invested are identical for the alternatives under consideration. Comparing the average return on two alternatives can only tell us that, if the rate at which money can be borrowed is i_A, equal to the rate of return on alternative A, the discounted income from alternative A is nil; whereas, if the rate on borrowed capital is i_B, equal to the rate of return for alternative B, the discounted return for alternative B is nil.

A second disadvantage of the rate-of-return criterion is its dependency on the investment base. A return of 15% on an investment of $1000 is not necessarily preferable to a return of 12% on a $10,000,000 investment.

BENEFIT/COST RATIO OF DISCOUNTED CASH FLOWS

This criterion is similar to the present-value criterion. The difference is that expenditures (costs) and income (benefits) are treated separately and an index is obtained by forming a ratio of the present values. Thus for alternative A with interest at 8%, we have

$$B/C \ (i = 0.08) = \frac{4278(0.926) + 3200(0.875) + 5000(0.735) + 7750(0.68)}{12,000 + 3500(0.794)}$$

$$= \frac{\$15,714.18}{\$14,779.00}$$

$$= 1.063$$

The B/C ratio is not unique, and different results are obtained depending on whether or not the benefit and cost values are net values. For example, suppose that the $3500 cost for alternative A in year 3 is in reality a net cost obtained by offsetting $2500 in benefits against $6000 in costs. The B/C ratio could be

$$B/C \ (i = 0.08) = \$17,699.18/\$16,764.00$$
$$= 1.056$$

Since any changes of this nature affect both the numerator and denominator of the ratio equally, it is clear that, if the ratio is greater (smaller) than unity, it will remain so after the change. If only one project is being considered or if several projects are being considered and there is no limitation on available funds, the decision should be to fund any project having a B/C ratio greater than 1.

The usual situation is, however, that several alternatives are competing for limited funds and only one is to be funded. In this situation the correct use of the B/C method is an incremental analysis. Consider again the alternatives in Table A.1. We first rank the alternatives by increasing costs as shown in Table A.4. After that, we eliminate all alternatives having B/C ratios below 1 (in

Table A.4 Benefit/Cost Ratios

Alternative	Discounted Benefit ($)	Discounted Cost ($)	B/C Ratio
C	7,703.55	7,500.00	1.027
B	9,719.70	10,000.00	.972
D	11,731.50	10,000.00	1.173
A	15,714.18	14,779.00	1.063

this case alternative B). Next we compute the incremental B/C ratios as shown in Table A.5. We delete alternatives with an incremental ratio less than 1 (in

Table A.5 Incremental Analysis of B/C Ratios

Alternative	Discounted Benefit ($)	Cost ($)	B/C	Incremental Benefit ($)	Cost ($)	B/C
C	7,703.55	7,500.00	1.027	—	—	—
D	11,731.50	10,000.00	1.173	3,887.75	2,500.00	1.555
A	15,719.18	14,779.00	1.063	3,982.68	4,779.00	0.833

this case alternative A) and, if necessary, recalculate incremental B/C ratios. We choose the last alternative having an incremental B/C ratio greater than 1 (in this case alternative D). The rationale of this approach is that it is desirable to invest as much as possible so long as the discounted incremental B/C ratio exceeds unity.

Advantages and Disadvantages

The advantages and disadvantages are much the same as those for net present value.

COMPARISON OF EVALUATION CRITERIA

Each of the above criteria is useful in certain situations. For comparison, the criteria of the payback period, net present value, internal rate of return, and

Table A.6 Capital Projects Profitability Evaluation

Alternative	Net Annual Cash Flows by Year ($)						Payback Period	Net Present Value ($)	Internal Rate of Return (%)	B/C Ratio
	0	1	2	3	4	5				
A	−12,000	4,278	3,200	−3,500	5,000	7,750	4.39	935.18	10.4	1.063
B	−10,000	3,200	2,700	2,200	2,000	1,800	3.95	−280.30	6.7	0.972
C	−7,500	2,350	2,350	1,750	1,500	1,500	3.70	203.55	8.9	1.027
D	−10,000	2,000	2,000	2,000	2,000	7,500	4.27	1,731.50	13.0	1.173

benefit/cost ratio have been applied to the alternatives in Table A.1. An interest rate of 8% was used, and the results are shown in Table A.6. Note that all methods except the payback period rank alternative D first.

BIBLIOGRAPHY

Baldwin, George B. "Discounted Cash Flow," *Finance and Development* **6** (Sept. 1968).

Grant, Eugene L., and W. Grant Ireson. *Principles of Engineering.* 5th ed. New York: Ronald Press, 1970.

McLean, John G. "How to Evaluate New Capital Investment," *Harvard Business Review*, **36**, No. 6 (1958).

Merret, A. J., and Allen Sykes. *The Finance and Analysis of Capital Projects.* London: Longmans Green & Co., 1963.

Netto, Roberto P. Lima. "Choosing Among Proposals: The Making of Investment Decisions," *Finance and Development*, **8** (June 1971).

Organization for Economic Co-operation and Development. *Manual of Industrial Project Analysis in Developing Countries.* Paris: Development Centre of the Organization for Economic Cooperation Development, 1973.

Ravenscroft, Edward A. "Return on Investment: Fit the Method to Your Need," *Harvard Business Review*, **38**, No. 2 (1960).

Thuesen, H. G., W. J. Fabrycky, and H. J. Thuesen. *Engineering Management and Accounting.* 4th ed. Englewood Cliffs, N.J.: Prentice-Hall, 1971.

Vernon, Thomas H. "Capital Budgeting and the Evaluation Process," *Management Accounting*, **54**, No. 3 (1972).

INDEX